Baseball Between Us

16 YEARS. 32 BALLPARKS. 43,000 MILES.

A Road Map to a Winning Father/Son Relationship

MIKE LUERY

with Matt Luery

Baseball Between Us
Copyright © 2011 by Mike Luery
Published by Sleuth Publishing
www.baseballbetweenus.com
mike@baseballbetweenus.com

ISBN 978-0-9832744-0-7

Printed in the United States of America

Contents

Foreword

I've known Michael Luery since he was 9 years old and I was 18. We became friends in part because we both loved the game of baseball. We were spending the summer in Wayne, Maine, where I was the assistant baseball counselor at Camp Androscoggin Jr. The year was 1965, and I was the coach of the "B" team, for the younger boys, and Mike was my shortstop.

By the time he was 11, I was coach of the "A" team, and Mike was a star on a team of stars. We were cocky and arrogant. We would practice during free play and even in the rain, and when we played other camp teams, we were hard to beat.

Mike comes from Stamford, Connecticut, which is also my hometown, and I became close with his parents, Bob and Anita, his brother, Russell, and his sisters Roberta and Andrea. He faced a terrible tragedy when Roberta at age 20 was killed in a car accident as she was driving back to college. After moving to California to go to college, he experienced great joy when he married Carol and again when they had two beautiful children, Sarah and Matt. I remember when they were born.

A few years ago Mike called to say he and his son were coming to St. Petersburg. He and Matt had embarked on a quest to visit every ballpark. I thought to myself, that's excessive—even for a guy who loves baseball.

Michael always had the baseball gene. At camp we never had a practice he didn't savor, never held a batting practice he didn't cherish. I could hit him ground balls for an hour, and he never said, "Enough." He and I were crazy Yankee fans, and we would talk about Mickey Mantle, Roy White and Mel Stottlemyre, even though the Yankees in 1967 no longer were champions.

Mike had made up his mind about making this trek, and he's a stubborn cuss. I had a hunch he would follow through on his journey no matter what. My only question was whether Matt, who was 17, would be with him when it ended.

The two couldn't have been more different. Mike was into structure. He liked to plan ahead and follow a schedule. Matt was a free spirit who liked to wing it. I thought it might be fun to be a fly on the wall to watch the fur fly as they traveled from ballpark to ballpark.

Turns out there were a lot of heated arguments, as Mike relates in this touching and often humorous memoir. Only a father and a "Me Generation" son could argue over who was more important: Teddy Roosevelt or 50 Cent. Both had been shot. Like most teens, Matt felt that nothing that had happened before he was born counted for anything, so Roosevelt lost by definition. Matt opined that 50 Cent held a hallowed place in the "Me Generation" universe. Mike's sputtering answer: "Rap isn't even music." I'd had the same exchange with my own son.

The trip from sea to shining sea was held in segments over many years. Mike and Matt experienced a lot of history. They were there when Barry Bonds hit his 715th home run to pass Babe Ruth for second place on the all-time home run list. They were in the Dakotas when they ran across the biggest buffalo in the world, saw a real T-Rex skeleton, rode to the top of the

St. Louis arch, visited both the Rock and Roll and the Baseball Halls of Fame, saw some important monuments like Boog Powell, Bernie Williams, Niagara Falls, and the Liberty Bell. (Mike provides photos of them all in the book.)

More than anything, though, this book is about parenthood and the pain of a father watching a son grow up and move away. It's not easy to do. Fathers want to keep their sons with them forever. I know I did. (My son is living in L.A.) But Mike and I both knew for their mental health and for their future, it was necessary to let go. And though it wasn't easy, Michael at last was able to do that. The old-time baseball fan who loved Mickey Mantle and the Beatles finally had to lovingly admit that his little boy, who loved rap music and who was wedded to his iPod, had grown into a man. In this book we get to watch that too.

Peter Golenbock
St. Petersburg, Florida

Introduction

*"Now batting, the center fielder,
number 7, Mickey Mantle, number 7."*
BOB SHEPPARD

With a crack of the bat, the San Francisco Giants leadoff hitter, Omar Vizquel, lined a fastball down the third base line. Tigers infielder Brandon Inge gloved it easily, then glided a step to his left. With a fluid motion, he fired the ball to first base, where Dmitri Young eagerly smothered it within his six-foot, two-inch frame.

"Out!" screamed the umpire to the delight of the 37,456 rabid fans at Detroit's Comerica Park. And with that, my baseball fantasy was on the fast track – the first game of a father-son road trip through the Midwest that would take me and my 16-year-old son Matthew to 4 ballparks, 8 states and 1 foreign country in 11 days.

The Road Trip Begins in 2005

The date on the calendar was June 18 and I probably should have been home in California, celebrating my 22nd wedding anniversary with my wife, Carol, but instead I was in downtown Detroit, running around the bleachers like a kid – with my kid

– and my trusty baseball glove. I was trying desperately to snag a batting practice home run. Capturing only the moment, but no ball, the calendar said it was 2005 – yet I felt myself flashing back in time to a far away memory tucked deep inside of me.

I looked around for my son, but quickly realized he was not in the ballpark. I did not panic, but instead felt a warm sense of calm surround me as I looked up and discovered a familiar face I hadn't seen in eight lonely years.

"Dad, is that you?" I said to myself.

In my vision, the kind and handsome man placed his arm around me. His face was silhouetted against the sun as he silently gave me a hug.

I felt childlike and small as I pressed myself against his belt, looking up at the man I missed so much in life. He smiled at me and then waved his arm to the crowd around us. The fans were dressed in old-fashioned clothing from a different era; in my flashback it was the fall of 1963 and my dad and I were together again at Yankee Stadium experiencing one of our happiest moments: at the very place where we truly bonded as a father-and-son team.

My lifelong passion for baseball was born on a crisp October day, when my dad, Robert Luery, took me to see my very first World Series game – in Yankee Stadium, the House that Ruth Built. Although I was only eight at the time, I can still vividly recall being mesmerized by the baseball monuments in center field and seeing the sun radiate against the brilliant green grass of the stadium. It was in Yankee Stadium where on many occasions, I would see my hero Mickey Mantle slug one out of the park. Mickey had massive muscles that rippled as he gripped the bat from either side of the batter's box. My favorite Yankee was also one of the most powerful switch hitters in the history of the game.

But it was more than the players who captivated me, for I quickly fell in love with the smell of the ballpark: the smoky roasted peanuts and the sugar-laden Crackerjacks mixed in with the aroma of fresh popcorn. Baseball is also about touch. I still love the tactile sensation of pounding that greasy Glovolium oil into my weathered mitt, to form the perfect pocket. The sounds of baseball are equally important: the crack of the bat, the cheers from the fans and the screams of excitement when a foul ball comes your way.

But the greatest sound of all was the rich and resonant tone of "the Voice of God": Bob Sheppard, the eloquent public address announcer for the Yankees, who inspired baseball fans for more than half a century with his player introductions. I can still hear Sheppard's powerful voice echoing off the canyons of Yankee Stadium with reverberation: "Now batting, the center fielder, number 7, Mickey Mantle, number 7." Sheppard pronounced "Man-tle" with a dramatic pause that bounced off the walls with a force so powerful it could make your spine tingle.

My dad was my baseball buddy. We traveled to Yankee Stadium as often as we could, studying the standings together and debating the intricacies of the game. We wondered who would be on the mound for our next ballgame and which player in pinstripes would be the hometown hero for the day. I always placed my faith on number 7, the Mick, although in many contests it was number 9, Roger Maris, who would lead the way.

⚾ ⚾ ⚾

I will never forget the moment it happened. Dad came home from work with a big smile – and holding two tickets.

"Michael," he said, "I got them."

"Got what?" I asked.

"I've got two tickets to the World Series!" he declared as I leaped three feet into the air in sheer excitement. "I'm pulling you out of school tomorrow," Dad said. "And we're driving to the Bronx to see Game One of the World Series."

"Woo hoo!" I screamed.

I was ecstatic about missing school but even more excited about going to my first World Series at the tender age of eight. Back in the early '60s, the World Series was actually played in the daytime, when fans could follow the action while the sun was still in the sky, unlike today's games, which routinely end after midnight on the East Coast.

But best of all, I would actually be witnessing history at Yankee Stadium, the epicenter of the baseball universe, while my third-grade buddies would all be stuck in school, forced to listen to the game on transistor radios hidden in their jackets.

"Be ready to go early tomorrow morning," Dad said.

"Don't worry, Dad," I said. "I'll get ready tonight."

I ran to my bedroom and quickly grabbed my navy blue Yankee warm-up jacket and slung it over my shoulders. I pulled up my dungarees and placed my Yankee hat on the pillow, then dug down deep into the sheets. Taking no chance of being late for the game, I decided to sleep in my Yankee outfit. I didn't want to miss a thing. By dawn's light, I was in the car, ready to leave my Connecticut home for the magic of New York City.

The 1963 World Series was a contest of baseball titans: on my side was the heavily favored American League Champion New York Yankees. On the other was the National League's Los Angeles Dodgers. Topping it all, my dad had scored two tickets to see one of the premier matchups in the history of baseball: Yankee ace Whitey Ford vs. the Dodger's lefty legend, Sandy Koufax.

I was absolutely convinced my Yankees would sweep the Dodgers in four straight games. After all, "we" had one of the greatest teams ever assembled. True baseball fans always use the term "we" to describe their team. Fans feel like they are an integral part of the club's success.

And in 1963, the Yanks had assembled one of the greatest lineups in all of baseball: Mickey Mantle, Roger Maris, Tony

Kubek, Bobby Richardson, Yogi Berra, Elston Howard and Rookie of the Year Tom Tresh, plus one of the best left arms ever – Whitey Ford, the Yankee "Chairman of the Board" who had defeated 25 opponents that year. The Yanks had run away with the American League pennant in '63, capturing the flag by 10¹/₂ games.

But the Dodgers were loaded too. They had Maury Wills and Frank Howard, along with Don Drysdale and Sandy Koufax. And on that sunny October day, Koufax was masterful in mowing down the first five Yankee batters he faced in the opening game of the Series. I watched in disbelief as one after another, Kubek, Richardson, Tresh, Mantle and Maris all fanned in frustration against the flame-throwing Dodger pitcher, a boy from Brooklyn, the original home of the team that now played in faraway Los Angeles.

The torment continued as the game entered the second inning, when Whitey Ford gave up an RBI single to former Yankee Bill "Moose" Skowron. No one at the park was expecting what happened next as the Dodgers put two more runners on base, setting the stage for John Roseboro to smack a three-run homer over the fence. Yankee fans were shell-shocked to see their best pitcher give up a home run, the first and only four-bagger Ford had allowed to a lefty batter all season. The Dodgers were up 4-0 before the Bronx Bombers could even hack their first hit against the lightning lefty who would strike out 15 Yankees on that October day. At the time, it was the most strikeouts of any World Series pitcher in history.

Even the mighty Mickey Mantle struck out twice that day, as Koufax teased and taunted him with a motley mix of curves and fastballs that turned my action hero into a mere mortal. Yankee second baseman Bobby Richardson struck out three times, leaving the crowd stunned. He had never even whiffed twice in a game all year – until he faced Koufax, the King of K's.

Only Tom Tresh was able to connect that day, socking a two-run homer in the eighth inning, but alas it was the lone bright spot in a dismal day that saw the Dodgers triumph 5-2. Sandy Koufax went the whole distance, hurling all nine innings to secure the victory for the visitors.

In those days pitchers routinely finished the game they started. It was not like today's game, where starters pitch a mere six innings before yielding to rocket-armed relievers who hurl six pitches and then limp off to the locker room, only to wrap ice around their strained biceps.

But back in the rough-and-tumble days of the 1960s, pitchers went the distance. There were no posers as closers, no micromanagers who needed a committee of four high-priced hurlers to get three outs.

It was a different era in 1963 and the crowd of 69,000 at Yankee Stadium was crestfallen by the loss – especially an 8-year-old boy from Connecticut who took it personally, crying the whole way home, heartbroken that his Yankees were no longer invincible.

The New Yorkers were eventually swept in four games and scored just four runs the entire World Series – the second lowest total by any World Series team at that point in history. Although the Yanks lost the Series, I gained a love for baseball and a deep bond with my dad, who got me hooked on America's pastime.

As a kid in love with baseball, I went to every game I could, attending dozens at Yankee Stadium. My dad also took me to the old Polo Grounds, which served as the New York Mets' first home until Shea Stadium opened in 1964.

I can remember how the New York fans rose to their feet to applaud Willie Mays, who was playing for the visiting San Francisco Giants against the hometown Mets. The partisan crowd jumped for joy when Willie launched a massive home run deep into the center field seats. As a kid, I couldn't understand why all those New Yorkers were cheering for an opposing player, until my dad explained that Willie Mays had played for the New York Giants before his team moved to San Francisco in 1958. While thousands of New Yorkers were crushed about losing their Giants, they never lost their love for the Say Hey Kid.

As I grew older, I saw the Mets play many times in Shea Stadium and traveled frequently to visit friends in other cities to catch a ballgame. In Baltimore, I loved seeing Brooks and Frank Robinson lead the Orioles to victory in the now-defunct Memorial Stadium. It didn't matter who was playing; I always rooted for the home team. Unless, of course, the visitors wore the gray flannel road jerseys of the New York Yankees.

Over the years, I visited half a dozen parks that have since been torn down or replaced, including Veterans Stadium in Philadelphia, the original Busch Stadium in St. Louis, the Astrodome in Houston and the Kingdome in Seattle. I also saw the Padres play at the old Jack Murphy Stadium in San Diego and the San Francisco Giants at Candlestick Park.

By the mid '70s, I had become a full-fledged baseball fanatic and promised myself that one day, I would visit every Major League stadium to see a game in person. But it was not until decades later that I would actually launch my plan into action, thanks to the help of my wife, Carol, and our two children, Sarah and Matthew. They all became my baseball companions – giving me both the chance to reach my boyhood dream – and to write this book, which I hope will capture my passion for the game of baseball and my love for life on the road.

Road Trip Preview

(1994 – 2005)

(Original) Busch Stadium, St. Louis Cardinals; Chase Field, Arizona Diamondbacks; Safeco Field, Seattle Mariners; Coors Field, Colorado Rockies; Wrigley Field, Chicago Cubs; Petco Park, San Diego Padres.

"It's déjà vu, all over again."
YOGI BERRA

"Get your beer here!" screamed the Bud Man as he vaulted his way up the steps of the old Busch Stadium in St. Louis.

He smelled of hops and barley as he shouted, "Ice cold beer!" to the inebriated crowd. "Bud and Bud Light here!" he chanted to the fans as they roared their approval by slapping him with high-fives adorned with pictures of Lincoln stuck to their beer-stained palms.

"Can't we get a non-alcoholic beverage at this stadium?" my wife lamented. "This beer man just bounces up and down those steps selling suds for buds. Can't I get some juice for my babies, or maybe even a bottle of water?"

I looked around but didn't see any babies at the ballpark. I did spy however, my 8-year-old daughter, Sarah and my 5-year-old son, Matthew. They were easy to spot, since they were sitting right next to us.

The Luerys were in St. Louis for a family vacation, mixed in with a business conference of Investigative Reporters and Editors. While my colleagues were exploring their sleuth-like tendencies, I was playing hooky at the ballpark with my family. The only problem was that my wife and kids didn't seem to be enjoying the experience.

The year was 1994, well before smoking bans were in vogue, and the air at the ballpark was filled with thick cigarette smoke. My kids were hungry but the hot dog man was nowhere in sight. Instead, Carol constantly reminded me, we were trapped in a bad movie, *Revenge of the Beer Vendors*.

"Why are they selling only beer?" she demanded.

"Why do you think they call it Busch Stadium?" was my sarcastic response.

Carol shot me a look that could have killed a bull moose. My only redemption was to do something dramatic.

"I'll get some food," I said proudly, hoping my wife would recognize the supreme sacrifice I was making by offering to hunt and gather instead of watching the game.

"Hurry up," was her short retort. "The kids are tired, hungry and thirsty."

I bolted for the concession stand.

Our first family trip to the ballpark was not a big hit. The only thing Sarah and Matt truly enjoyed was the fireworks display following the game, in celebration of the Cardinals' victory.

But I was determined not to give up so easily. So as my kids got older, I would insist on taking them to ballgames in whatever city we happened to be visiting.

In 2001, we were in Arizona for Spring Break – a perfect opportunity, I told my family – to see the Diamondbacks play in their new downtown Phoenix stadium, which is now known as Chase Field.

"This is even more boring than watching paint dry," Carol declared in the very first inning.

"Just look around you," I said. "This is the very first ballpark to feature a swimming pool in the outfield."

Suddenly, the kids came alive.

"Where's the pool, Dad?" Sarah asked.

"Can we jump in?" Matt wanted to know.

"It's over there," I said, pointing toward the center field fence. "And no, we can't go swimming. We didn't bring our bathing suits."

The swimming pool sits just 415 feet from home plate – and over the years many batters have launched "splash hits" into the water. The first to do so was Mark Grace of the Chicago Cubs, who homered against the Diamondbacks on May 12, 1998, the year the ballpark opened.

Attending a game at Chase Field is a visual experience. The park features an electronic video display board with a Light Emitting Diode (LED) ribbon that runs 1,119 feet around the park, the largest ribbon display in all of baseball. But the most prominent part of the park is the retractable roof, which opens (and closes) to its own musical beat in just four and a half minutes. On most day games, the roof is closed to shade the fans from the triple-digit heat – but at night you can see the desert sky above.

And on this early April evening, it was 85 degrees at game time – a perfect night for an open roof, as more than 36,000 fans entered the park to see the Diamondbacks host the Milwaukee Brewers.

While I was engrossed in the game, the rest of my family was focused on eating – and the fact we could order hot dogs, submarine sandwiches, or even Chinese food without ever having to leave our seats in the upper deck.

As for me, the game was food for thought — a scoreless tie until the top of the third inning, when the Brewers beat up on Arizona ace Curt Schilling, hitting him hard for two runs and a lead they would never relinquish.

The Brewers slid past the D-backs to win the game 3-2. As the game ended, my 12-year-old son gave me a big smile and declared, "Hey, Dad, this was fun. Let's do it again sometime."

I smiled and nodded.

Turns out our next time would be two years later — on a college road trip to Seattle, home of the University of Washington. The academic setting was spectacular and Sarah, now a senior in high school, was impressed with the scenic beauty of the school. But to me, the real gem of the Puget Sound is the diamond known as Safeco Field.

Since it opened in 1999, Safeco has offered scintillating views of Seattle's skyline, thanks to the retractable roof that takes just 15 minutes to close, thereby saving the Mariners from what would likely be a sea of rainouts. The roof weighs 22 million pounds and as the Mariners say, enough steel to build a 55-story skyscraper.

The park features a multitude of electronic displays, but best of all is the retro-style, hand-operated scoreboard in left field, reminiscent of Fenway Park. You can also check on games in real time from around the Majors on the out-of-town scoreboard. But if you want to focus on the game in Seattle, you can survey the play-by-play boards of the Mariners' game, located just along the first and third base lines.

The field is natural grass with four different kinds of Kentucky bluegrass, blended immaculately with ryegrass to create an artistic green checkerboard on the diamond.

At game time it was cloudy on this chilly afternoon. It was April 17, 2003, and the swirling wind made the 54-degree temperature feel even colder. But Carol was so struck by the beauty of the ballpark that she never complained about the weather. Secretly, I thought she might even be enjoying the game.

Then I opened my mouth, and ruined everything. "Are you having fun?" I asked her between pitches.

"Still looking for my paint brush," she said.

"What are you talking about?"

"You know – the brush I'll need to paint this picture. It's called 'Baseball is Boring.'"

"Anything would be more exciting than this game," she added with a twist of the dagger, before adding the fatal blow. "Football and basketball are so much more exciting. At least there's scoring."

All I could do was bury my head in my hands.

But at least Sarah and Matt seemed to be enjoying the game.

"Sarah, U Dub would be a wonderful place to go to college. You could be a Husky," I suggested.

"You mean *you* could become a Mariners fan," my daughter boldly stated. "Isn't that what you really want?" she inquired. "Your hidden agenda is to attend dozens of games in this beautiful park while I'm in school nearby," she stated with emphasis, her words jabbing me in the heart.

"Well, I'm only thinking of your academics," I said. "Cloudy days make you want to study more."

"Dad, give it up," Sarah countered. "I want to be the one making the choice here – and it has nothing to do with baseball."

"Yeah, Dad, it's Sarah's decision," Matt echoed, deliberately joining sides with his sister in a show of force.

"Well, I'm glad I won that argument," I chuckled.

On this cloudy day, the Mariners attracted 33,412 faithful

fans to see the home team defeat my favorite West Coast team, the Oakland A's, by a score of 4-3, thanks to an RBI double from John Olerud.

By late afternoon, the sun finally emerged and as the game ended, we met with my good friends Herb and Deb Weisbaum. Herb is a veteran TV and radio anchor in Seattle and he knew exactly where to take the out-of-towners.

We drove to a wonderful seafood restaurant in West Seattle called Salty's, where we saw the sun peek majestically between the clouds. In a transcendental moment, the setting sun reflected on the mirrored windows of the city, lighting up the skyline with a golden glow.

"It would be very easy," I told Herb, "to fall in love with this spectacular city and the beautiful ballpark here."

"Doesn't Sarah get to make her own choice?" Herb demanded.

"Yes," I countered. "She can go anyplace there's a Major League ballpark nearby."

Herb just rolled his eyes.

"Sarah," he said. "Tell your dad it's your decision, not his."

Alas, it seemed that everyone was conspiring against me.

But I would carry on – and couldn't wait to visit the next school on Sarah's list – the University of Colorado. Somehow I just knew we'd find a way to visit the Rockies – not the mountains, but the baseball team. Sure enough, my dream came true just three months later.

⚾ ⚾ ⚾

Our visit to the college campus in Boulder convinced me that everyone in Colorado was trim and athletic. There were people in motion everywhere you looked – jogging, hiking, mountain biking. And of course, nearly everyone seemed to be enjoying the ultimate elbow exerciser, beer drinking.

That's why Coors was invented in Colorado – to wash down

all that healthy exercise with some nutritious barley and hops. It's well known in Colorado that beer is good for the palate and good for the soul. And I wanted to make sure I had my fill of inspiration at Coors Field – to savor the local flavor and get a taste of what the ballpark has to offer – which is to say, plenty of offense.

Since Coors Field opened in 1999, it's been one of the most prolific parks for home runs anywhere in baseball. Inspired by the mile-high air, the Rockies and their opponents clubbed 303 homers in the inaugural season, the most ever at any ballpark. Turns out the atmosphere really does make a difference, with a ball traveling 9 percent farther at a mile high compared to sea level, according to the Rockies. By way of comparison, a 400-foot four-bagger in Yankee Stadium would soar 440 feet in Denver.

Fastball hurlers loved Coors Field because their pitches seem to have more pop – coming in faster, thanks to the thin air. But curveball hurlers hated the park, because the mile-high elevation caused the ball to lose its lift, forcing it to hang up in the air, where a batter could more easily slug it over the wall.

That was in the early days of the park – but now the Rockies keep the game balls in a climate-controlled humidor, so the spheroids don't behave as if they're on steroids.

Coors Field is just two blocks from Union Station in the trendy LoDo (Lower Downtown) section of Denver. The city skyline is located behind home plate, plainly visible from the outfield bleachers, which offer a picturesque view of the Rocky Mountains.

The park is asymmetrical with the deepest part 424 feet from home plate in deep right-center field. It's at precisely that point where the out-of-town scoreboard is situated, enabling partisans to root for their hometown teams from across the Major Leagues. Coors Field is a retro park, built just for baseball with hand-laid brick and an old-fashioned clock tower to keep track of the time for up to 50,381 fans at full capacity.

For our game, 31,139 people marched past the turnstiles to see the Rockies host Barry Bonds and the San Francisco Giants. Bonds was on fire, going three for four, with four runs batted in, including a line drive home run into the right field bullpen with two men on board. Nevertheless, the Rockies outslugged the Giants 11-7 in a battle that took eight pitchers and 185 minutes to complete.

And yet I heard nary a complaint from the Luery family.

"Dad, this park is awesome," Matt said.

"Yes," I agreed emphatically. "We can see many games in this park if Sarah chooses to enroll at CU. But there's no pressure, Sarah," I said to my daughter.

As a dad, it was my job to let her know she could pick any school near a ballpark. "I think the University of Colorado is a great school," I said with enthusiasm.

"Ha, Daddy, I love you," she laughed.

At that moment I felt everything was right with the world. My daughter had lots of exciting choices for college and in just four days, we would be sitting in one of America's most historic ballparks: Wrigley Field.

The road to Wrigley would be paved with yet another obligatory campus visit. Now don't get me wrong. Northwestern University is a beautiful school nestled on the shores of Lake Michigan in the picturesque town of Evanston, Illinois – but it's no Wrigley Field. Yes, Northwestern does have an outstanding journalism school and deep inside I was hoping my daughter, as an aspiring writer, would be eager to apply. In my dream world, Sarah would become a reporter like her dear old dad and learn the nuances of journalism. And of course, having Sarah enrolled at Northwestern would give me just the excuse I needed to become a frequent flyer to Chicago, where I could take her to a multitude of Cubs games.

But first I had to get her hooked on the park. So on July 13, 2003, the Luerys visited Wrigley Field, the second oldest ballpark in the Majors.

"When was it built, Dad?" Sarah wanted to know.

"It opened in 1914," I said.

"Wow, Dad," Matt chipped in. "That's even older than you."

"That's funny," was my verbal retort. "Yes, there are a few things on Earth older than I am and Wrigley Field is certainly one of them."

The walls of the stadium are dripping with history, including the ivy-covered vines that have been hugging the outfield fence since 1937. Wrigley Field is the site of Babe Ruth's famous "called shot" from the 1932 World Series, when the Bambino pointed toward the outfield bleachers before slugging the next pitch out of the park.

The original scoreboard, also from 1937, is still in use today, signaling balls and strikes, hits and errors, with human hands constantly changing all the numbers. And the Cubs still hoist a white flag decorated with a blue "W" atop the scoreboard following a win, while North Siders know there is nothing to celebrate when a blue flag with a white "L" flies overhead. In 1941, the Cubs introduced organ music to baseball and the custom has spread now to every Major League park in the country.

Wrigley was also the first field to let fans keep foul balls as a souvenir. On the north side of Chicago, the locals love to throw back home run balls hit by opposing players. However, I have vowed to keep any home run ball I'm lucky enough to catch in the bleachers, no matter who hits it.

But the best thing about Wrigley Field is the crowd. The fans are passionate about their Cubbies and not afraid of drinking eight or ten beers just to prove it. On the night of our game, the Cubs were hosting the Atlanta Braves. The Luerys were hoisted high up above in the rickety, wooden right field stands, where we could see fans from neighboring North Sheffield Avenue pop open their Budweisers as they lounged in lawn chairs to watch the game from their rooftops.

Softly, at first, we heard a murmur in the crowd.

"This field rocks," they seemed to say.

"What's that sound?" my wife wanted to know.

Then it got louder.

Carol poked me in the ribs. "Are they saying, 'Eat my Socks'?" she demanded.

I nearly choked on my hot dog. "No, they're saying something else," I said with a devious smile.

"Left field sucks," they chanted softly.

And from the opposite side of the field we heard, "Right field sucks," in perfect cadence, as if we were in an echo chamber.

Now hundreds of people in the right field bleachers were on their feet screaming, "LEFT FIELD SUCKS! LEFT FIELD SUCKS!"

Within seconds, we heard a booming echo rocking the stadium from the bleachers above West Waveland Avenue. "RIGHT FIELD SUCKS! RIGHT FIELD SUCKS!"

Each side was trying to drown out the other in a battle over who could be more rowdy.

"That cheer is moronic," Carol stated. "There are children in the crowd and it's totally inappropriate."

You'd never guess my wife is an elementary school teacher. Clearly she didn't appreciate the humor of the situation, but Sarah and Matt were busting a gut.

"Dad, I hope Sarah gets into Northwestern," Matt said. "We could have a lot of fun in this park when I get older."

"Yes," I quickly agreed. "I could teach you some drinking songs."

Carol shot me another dirty look.

"I mean, when you're 21, of course," I added.

Matt chuckled, but Sarah was insistent on making a point: "Dad, I'm not picking a school based on a ballpark."

"Of course not," I responded. "You can go to the college of your choice. And fortunately, all of them are near a baseball stadium, so we're covered no matter what."

She just turned the other way and pretended not to know me. But it was hard to ignore the Atlanta Braves, who were on fire that July night, lashing out 13 hits en route to a 7-2 pasting of the Cubs before a partisan crowd of 39,832. Shane Reynolds got the win for the Braves, while the Cubs ace Carlos Zambrano took the loss.

The hometown team had come up short, but my family was starting to get the baseball bug. Or at least, they seemed willing to join me at the games without too much of a fight.

Following the game we caught the "L" train back to the Loop for a stroll along the Chicago River. Vincent, a Chicago institution known for his friendly demeanor, multicolored suits and shock of white hair, provided our evening entertainment.

Vincent, the Man of a Thousand Suits, is a jumping bridge greeter – not to be confused with a bridge jumper. Rather, he serves as an unofficial goodwill ambassador to the Windy City. The whirling dervish is in reality Vincent Falk, who is world renowned for his spinning, twirling acrobatics above the State Street Bridge. You can see him perform pirouettes in the air on warm summer evenings while waving to the boats passing by on the Chicago River.

Vincent was a tireless entertainer and easy to spot on the Chicago skyline with his flamboyant suits, which sparkle in ever-changing hues of fuchsia, peach and banana yellow. He is also the star of a movie called *Vincent: A Life in Color*. The film is a tribute to the fashion maven known as the "Suit Man" and "Riverace," a name that rhymes with "Liberace."

Vincent was a man in motion and performed passionately to the joy and delight of hundreds of waving pedestrians. He never said a word, although I could swear he was muttering something under his breath. As I walked closer to Vincent, I thought I heard him say, "Right Field Sucks" – but perhaps that was just another Chicago legend.

Two years later, the Luerys were on the road again, this time to San Diego to visit Carol's family. And for me it was the perfect opportunity to attend Petco Park, home of the Padres.

◎ ◎ ◎

Petco Park opened in 2004 and is a beautiful made-for-baseball stadium, with a natural stone exterior and distinctive left field foul pole that's actually attached to a four-story building, which opens up to the field.

The Padres team store is conveniently located on the first floor of the newly renovated Western Metal Supply Company Building, which also features a restaurant on the top floor. But the coolest part of the park is the see-through fence in right field, next to a huge sandbox called "The Beach," where kids can dig for hours while their parents are digging the game. But if you fancy a seat with a view, the two upper decks are uniquely engineered to bring you very close to the action.

Like all modern ballparks, there is a huge bank of video screens and scoreboards to keep you up to date on every out-of-town game. For our game (on May 14, 2005), we saw Padres pitcher Jake Peavy strike out eight batters in a 2-1 victory over Al Leiter and the Florida Marlins. All the scoring was finished by the sixth inning, which made Carol and Sarah want to head for the exits, but Matt seemed to be enjoying the pitching duel. He was impressed with the musical mayhem greeting Trevor Hoffman as he entered the field in the ninth inning to a stadium-rocking rendition of "Hells Bells" by AC/DC. The Padres ace reliever came in to reel in three Marlins in succession, spear fishing his 404th career save in the process.

"You're looking at one of the greatest closers in the history of the game," I told Matt.

"Better than Mariano Rivera?" he demanded. "Rivera has more World Series saves than just about anyone."

"That's because Rivera plays for the Yankees," I stated. "It's an unfair advantage."

"But New York's a pressure cooker," he insisted. "The fans demand excellence and Rivera has never disappointed them."

"Except for the 2001 World Series when Rivera lost Game 7. Remember when Luis Gonzalez flared a ball to short center to single in the winning run for the underdog Diamondbacks?" I asked Matt. "Arizona actually trailed 2-1 in the ninth."

"Dad, I can learn a lot about baseball from you," Matt said. "You've been teaching me the game ever since you showed me how to switch hit when I was five. And then, as my Little League coach, you guided me on the mound and taught me how to pitch."

"And now it's time for the next lesson," I stated. "That's why I'm taking you on a cross-country baseball trip this summer, just the two of us. This is our warm-up game."

It was, as Yogi Berra once said, déjà vu all over again. Just as my dad had introduced me to the timeless game of baseball, it was now my turn to share the tradition with my son, a skinny but athletic 16-year-old kid with green eyes and a mop of blonde hair. He barely tipped the scales at 100 pounds soaking wet. But Matt proved himself to be a fierce competitor on the diamond, soccer field or tennis court against athletes twice his size. He used his quickness to his advantage against opponents, who constantly underestimated his abilities.

Matt was already in love with baseball – so what better way for father and son to bond than to hit the road and explore the national pastime through America's heartland?

This is the ultimate road trip – the story of how a father and son discovered each other on a cross-country journey made possible through the magic of baseball.

The Road Trip Begins

Saturday, June 18, 2005

Comerica Park, Detroit Tigers

*"You Tiger fans, you've given me so much warmth,
so much affection and so much love."*
ERNIE HARWELL

Life-sized replicas of Al Kaline, Ty Cobb, Hank Greenburg, Charlie Gehringer and Willie Horton surrounded us. The home of the Tigers is bursting with Bengals.

"Look, Dad, there are Tigers everywhere," Matt observed as we walked along Brush Street, home of the Detroit Tigers and Comerica Park. And indeed there are giant Tigers carved into the stadium itself, but these concrete cats are chewing baseballs with their oversized fangs, serving as a Motor City mosaic of modern culture, an ornate shrine to the secular religion of baseball.

Giant striped tiger replicas, radiating their orange and black aura into the night, surround the stadium. But the most impressive Tigers of all are the ones named Cobb, Kaline and Greenburg, who form a statuesque parade of baseball greats that include Gehringer and Horton — a living tribute to the legends of the game. Ty Cobb's statue shows him sliding into third, spikes up, of course, hoping to draw blood from his intimidated opponent.

"Ty Cobb was one of the most feared and most hated players ever," I explained to Matt. "He was a conniving, tobacco-spitting racist with a personality so abrasive that even his own teammates couldn't stand him. And when he died, only two ballplayers attended his funeral."

But Cobb's lifetime stats tell a different story, a chronicle that shows the fierce competitor who dominated the diamond for two decades. Ty Cobb had a lifetime batting average of .367 – the best of any hitter who ever played the game. Cobb won 12 American League batting titles and hit over .400 in 1911, 1912 and 1922. The Georgia Peach also hit at least .300 for 23 seasons in a row, showing his consistency as a competitor.

It's only fitting that Ty Cobb, a segregationist son of the South, would find his final metallic resting place at Comerica Park right next to the statue of Willie Horton, a beloved black player who epitomized the passion and soul of Detroit from 1963 to 1977. Only baseball could integrate two men from two different eras and make them statuesque teammates, baseball brothers bonded in bronze and the love of the game, forging a fantasy friendship that will last forever at Comerica Park.

Fatefully, the home team was victorious for our opening game, with Brandon Inge hitting a home run and double to lead the Tigers to an 8-2 victory over the San Francisco Giants, who competed without their best player and superstar Barry Bonds, a DNP (Did Not Play) on this warm Detroit night. Matt and I were jetlagged from our early flight and happy to settle in to our room at the Hilton Garden Inn – conveniently located just five minutes from the ballpark.

⚾ ⚾ ⚾

We woke the next morning and grabbed a quick breakfast in the hotel lobby. It took only a few minutes to load our rented Chevy Trailblazer with our two travel bags for the day's journey. Our first destination: Windsor, Ontario, a gleaming Canadian city just across the Detroit River through the Detroit-Windsor Tunnel, the second busiest crossing between the United States and Canada.

Windsor's pristine, sparkling beauty contrasted sharply with the grittier, grimy feeling of downtown Detroit. It was Matt's first time in Canada and so we drove along the waterfront on Riverside Drive, a scenic roadway meandering along the banks of the Detroit River. The steel monoliths of the Motor City shone in the distance, with the Renaissance Tower serving as our beacon.

We headed back to Michigan over the Ambassador Bridge, only to be stopped by border security.

"Purpose of your visit?" asked the border guard.

"A baseball trip," I said. "My son and I are on a road trip and he's never been to Canada before," I blabbered.

"I'm really more of a hockey fan," said the border guard. "Enjoy your trip," he said before waving us through to the United States.

Back in the Wolverine State, we drove on to Grosse Pointe Shores, a town nestled on the banks of Lake Michigan, where my wife had lived as a child. We wandered up to the house where she resided for two years before moving to Arizona.

"Wow, Mom lived here in this house?"

"Yes," I said. "Let's call her and tell her what it looks like now."

"No, Dad. Why do you have to ruin everything with a phone call? Can't you just enjoy the beauty of the moment and keep it in your mind?"

"No," I said. "My memory isn't what it used to be."

"Dad, you're impossible! How am I going to survive this trip?"

"Here, talk to your mother on the phone; tell her about the house."

Matt just rolled his eyes and stared daggers at me.

I decided to ease the tension by hitting the gas. From Grosse Pointe, we traveled west to Ann Arbor, home of the University of Michigan, my dad's alma mater – conveniently located just an hour west of Detroit.

$$\oslash \ominus \oslash$$

Dad was a proud Wolverine, always rooting for the Maize and Blue in the Rose Bowl, where his favorite football team was pummeled year after year it seemed, by the opponent from the Pacific Ten Conference champion. The Pac Ten had mastered the aerial attack, while the Big Ten was endlessly trying to grind out three yards on the ground with a cloud of dust, often falling short of the first down.

At the university bookstore, I purchased a Maize and Blue Michigan T-shirt in honor of my dad, who had passed away in 1997, well before Matt could really get to know him. So Matt and I walked the campus to get a feel for the school my father had loved and the place where he had worked as the equipment manager for the University of Michigan swim team before joining the Reserve Officers Training Corp to help pay for school.

"Grandpa Bob would be happy you visited his school," I said to Matt. He nodded.

"You know you can go here too if you want," I said with encouragement. "I can see you as a Wolverine."

"No, Dad, I see right through this whole charade."

"What charade?"

"The charade where you parent-bomb me with frequent visits to Ann Arbor, while secretly becoming a wannabe Tigers fan. What you really want is to visit Comerica Park."

26

"Busted," I said to myself.

"Well, Comerica is a beautiful park," I countered. "You can see the whole skyline of downtown Detroit from the upper deck behind home plate."

"Yeah, Dad, but I want to pick a college that's right for me – not because it's conveniently located near a ballpark."

"You sound just like your sister."

"She's right. I want to have my independence. And sometimes that means being away from you."

"But..."

"Keep it up and I'll be sure to pick a school that's far, far away from home," said the mouth that roared.

I ducked from the brushback pitch. "Wow, I didn't see that coming," I said.

"Well, I'm growing up."

Deep inside I knew he was right. Still, it's hard for a father to let go of a child – especially one who was obviously very eager to become a man.

U.S. Cellular Field, Chicago White Sox

Sunday, June 19, 2005

"Just chill, Dad.
We'll get there when we get there."
MATT LUERY

I could tell Matt's circuits were getting overloaded on Memory Lane. So we left the University of Michigan and took a lunch break in downtown Ann Arbor, where the sweet sounds of native son Bob Seger lit up the radio airwaves. I rocked to the rhythm of "Travelin' Man" as we ordered our sandwiches.

"Hey, this guy's not half bad," Matt said. "Who is he?"

"That's Bob Seger – a true rocker who grew up here in Ann Arbor." I said. "Seger's raspy vocal style is inspired by Little Richard. You can even detect a little bit of Elvis Presley," I stated in full nostalgia mode, recalling my years as a rock radio disc jockey.

"Oh."

"One day," I told myself, "this will all sink in."

We hopped in the car and turned on the local radio station where Don McLean's "American Pie" was playing. I cranked it to the max as McLean belted out his tale of a king losing his crown.

"The King is Elvis Presley," I explained to Matt. "And the Jester is Bob Dylan – who symbolically took rock in a different direction. You're listening to rock history here."

"And what about Lennon and Marx?"

"That's John Lennon of The Beatles and a reference to their song, 'Revolution,'" I clarified. "Ultimately, Lennon rejected Marx and his philosophy of Communism.

I was on a roll now, as Matt listened with a look of awe, as if maybe I did know something after all. "Back to 'American Pie,'" I continued. "The three men he really admires are Buddy Holly, Ritchie Valens and the Big Bopper, J.P. Richardson. They died in a 1959 plane crash in snowy Clear Lake, Iowa. They were en route to a concert in Moorhead, Minnesota, when their plane iced up and went down," I said. "Waylon Jennings was supposed to be on that flight, but gave up his seat to the Big Bopper, who was fighting a fever. That act of kindness saved his life but haunted him forever."

"Dad, sometimes you can actually be halfway cool, when you're not bossing me around."

I smiled as we headed south to the Hoosier State. We were destined for Indiana Dunes State Park, a sandy beachfront on the shores of Lake Michigan.

♖♗♘

Indiana Dunes offers a panoramic view of the Chicago skyline across an inland sea of fresh water. We took a quick stroll along the shoreline and I stole a furtive glance at my watch.

"Oh no!" I cried.

"What's wrong, Dad?"

"We're gonna be late for the game."

"Just chill, Dad. We'll get there when we get there."

"There's nothing worse than missing the first pitch," I pleaded.

"That's my worst fear in life."

"What's so special about the first pitch?"

"Because the game is perfect when it starts – with only zeros on the scoreboard. No hits, no runs, no errors. It's like a blank canvas that takes on color with every swing of the bat," I explained. "And every pitch is like a dot from the brush of an Impressionist master, painting the canvas with movements that are unique. And no two games, just like no two canvasses, are alike."

Matt nudged me. "Dad, I don't know much about painting. But if missing the first pitch is your worst fear, then my impression is that your life is pretty good," he said with a laugh.

"Smart kid," I said to myself, while suppressing a smile. Then I shouted, "We've got to make tracks!"

⚾ ⚾ ⚾

So we raced across the Illinois state line only to get caught in a huge traffic jam. The freeway was a sea of chrome, and traffic had slowed to 20 miles per hour. I had banked on gaining an hour by crossing from the Eastern to the Central time zone, but our freeway follies were too great a force to overcome – and by the time we reached the south side of Chicago to enter the ballpark, it was already the fourth inning.

As a baseball guide, I was destined for reassignment; surely I would be sent down to the minor leagues, forced to drive a golf cart the rest of my life. But Matt didn't seem to mind being an hour late.

"I'm hungry," was all he could say.

I stuffed a hot dog into his face and he seemed content. I settled back into my seat and tried to relax.

The White Sox were hosting the Los Angeles Dodgers for an interleague game at U.S. Cellular Field. The ballpark is directly across the street from the old Comiskey Park and opened in 1991 with an exploding scoreboard and a façade with arches to create a "retro ballpark" look.

Aaron Rowand drove in the winning runs for the Sox in the bottom of the eighth inning, with a screaming single to left that brought in runners from second and third. My son was excited because Rowand, with his productive at bat, had scored points for Matt's fantasy baseball team – a competition based on the statistical performance of the players on your roster. We were both thrilled by the fireworks that erupted after the White Sox victory. Chicago was having a charmed season that would eventually lead them to the World Series in 2005 – and the team's first championship since 1917, the year my father was born.

After the game, Matt and I rode the L train back to the hotel. We decided to celebrate by ordering sirloin steaks smothered in grilled onions at Smith and Wallensky, the famous steakhouse located above the Chicago River. We both looked around for any signs of Vincent, the iconic bridge dancer, but he was a no-show on this warm Chicago night.

⊗ ⊗ ⊘

No trip to Chicago would be complete without a visit to the John Hancock Observatory, so the next morning, Matt and I took the tour, which lifts you high above the waterfront. The Hancock opened in 1970, weighs 46,000 tons and rises 1,456 feet above the Chicago skyline (including antennas). The building promoters boast that the 2.5 million pounds of aluminum construction is enough to fill Lake Michigan as a skating rink.

As a budding architect, Matt was impressed by the view from the Observatory, where you can see the entire city below you – and on a clear day, landmarks as far away as Wisconsin, Indiana and Michigan. Chicago's skyline is magnificent and I couldn't help but notice that Matt's height was changing too. He had grown 6 inches in 2 years, stretching out to 5 feet 9. I had just an inch on him at this point and knew that soon he would be looking down at me.

We walked along Michigan Avenue and discovered a portion of the street was roped off for a movie scene. Crowds were lining up to see Jennifer Aniston and Vince Vaughn perform in *The Break Up*, a romantic comedy, in which the two characters first meet at the baseball mecca of Wrigley Field, home of the Cubs. "Should we hang out here to see Jennifer?" I asked my teenaged son.

"No," he said. "I'm hungry now."

I was a bit disappointed, but decided the best course of action would be a break for lunch at Bandera's. We scored a window seat two stories above Michigan Avenue, a perfect perch for people watching. We were hoping to spot Vincent the bridge greeter, but once again he was nowhere to be seen. Sometimes disappointment is part of the journey, but in the morning, Matt and I would be on the road to Milwaukee.

Miller Park, Milwaukee Brewers

Tuesday, June 21, 2005

"It takes more than that to kill a Bull Moose!"
TEDDY ROOSEVELT

Matt and I were cruising north along Interstate 94 in our rented Trailblazer when we noticed them. Conspicuous in their bright blue caps with the ruby red "C" in the middle, they were pledging their allegiance to the Chicago Cubs. By the thousands, the Cubs faithful were crawling along the freeway with us for 90 miles from Chicago to Milwaukee to see their beloved team play on the road. We were deep into the Dairy State, but Matt and I were surrounded by Cubs fans, and they were very intent on cheering loudly for their team against the hometown Milwaukee Brewers.

The Brewers play in Miller Park, named after the famous Milwaukee beer maker. Outside the stadium is a life-size statue of Henry Aaron, who played for the Milwaukee Braves before the team moved to Atlanta. Baseball purists say that Aaron was the greatest natural home run hitter in the history of the game. Hammerin' Hank smacked 755 home runs in a career that spanned 23 years – and every single one of Aaron's homers was man-made, with no cheating on steroids.

There's no argument about the beauty of Miller Park. It has a retractable roof to shut out the cold, but on this June evening (the first day of summer) the baseball gods let the stadium soak in the natural light with the roof wide open.

There's a great sense of Brewers history surrounding Miller Park, which honors Milwaukee's greatest players, including Rollie Fingers (number 34), Robin Yount (number 19) and Paul Molitor, who wore number 4. All the Milwaukee legends have their jersey numbers memorialized on the outfield wall.

Of the 40,000 people in attendance for the game, at least half of them were Cubs fans. They screamed loudly for Derek Lee, who crushed the ball over the left field fence his first time up. Lee also walked twice (once intentionally) and skied one deep to right field on his second time up. Lee was hitting .390 with 19 home runs and 10 stolen bases. I felt he deserved to be selected to the All-Star Game, but Lee trailed in the voting to fellow first baseman Albert Pujols, the slugger from the St. Louis Cardinals.

Brady Clark from the Brewers was Matt's fantasy league player. Clark hit a single down the line to left his first time up, but was thrown out by the left fielder while trying to stretch it into a double. He got another single later and walked, but the Cubbies ended up winning the game 5-4, much to the delight of the visiting fans from Chicago.

I had seen the home team out-rooted by the visiting team's fans only twice before: in Philadelphia at the old Veterans Stadium, where thousands of New York Mets fans drowned out the Philly faithful. And before it was torn down, the Polo Grounds in New York was the site of a game where I saw Willie Mays blast a home run to straight-away center field, nearly hitting the billboard at the top of the stadium. That was back in 1962, when the Say Hey Kid played for the San Francisco Giants in a day game against the New York Mets. The Mets were born in the Polo Grounds and played their first two seasons there – the very place Willie Mays had roamed center field for the then New York Giants.

On the day I visited the Polo Grounds, there were more Willie Mays supporters in attendance than Mets fans, so the crowd cheered heartily for the visiting player who had returned home.

My fond recollection of the old Polo Grounds sparked a lively debate with Matt. I told my son I had visited 26 ballparks, including seven that had since been demolished or abandoned.

"Those seven don't count," Matt insisted. "They don't exist anymore so it's deceptive to add them to your running tally of ballparks."

"No way!" I exclaimed. "Of course I can include them. I saw real baseball games there. They absolutely count."

"No, Dad, you can only count the parks that are currently in use."

I was not about to give away my baseball memories. I will never forget watching Willie Mays hit that towering home run at the Polo Grounds, or seeing Mike Schmidt smother a hot shot down the third base line for the Phillies at the old Veterans Stadium in Philadelphia.

And I can certainly remember watching Brooks Robinson and Frank Robinson play for the Orioles at Memorial Stadium in Baltimore and the Astros taking the field at the Houston Astrodome.

"You can't take that away from me!" I yelled. "And you can't erase the Padres games I watched at Jack Murphy Stadium in San Diego or witnessing the Giants at Candlestick Park in San Francisco."

I kept my mouth shut about seeing the Seattle Mariners play at the Kingdome, a concrete bunker masquerading as a ballpark, but I was in no mood to give up any stadium.

"But those parks date back to when dinosaurs roamed the earth," Matt countered. "Maybe you were there, T-Rex, but those parks are ancient history and I'm not allowing you to count them."

"Well I *am* counting them," I insisted. "My list will not be sacrificed to revisionist history!" It was pure playground rules: If I couldn't be the pitcher in this road trip fantasy, then I was taking away my ball so no one could play. End of discussion.

Our next argument flared up over the hot topic of All-Star balloting, which as it turns out, is a great way to have a dialogue with your teenager. You may never get him to reveal which girls he likes or what he does with his friends, but he will open up to a debate over which National League first baseman deserves to go to the All-Star Game. I insisted on voting for Derek Lee from the Cubs, while Matt favored Albert Pujols from the Cards. We compared the stats and found Lee leading all hitters by 60 percentage points in batting average, complementing his 19 home runs and 10 stolen bases. By contrast Pujols, while a great hitter, had much lower numbers.

I convinced Matt that the Cubs candidate was the better choice – so we grabbed a dozen All-Star ballots at Miller Park and voted for Derek Lee. We might have been in Milwaukee, but we intended to follow a hallowed Chicago tradition, where politicians for generations urged their patrons to "vote early, vote often."

Mentally fatigued from our divisive dialogue, we headed back to the hotel for a shower and a good night's sleep.

◈ ◈ ◈

In the morning, the blinking red numbers on the hotel alarm clock woke me up – it was 10:48. I looked outside the Hyatt window to see the Milwaukee Sentinel Journal and Usinger's Famous Sausage buildings. In the distance was the old Pabst brewery plant and in the foreground was U.S. Cellular Arena, home of the Milwaukee Bucks.

"Matt, it's time to get up," I said.

Silence.

"Matt, we need to get going if we want to make breakfast; the hotel restaurant stops serving at 11. Plus we've got to make Minneapolis today. It's 336 miles away."

Silence.

"Don't pretend you don't hear me!"

No response.

Then I realized Matt was completely plugged into his iPod. All I could see was a pair of white earbuds leading to this Stinkbug under the covers. Carol had dubbed Matt the "Stinkbug" early in life because of this post-natal predilection for burying his face in the pillow while planting his butt high in the air. He looked like some sort of prehistoric creature, a reverse praying mantis of the human kind; hence the moniker "Stinkbug," which we employed whenever he behaved badly. And now was one of those times.

Matt was totally tuning me out and couldn't hear a word I was saying.

This is how teenagers deal with dads when they don't want to hear what you have to say. They simply jack up their music so they literally can't listen and couldn't possibly hear you even if they wanted to – which they don't. We were having our third real argument on the trip, but I had the ultimate weapon.

"Matt, we're having a fight and I'm writing about it in my book. Everyone will know what a Stinkbug you are."

Groan.

Aha! There was life there under the blankets.

"You said I could sleep in today," said the voice from under the covers.

"I did let you sleep," I said. "Now it's nearly 11 o'clock and I'm hungry."

Silence again.

The Stinkbug rolled into a ball under the blankets.

The music from under the sheets was getting louder. I could see I was losing this fight – and feeling the need to bring out more weaponry. Suddenly, the phone rang.

It was my cell phone blaring "When the Saints Go Marching In," a clear signal that my wife was on the line.

"Carol," I pleaded, "Matt won't get out of bed and he's being a Stinkbug."

"Oh, let the poor kid sleep in," she said. "You've exhausted him visiting four states in three days. Give him a break."

Game, set, match.

Matt got to sleep in.

"Minneapolis will still be there no matter what time we arrive," I told myself in consolation.

But before leaving the downtown Hyatt Regency in Milwaukee, I discovered a little slice of American history in the lobby. As it turns out, our hotel was built on the very same spot where former President Teddy Roosevelt was shot and nearly killed by a deranged man during a campaign rally for a re-election run in 1912. According to the plaques on the wall, the would-be assassin's bullet stopped just short of Roosevelt's heart. TR's 50 page speech was so thick that it actually stopped the bullet from penetrating further into his body.

"It takes a lot more than that to kill a Bull Moose!" declared Roosevelt, who insisted on finishing his speech before being rushed to the hospital. His doctors decided it was safer to leave the bullet inside his body rather than run the risk of removing it. And indeed, that bullet stayed inside Roosevelt's chest until he eventually died of natural causes many years later.

As a dad, you're always looking for ways to make history come alive for kids, and I was delighted our baseball road trip had imparted such an important chapter of history.

"So what did you think of that?" I asked Matt.

"Dad," he declared, "Teddy Roosevelt was shot only one time, but 50 Cent was shot nine times. And 50 Cent is one of the greatest rappers ever. That's much more important."

"Matt!" I shouted. "How could you compare the shooting of a former president to some 'gangsta' who's worth only half a dollar? Besides, all he does is scream obscenities for a living."

"You're right," Matt said. "50 Cent is way cooler than Teddy Roosevelt."

Ugh.

God help the Millennium kids, the children of the '80s. They actually think rap is music. But to me, rap "artists" are nothing more than foul-mouthed felons spitting insults into a microphone. That's not singing. If tattoos were talent, they'd take the prize – but most rappers don't even know how to play an instrument. That's not music. End of argument.

Now when it comes to My Generation, we had The Who to show us the way. Of course they were foul-mouthed too, and yes a bit violent when smashing guitars, but I wish I could get Matt to understand how they were way cooler than Nelly and 50 Cent. Fortunately I would have my chance.

One of the great joys of being on the road is cranking up the right music mix of travel tunes to help glide you and guide you down the highway. In preparation for the road trip, I had picked out a dozen CDs from my classic rock collection – featuring Eric Clapton, Dire Straits, Emerson, Lake and Palmer and of course, The Who to serve as a our musical guides. I couldn't wait to turn up the car stereo to belt out "Ramblin' Man," one of my favorite tunes from The Allman Brothers.

"Matt, I've got the best road album to turn you onto," I declared.

"Dad, I don't want you to turn me on to anything. I don't want to be your musical lab rat."

"What do you mean, 'lab rat'? Just listen to the great guitar licks on this song," I insisted as I cranked up the volume to the melodic sounds of "Melissa."

Greg Allman's sweet serenade filled the car with a sense of soul. Next, we listened to the magical guitar work of Dickey Betts wailing on "Blue Skies," a song that perfectly described the bucolic Wisconsin summer day.

When the final notes faded, I asked Matt, "What did you think of that great fingerpicking?"

Matt just shrugged. "It was alright."

"What do you mean, 'alright'?" I asked defensively. "The Allman Brothers were more than just alright – they mixed Southern rock with rhythm and blues better than anyone."

"Well, I've heard it before."

"You've heard those tunes before?"

"No, but music that sounds just like it," he said. "It all sounds the same to me."

"How can you say it all sounds the same? Can't you just hear the way Dickey Betts makes that guitar scream with passion? It's inspirational."

"Yeah, Dad, whatever."

It was a crushing blow to learn that Matt didn't really appreciate my music. The only salvation was baseball. At least we shared America's pastime together, as fathers and sons have done for generations. As a dad you can take your teenager to a baseball game and never have to worry about being uncool.

The Hubert Humphrey Metrodome, Minnesota Twins

Wednesday, June 22, 2005

"Dad, you're going the wrong way!"
MATT LUERY

Thanks to our late start, it was pitch dark by the time we got to Minneapolis. Unfamiliar with the city, I found myself driving the wrong direction down a one-way street downtown, where another car was accelerating on a collision course.

"Dad, you're going the wrong way!" Matt warned.

I pulled into an alley and quickly corrected course. "Wrong Way Mike," I said to myself. My sense of direction is terrible, and how embarrassing is it to prove this to the whole world, with my son as a witness.

I quickly checked us into the hotel to avoid further damage and hid under the covers, hoping a good night's sleep might change my fortune.

Upon waking in the morning, we decided to explore the Twin Cities, heading over to St. Paul to see the State Capitol, where the marble dome radiates into the Minnesota sky. Just the day before, I had dragged Matt through the majestic granite statehouse in Madison, home of Wisconsin's State Capitol. Even though it was our second "statehouse" visit in as many days, Matt was actually interested to see the architecture of the buildings. And I was fascinated by the political intrigue inside the domes.

Next it was on to Bloomington for some Midwestern fun: riding the rollercoaster inside the Mall of America, which is so big that seven Yankee Stadiums would actually fit inside it, according to its promoters. Matt was like a little kid again, racing around on the rides.

We were hungry, of course, and Matt insisted on wolfing down a burger at Johnny Rocket's, where we listened to oldies on the jukebox. I fed the machine with plenty of coins, but my selected songs never seemed to get played.

"Dad, the songs are on a continuous loop – they play in sequence regardless of what buttons you press."

"How do you know that?"

"Sarah told me," he said.

My daughter Sarah had the inside scoop. She had worked as a waitress at the Johnny Rocket's in Los Angeles to help support herself through college.

"Yes," she would inform me later. "It's true, the songs are on a rotation. That's why they give you nickels to feed the jukebox – eventually, your selection will come up."

Heartbroken by the pay-to-play game, I knew it was time to leave hamburger heaven and head back to downtown Minneapolis for the main event: our visit to the Hubert H. Humphrey Metrodome, where the hometown Twins were entertaining the very same Detroit Tigers we had seen just four nights earlier.

The Metrodome was a concrete monstrosity posing as a ballpark. The Minnesota Twins proudly proclaimed that the "Dome" contains 40,000 cubic yards of concrete and a million pounds of steel! But to baseball purists like me, the game is supposed to be played outside on natural grass, not under a fabric roof that blows 250,000 cubic feet of air pressure per minute just to keep the darn thing inflated.

The only thing I liked about the "Dome" was the name. Hubert Humphrey was the nation's vice president under Lyndon Johnson and ran for president in 1968 in a hotly contested election against Richard Nixon. In the heat of the campaign, I somehow convinced my rock-ribbed Republican grandfather to vote for the Democrat from Minnesota. This was no small task, since the last Democrat my grandfather had voted for was Franklin Roosevelt in 1936. But when I asked my grandfather whom he voted for on Election Day in 1968, he smiled and said, "Michael, I didn't vote for Humphrey – I voted for you." Tears welled up in my eyes as I realized my grandfather had just sacrificed his vote for me.

I was honored that my grandfather had actually voted for the candidate of my choice, but the Hubert H. Humphrey Metrodome didn't live up to the billing. I was disappointed to see that Humphrey's namesake stadium was a baseball morgue filled with fake grass and a sterile, pressurized environment; it was similar to playing baseball in a tennis bubble.

However, the scenery surrounding the park was enticing. As we walked to the stadium from our downtown hotel, I couldn't help but notice a voluptuous blonde woman wearing a revealing T-shirt proclaiming, "This is Twins Territory."

"Yes it is," I said to myself while chuckling at the double entendre.

"What are you laughing about?" Matt wanted to know.

"Nothing," I insisted. "One day you'll find out for yourself."

"Find out what?"

"The mystery of life."

"What is the mystery?"

"If I told you, Matt, it wouldn't be a mystery, now, would it?"

"Dad, you've lost it," was Matt's response.

Inside the domed stadium, thousands of fans were decked out in blue Twins jerseys highlighted with red letters. In the outfield there were giant pictures of Twins legends

Harmon Killebrew, Tony Oliva, Rod Carew, Kent Hrbek and Kirby Puckett.

Tony Oliva was on the 1965 Twins team that lost to the Dodgers in the World Series, but he won great praise from Wes Parker, the Los Angeles first baseman. Known for his defensive prowess, Parker was named by Rawlings as one of the 50 Greatest Gold Glove players of all time. In 2011, I met the Dodger legend at a convention of the Society for American Baseball Research in Long Beach, California. It was there he told me that Tony Oliva was a "great player." Parker seemed in awe of the three time batting champ from the Minnesota Twins.

"If you saw Tony Oliva before his knees ran out, he was as good as anybody. Like a Clemente but a lefthanded hitter," he stated.

Parker continued in his praise of Oliva, "In fact, he was a Rod Carew with power – same type of hitter with power. Great ballplayer, great arm, good outfielder."

But despite the legend of Tony Oliva, the Tigers won the game 8-1, with Omar Infante parking one deep into the left field bleachers. The Tigers' catcher, Ivan Rodriguez, banged out two big hits, while the Twins' Torri Hunter, Matt's fantasy league center fielder, went hitless.

Matt's other fantasy player, Dmitri Young, the Tigers' first baseman, bobbled a play at first and had to leave the game with an injury. Despite the unnatural playing atmosphere, the game was fun and we really enjoyed getting great seats and sitting so close to the action.

The Twins would eventually retire their sterile stadium at the end of the 2009 season and move to a new outdoor venue in 2010. But that night at the hotel, I fell asleep to the fantasy of visiting the Twins again in their new park during a future road trip with my son.

The next morning, I was catching up on the TV news in our hotel room when Matt sauntered in for breakfast. We now had our road routine down pat. I would wake at 8 and eat downstairs, then head up to the room armed with fresh fruit, cereal and some blueberry muffins for Matt, once the Stinkbug was awake. Teenagers hate getting up early and I could see that Matt really needed his sleep.

I started watching CNN and witnessed a heated exchange between Ted Kennedy and Donald Rumsfeld. The senator questioned whether the secretary of defense was waging a competent war against the insurgents in Iraq. Kennedy grilled Rumsfeld and challenged his competency in running the military campaign.

Kennedy then accused Rumsfeld of supplying Congress with overly optimistic data designed to sugarcoat the true effects of the war. At one point Kennedy asked Rumsfeld when he was going to resign.

Rumsfeld seemed stunned by the question and finally blurted out that he had offered his resignation to President Bush on several occasions, but the president wanted him to continue his mission.

Matt was energized by the proceedings and said, "Dad, that guy Kennedy should run for president."

"He already did," I informed him. "Ted Kennedy ran in 1980 for the Democratic nomination against President Jimmy Carter and lost. His brother was President John Kennedy."

"Kennedy was a great President," declared Matt, before adding, "and so was Bill Clinton."

"Well, both Kennedy and Clinton were morally challenged," I countered.

"What do you mean?"

"Kennedy had numerous affairs while in the White House," I explained in my best paternal tone. "And Clinton failed to set a good example of how to behave as president."

"What are you talking about?" Matt asked.

"Well, Bill Clinton had an affair with Monica Lewinsky, a White House intern. She had oral sex with him inside the White House."

"Well, that's not really sex. Sex means, you know, having intercourse. You have to be able to create life to call it sex," he declared.

"Oh really, Mr. Smarty Pants? You can get a sexually transmitted disease from oral sex. Why do you think they call it sex?"

"Well, that's something your generation made up. Oral sex is not really sex. It's just foreplay."

Grrr!

"Matt, the bottom line is, he cheated on his wife and that's wrong. And if he cheats on his wife, that means he's not very trustworthy, and do you want someone like that running the country?"

"Clinton did a good job of running the country. At least we weren't at war. As for the other stuff, that's his private affair and I just don't care what he did with Monica—that's none of our business."

"None of our business? I'll have you know the White House is supported by taxpayers and everything that happens there is definitely our business. And I don't think it's right for a head of state to be getting, uh, well, to be representing America in that way."

"But Kennedy did it too!"

"Exactly," I said, realizing the argument was going nowhere.

"Thank you, Bill Clinton, for keeping us out of war!" Matt shouted with enthusiasm.

Yes, thank you so much, Bill, for changing the definition of the word "sex." You've given hormonally crazed teenagers a free pass to fool around and not feel guilty about it. And in so doing, you've provided parents and kids with plenty to talk about for generations to come.

Roger Maris and Maury Wills
Fargo, North Dakota

Thursday, June 23 – Friday, June 24, 2005

*"Roger Maris was as good a man
and as good a ballplayer as there ever was."*
MICKEY MANTLE

It was good to hit the road again. We drove west along
Interstate 94, meandering through Minnesota's prairie lands.
Native son Bob Dylan served as our musical guide,
accompanying us on the radio. I cranked up the volume on
our Chevy Trailblazer to hear the heartfelt harmonies and
soulful serenade from my favorite Dylan tune, "Knockin' on
Heaven's Door."

My daughter, Sarah, adores Bob Dylan. She's got a poster of
him on the wall above her bed. For Sarah, Bob Dylan is like
a religion – someone she listens to faithfully each day and
trusts implicitly – a god of the rock world. While Dylan was
clearly my daughter's idol, by contrast, my son was not yet a
resident of Planet Bob. In fact, Matt seemed bored.

"Bob Dylan was from Hibbing, Minnesota," I explained to
him. "It's a small town way up north, past Duluth."

Silence from the Stinkbug.

Matt was oblivious to my rock history lesson. His head was

nodding in motion to his own tunes on the iPod. I silently prayed that one day Matt would appreciate Dylan for his revolutionary impact on modern music.

But Matt was lost in his own world as we drove through 240 miles of Minnesota and crossed into North Dakota, my 49th state. I was now one step closer to completing my bucket list: essential things to accomplish before you kick the bucket. And topping my list was my dream of visiting all 50 states before reaching my 50th birthday – which was approaching fast.

I was anxious to explore the Peace Garden State – so named because the International Peace Garden forms the boundary between North Dakota and Manitoba, Canada. We checked into the Holiday Inn Express in North Dakota's largest city of Fargo, with a population of just 105,000.

Our first stop was the Roger Maris Museum, situated in the West Acres Shopping Center, conveniently located in plain view from our hotel room. The renovated Maris Museum is actually located inside the mall and features more than 150 artifacts from Roger's illustrious career including bats, balls and even the spikes he wore in the early '60s. Maris was from Fargo – a reluctant hero who never was really comfortable in the Big Apple, while remaining true to his rural roots.

The Maris Museum features Roger's old-time baseball jerseys, starting with the Cleveland Indians, then the Kansas City Athletics and, of course, the legendary pinstripes of the New York Yankees. At the museum, you can watch a video of Roger Maris' life from a viewing room while actually sitting in the right field seats from the original Yankee Stadium (before it was remodeled in 1975).

I wanted to take a picture of Matt – much to his dismay.

"Dad, why do you insist on taking pictures every place we go on this trip?" he asked with venom.

"Because I want to capture the moment."

"But I hate getting my picture taken. It ruins the shot and interrupts the natural flow of events."

I felt like he had just thrown a brushback pitch to knock me down. As it turned out, Matt wasn't done making his point.

"By taking a picture," he argued, "you are altering the authenticity of the moment."

"Matt, they're just empty seats unless someone is sitting in them. So park your fanny in one, since you're the only person I actually know here in Fargo."

Matt just rolled his eyes, then glared at the camera.

"I'm not smiling for you," he stated emphatically.

"Don't bother. Just be your grumpy self. I'll capture the realism you so desperately seek."

Click.

At the very same moment Matt and I were seated in those historic seats, my brother, Russell, was sitting in the real Yankee Stadium with his 8 year-old son, Shane, who was about to experience his first Yankee game. Russ called me from his cell phone to say he was at the ballpark.

"Really?" I responded. "That's amazing, because at this very moment, Matt and I are visiting the Roger Maris Museum in Fargo."

We were both caught up in the symmetry of the moment. The baseball gods, we believed, were surely with us today.

The Roger Maris video was a tearjerker. It brought back wonderful memories from my youth, as I watched the handsome, crewcut ballplayer circle the bases for his historic run at Babe Ruth. Maris eventually broke the Babe's record of 60 homers in a single season, on the very last day of the 1961 season. Maris was so frazzled from all the constant media madness that his hair began falling out in clumps, but he persevered to hit 61 homers in '61. Tears fell while I viewed the video of that historic homer sailing over the Yankee Stadium right field fence, with legendary Yankee announcer Phil Rizutto describing the action.

Roger Maris peaked as a player in 1961 and after that wonderful year, he would never again hit more than 40 home runs in a single season. Maris ended his career with 275 career four-baggers, not quite enough to earn him a ticket into the Baseball Hall of Fame. But in Fargo he is still a hero and every summer, the city holds a celebrity golf tournament in his honor. The proceeds benefit Shanley High, where Maris went to school.

The money raised from the golf tournament also helps Hospice of the Red River Valley and the Roger Maris Cancer Center. Maris died of cancer in 1985, when he was just 51. Many of his former Yankee teammates attended the funeral, some of them breaking down in tears.

Maris' good friend and Yankee teammate Mickey Mantle flew to frigid Fargo for the funeral in the middle of December. Mantle spoke from the heart – stating how unfair it was that Maris should die first, because Roger had been such a great family man and dedicated dad to his six kids. By contrast, Mickey was a playboy, a perennial magnet for wild women and alcohol.

"Roger Maris was as good a man and as good a ballplayer as there ever was," Mantle was quoted as saying at the funeral.

As a competitor, Roger Maris was tough as nails and frequently played with injuries. During the 1966 season, he hurt his right hand sliding into home and could barely grip the bat because the pain was so intense. He had multiple X-rays, yet the Yankee management never told Maris his hand was actually broken. The Yanks were more concerned that pulling Maris from the lineup in a year when the team was terrible would result in a massive fan exodus. After all, in 1966, Maris and Mantle were the only reasons for Yankee fans to go to the games because the Bronx Bombers bombed, finishing in last place, $26^{1}/_{2}$ games behind the Baltimore Orioles, the team that would win the World Series. Roger Maris hit only

.233 in 1966 and told the Yanks he wanted to retire at the end of the season.

The Yankees told him to wait until spring training, then traded him to the St. Louis Cardinals. While disappointed with the way the Yankees had treated him, Maris was happy to move back to the Midwest, far away from the New York media and the maddening crowds. In St. Louis, his teammates admired him as a fierce competitor and team leader. Cardinal outfielder Mike Shannon even gave up his coveted right field position and moved to third base to accommodate his new teammate. Maris helped the Cardinals win the World Series in 1967 – and after two years in St. Louis and a new World Series ring, Roger Maris hung up his cleats, never playing professional baseball again.

Maris' relationship with the Yankees was always strained until George Steinbrenner took over the team and invited Roger back for an Old Timers Game. Maris was reluctant to return until Steinbrenner magnanimously offered to pay for the construction of a youth baseball field named after Maris in Gainesville, Florida, where he had retired. Roger Maris attended the 1984 Old Timers Game and was overwhelmed by the accolades and adoring cheers of the Yankee fans. Roger Maris' spirit will live forever in Yankee Stadium, but he is buried in Holy Cross Cemetery on the north side of Fargo, on 32nd Avenue North, near North Dakota State University.

Matt and I felt compelled to visit Maris' final resting place. We pulled into the cemetery, not knowing where to find his gravesite.

"What do you think we should look for?" I asked Matt.

"I don't know, maybe a baseball diamond."

We scanned the cemetery and within minutes, Matt had picked out Maris' grave halfway across the grounds by spotting a diamond-shaped gravestone. As we got closer, I noticed it said "Maris" on it, with the words "61 in '61" etched into the marble, along with the phrase, "Against All Odds" – the same words inscribed on a plaque honoring him at Yankee Stadium.

As I walked closer I noticed a dozen baseballs at the base of the grave, each of them a gift from fans, offering a simple tribute to the man who symbolized Fargo in death as in life.

Kneeling at the gravesite, I was overcome with emotion. Here was the burial spot of the man who had won the American League MVP award in 1961. As a right fielder, Maris had a powerful arm that could gun down any runner who tried to score from second base. More than anything, Maris wanted to be known as a complete ballplayer and not just a home run hitter.

I silently thanked Roger for all the great baseball memories he had provided me in my youth – how he and Mickey, "the M & M Boys," had enriched my life with the love of baseball.

"Thanks for giving me a passion for the game," I whispered to Roger's grave. "And thanks for being a dedicated dad and devoted family man – that's truly the greatest accomplishment any man can achieve," I said silently.

I said my final goodbyes to Roger Maris and marveled over how he had battled adversity to become the single-season home run king. It would be 37 years before he was eclipsed at the plate by sluggers Mark McGwire and Sammy Sosa – both of whom are now tainted by the stigma of performance-enhancing drugs.

But for every heroic deed, it seems there must be an anti-heroic force trying to undermine it and in 1961 it was Ford Frick, the all-powerful commissioner of baseball. Frick was a baseball traditionalist who idolized Babe Ruth, the player who had hit 60 home runs in 1927, when the baseball season was just 154 games long.

Baseball expanded its season from 154 games to 162 games in 1961 in order to add two new teams, the Los Angeles Angels and the Washington Senators. But because Roger Maris hit his 61st homer on the last game of the season, Frick declared his record should be marked by an asterisk * to indicate that Babe Ruth – and not Roger Maris – was the real home run record holder.

Never mind the fact that Maris had missed a couple of games and ended up with only seven more at bats in 1961, Frick was determined to slight the Bronx Bomber with a lesser achievement. It wasn't until many years later that a new baseball commissioner by the name of Fay Vincent would remove the asterisk from the record books forever, crediting Roger with the glory he so justly deserved.

But Ford Frick and his frickin' asterisk would play a similar role one year later in robbing another baseball legend of a record-setting achievement.

In 1962, a National League player by the name of Maury Wills was tearing up the base paths for the Los Angeles Dodgers. Wills, one of the greatest base stealers of all time, was approaching the single season record of 96 stolen bases, a mark set by the legendary Ty Cobb. But Baseball Commissioner Ford Frick announced that Wills would have an asterisk by his name, along with Maris, unless Wills broke the record in 156 games, just as Cobb had done years earlier.

Maury Wills learned of his impending fate from sportswriters who were covering his every move. In an interview with broadcaster Jack Michaels many years later, Wills would recall the tension of the race, after swiping his 95th bag, late in the season.

"Maury, we just talked to the Commissioner Ford Frick and he said that unless you break Cobb's record in the same amount of games Cobb played, they're not going to recognize it," a sportswriter informed the astonished Dodger speedster.

Maury's response was to focus on his team's achievements. "I said, 'OK, we're just trying to win ballgames. We're in a tight pennant race.'"

Then Wills' competitive streak came alive in the battle with Ty Cobb.

"How many did he have?" Wills chuckled.

"Cobb had 96," stated the sportswriter.

"How many games did Cobb play?" Wills demanded.

"He played 156 games," the scribe clarified before adding, "It was a 154-game schedule and he played two extra games, got a stolen base in each game, so it goes to 156 games."

"How many have we played?" Wills wanted to know.

The sportswriter told him, "One hundred fifty-five."

Wills instantly realized he would have to swipe two bags in his next game to break the record.

"Why didn't you tell me this two weeks ago?" he laughed.

The starting pitcher for the St. Louis Cardinals that next game was Curt Simmons, a southpaw who could never stop Maury Wills on the base paths. Wills considered Simmons to be the easiest pitcher to steal a base against, while the toughest was Cardinal teammate Larry Jackson, a righty who did "some tricky stuff on the mound," according to Wills.

Wills was elated to hear he'd be facing the slack-armed Simmons in the battle for baseball's prize for stolen bases.

As Wills told sportscaster Jack Michaels, "I went back to the hotel, got my rest anyhow and got to the park early. Got the trainer there to give me a little rubdown and got into a whirlpool.

That was sophisticated in those days," Wills recalled. "You jumped in the whirlpool, a tub, to get started. And I got a little rubdown and went out and ran a little bit. Well, I felt great. I felt so light I was just kind of hovering over the ground. And Curt Simmons, he can't even get me out anyhow."

But Wills' luck was about to change. Somebody came running out of the Dodger clubhouse screaming that Larry Jackson —

and not Curt Simmons – would be taking the mound that night for the Cardinals. Wills figured that Simmons had gotten hurt, but later learned, Simmons simply didn't want the ball for fear of giving up the history-making stolen base to Wills.

But Larry Jackson did want the ball. "Give it to me," Jackson told Wills years later. "I'll get the little so-and-so," he said with an evil laugh.

But it was Maury Wills who prevailed that September night in 1962, stealing not one, but two bases at the old Busch Stadium in St. Louis to break the record set by Ty Cobb 47 years earlier. Not only did Maury Wills shatter the stolen base record with 104, he did it with amazing efficiency, getting thrown out just 13 times all season. By contrast, Ty Cobb was nailed 38 times while swiping 96 bags in 1915. But in 1962, Wills also led the National League in triples with 10. And he won a Gold Glove to clinch the Most Valuable Player Award in 1962.

The Maury Wills Museum in Fargo recaptures that historic season and his legendary career with pictures, posters and stolen bases from the ballparks. The museum is located at Newman Outdoor Field, on the North Dakota State University campus. Newman Outdoor Field is also home to the Fargo-Moorhead RedHawks, a minor league team. Fargo may be small, but it's a virtual baseball paradise and the only American city with museums featuring both the 1961 and 1962 Most Valuable Players.

How did Maury Wills end up with a museum in North Dakota? He never played there and he didn't grow up there, so I was curious to find out.

Matt and I visited Newman Outdoor Stadium and ran into baseball broadcaster Jack Michaels, who was the voice of the Fargo-Moorhead RedHawks, from the independent Northern League. Jack did the play-by-play for the RedHawks games and Maury Wills was his color commentator, offering inside-baseball stories to help pace the broadcast.

"Maury's connection here is through the Dodgers," Jack explained in a reverential tone.

"One of our former general managers was friendly with an old Dodger scout who actually signed Maury Wills for $500," Michaels added. Matt and I listened intently.

Then Michaels continued, "So when the RedHawks came into existence in 1996, the owners were looking for a way to generate some excitement here in Fargo. They invited Maury Wills to meet with the guys on the team. He came up and loved it so much, he decided to work with the guys for another season and before you know it, Maury was joining me in the broadcast booth, where he weaves his wonderful baseball stories into the game. And he's been here ever since. Would you like to meet him?" Jack asked.

My eyes lit up. "Wow, I'd give anything to meet Maury Wills!"

"Well, why don't you come back around 4 this afternoon? He's playing in the Roger Maris Annual Golf Tournament and he should be back by then," Michaels said.

Jack gave us carte blanche to tour the stadium and see anything we wanted to see.

"I've got to do some interviews now," he said, "but if anybody questions you, just tell them you're with me."

Wow, I couldn't believe it. Could it really get any better than this?

It did.

We returned to the stadium three hours later and found Maury Wills in the broadcast booth. I felt my knees quiver. He was much smaller than I expected, standing just 5 foot 8 or so and weighing maybe 155 pounds.

"Maury," I exclaimed as I introduced myself, "it's a pleasure to meet you! This is Matt – we're traveling on a father-son road trip to visit as many baseball parks as we can. I saw you play in the 1963 World Series against the Yankees at Yankee Stadium. That was the game Sandy Koufax struck out 15 Yankees that day."

"We had a great team that year," Maury declared. "We had Sandy and Don Drysdale, Willie Davis and Tommy Davis."

"And you," I interjected. "you were the catalyst who made it all happen that year."

Maury just grinned.

"Would you like me to sign that baseball, Matt?" Wills said softly.

Matt's eyes lit up as he held out his brand new RedHawks baseball – the very same one we had just purchased in the team gift store. And with that, Maury signed it, "To Matt: Thanks for being a baseball fan. Maury Wills #30. L.A. Dodgers. 586 steals."

"Would it be OK, Maury, if I took a quick picture with you?" I asked the Most Valuable Player from 1962.

"Of course," he said. And with that, Matt quickly snapped a shot of Maury and me.

"How 'bout if you take one with me and Matt?" Maury said.

"Now, Matt, come on over here and put your arm up on my shoulder like we're old friends."

Click.

I got it.

"And Maury, would you mind signing this T-shirt for my best friend, Marty Gonzalez. He's a true Dodger fan from California and watched you play many times at Dodger Stadium. It's a Maury Wills T-shirt. I bought it at your museum."

"Well, let me get a blue Sharpie – I want to make sure it writes with Dodger Blue."

And so Maury signed Marty's T-shirt, "To Marty – Maury Wills #30. L.A. Dodgers. MVP NL '62. 2,134 Hits. 586 Steals."

"Maury, thank you so much for everything. You've been such

an inspiration to so many people. The video in the museum talks about your battle with alcoholism and how you've overcome that to celebrate many years of sobriety. Congratulations – that's such a great achievement," I gushed.

"That's my greatest victory," he said.

Matt and I thanked him for spending time with us and we shook his hand goodbye.

Two months later, on August 22nd, I would meet Maury Wills again, this time in my adopted hometown of Sacramento, where the California Legislature was honoring him with a resolution urging the Dodgers to retire his number. I met Maury just outside the crowded Capitol chambers. Fortunately, he remembered me from our North Dakota adventure. Armed with tape recorder in hand, I asked him how he felt about the Capitol resolution, urging his "overdue induction into Baseball's Hall of Fame."

"Well I'm very grateful, appreciative, somewhat overwhelmed even," Maury said quietly. "And I think of it like other millions of fans around the country. I don't know if it's gonna work, but it's a nice thought. And hopefully it does because I would like to be there."

"Do you think, Maury, the Dodgers should have retired your number a long time ago?" I asked.

"Well, maybe, maybe not," Maury said. "It would have been nice if that happened. But it's gotten to the point in life I'm grateful for where I am today, without any resentments or ill feelings about anything," he said. "But when I go to Dodger Stadium," he added, "and I look up and see all those numbers up there, that are retired, I do. I'm being honest, I do say to myself, 'Why not me?' And maybe that'll happen now."

"Why haven't the Dodgers retired your number?" I inquired further.

Maury calmly explained the Dodger tradition for retiring

a number. "In the past," he said, "they've had a policy that only when you make the Hall of Fame, that was under the late Walter O'Malley's regime. But since then Fox has owned the club, then the McCourts, and they've changed some of the things. Jim Gilliam's not in the Hall. Hey, at least I was there with them and on the field with most of them and I enjoyed those memories."

I recalled that after the 1966 season, the Dodgers organized a trip to Japan to play some exhibition games there against the top Japanese teams. But Maury Wills did not make the trip.

"Was it possible," I asked the All-Star shortstop, "that the Dodgers didn't retire your number out of spite for your absence on that trip?"

Maury laughed. "Oh no, that's far-fetched," he said. "That doesn't even come into play. In fact the Dodgers brought me back for the last three and a half years of my career. So I'm sure that has nothing to do with it."

Later I would call the Dodgers to ask for the official explanation for excluding Maury Wills from the retired numbers at the stadium.

"The numbers are reserved only for Hall of Fame players," the Dodger official told me.

"But what about Jim Gilliam?" I asked.

"He was an exception," I was told.

Well, if the door is open for exceptions, then certainly Maury Wills, one of the most electrifying players in baseball history, should have his number retired at Dodger Stadium.

That's my story and I'm sticking to it.

And Maury's fellow teammate Wes Parker is supportive too. In an interview with the six-time Gold Glover, Parker told me that Wills was "the leader" in the Dodger clubhouse, along with Don Drysdale.

"Maury Wills did not make the Hall of Fame," I noted, "But

a lot of people think Wills should have made it in. What are your thoughts?"

"He's deserving," Parker asserted. He agreed that Wills should be elected into the Hall of Fame. And that would be the ticket of course, for Wills' number 30 to be retired at Dodger Stadium.

Few baseball fans – not even the hardcore ones who check the box scores every day – would know that Maury Wills and Roger Maris share both the curse of the asterisk and the blessing of having museums that honor them just 10 minutes apart, in the secret baseball mecca of Fargo, North Dakota.

The Dakotas

Friday, June 24 – Tuesday, June 28, 2005

*"Always go to other people's funerals.
Otherwise they won't come to yours."*
YOGI BERRA

With 49 states under my belt, I was eager to complete my American journey by entering my 50th state: South Dakota. But to get there, we discovered there was still plenty of North Dakota to explore. Matt and I headed west from Fargo along Interstate 94 and drove across the grassy plains of the Peace Garden State. We stopped in Jamestown to see the world's biggest stuffed buffalo, which stands 26 feet tall, 46 feet long and weighs 60 tons, dwarfing any human in its path.

"Let's get out and take a picture," I said.

"Why do that?" was Matt's retort. "I can see it from here in the parking lot."

"But if you don't get out, no one will believe how big this buffalo is."

"So what am I? Just a prop for your pictures? I am tired of being a pawn in your little game of Mapquest. I just want to have my own space."

"Matt!" I shouted. "You've got MySpace on your computer. Get out of the car now! Later we can stop anywhere you want to get something to eat."

"Deal," Matt said as he bolted for the buffalo.

I felt guilty about using food as a weapon. Instead, I tried to view it as a simple psychology experiment to produce good behavior. Either way, it seemed to work. Pavlov was right.

Click.

Within minutes of taking the picture, Matt had his sights set on a neighboring convenience store where he munched on Pringles before washing them down with a Dr. Pepper.

"You're lucky your mother is not here to see this."

"Don't rat me out," he begged.

"One day, she'll read about it."

"Ha, that'll be the day!"

I laughed, recording his words silently into my memory bank.

Just 20 miles shy of Bismarck, we left the interstate and headed south along Highway 83, a two-lane country road that meanders through a pastoral paradise, where we witnessed a spectacular sunset that painted the prairie in shades of purple and gold.

The last radiant rays of sun created a pink canvas in the sky as we crossed the border into South Dakota, my 50th state, allowing me to achieve my top goal of visiting all 50 states before joining the Half Century Club. I was ecstatic about notching number 50 on my belt, just a month before turning 50. I had beaten "The Bucket List" – a litany of the most important things to accomplish before you "kick the bucket." Years later, Morgan Freeman and Jack Nicholson would star in a hilarious movie with the same name.

"Dad, what is it about this Bucket List that's so important to you? Do you have some terminal illness you haven't told me about?"

"No, but the Bucket List reminds me of the old Yogi Berra line: 'Always go to other people's funerals,' Yogi would say. 'Otherwise they won't come to yours.'"

"Ha, that's funny," Matt said. "But what was Yogi talking about?"

"I think it's about closure. You know, accomplishing everything you can before you time is up," I stated.

"Or maybe Yogi just mixed up his words," Matt said with a smile.

We found a convenient hotel in the capitol city of Pierre and bunked down for the night. Now that I was knocking on the door of history, it was important for me to get my sleep.

Pierre is located on the banks of the Missouri River. The name Pierre is not French in origin, but actually pronounced "Peer," as we learned from our visit to the State Capitol. Matt didn't fight me about visiting yet another statehouse. In fact, he actually seemed to enjoy exploring the building. The South Dakota Capitol is 161 feet tall and made from native fieldstone, Indiana limestone and Italian marble. The South Dakota Capitol building was built by Minneapolis architects C.E. Bell and M.S. Detwiler for less than $1 million, according to the state Web site. South Dakota's dome is modeled after the Montana State capitol in Helena.

From Pierre, we drove south to Interstate 90, then west to Badlands National Park. We found the Badlands enchanting and loved walking along the fossil beds, which date back millions of years.

"Dad, do you feel at home here?"

"Yes, I love this landscape. Why do you ask?"

"Because there are so many fossils here – you just fit right in," he laughed.

"I guess I walked into that one. But it's great not being the oldest thing around – at least just once."

The terrain looks like a modern-day moonscape with its crusted canyons and jagged buttes pointing sharply into the South Dakota sky. Today the Badlands are home to thousands of bison, bighorn sheep and one of the most scenic grassland prairies in the United States.

The natural wonder of the Badlands could not have been a more jarring juxtaposition to our next stop, the tiny town of Wall, South Dakota, population 883. Some people might call it a tourist trap but to me, Wall is a wonderful place to visit, thanks to Wall Drug, one of the top roadside attractions in the country.

Upon arriving in Wall, Matt and I spotted license plates from at least 30 states on the town's main drag. Wall Drug, the main attraction, is not just one store, but 76,000 square feet of gift shops, ice cream parlors and restaurants. Wall Drug is famous, thanks to the 500 miles of billboards along Interstate 90 and its tradition of giving away free ice water – a brilliant marketing maneuver to entice thirsty motorists to stop and shop for merchandise that is not free. Wall Drug is a slice of Americana that's a must-see for anyone traveling across the Great Plains.

From Wall we headed west to Rapid City, South Dakota's second largest city, with roughly 68,000 residents. Only Sioux Falls is bigger in size, with nearly 160,000 people. We ate a casual dinner at Murphy's Sports Bar and then headed to Mount Rushmore to see the majestic presidential monuments lit up at night. The granite faces of George Washington, Thomas Jefferson, Abraham Lincoln and Theodore Roosevelt overlook the pine and spruce trees of the beautiful Black Hills.

A sculptor named Gutzon Borglum began drilling with dynamite in 1927 and after 14 years of intensive labor, he carved the 60-foot tall heads into the mountainside, which now draws 3 million visitors each year. The patriotic show was spectacular, offering a living chapter of American history, capped off with fireworks–a spectacular ending to a perfect day.

⊘ ⊖ ⊘

The alarm blared at 3:30 the next morning and for once Matt was not complaining about the early wake-up call; on this day we planned to go soaring into the sky in a hot air balloon. We met our group at the Flintstones Camping Grounds in Custer, South Dakota. The park is named after the cartoon caveman characters of Fred Flintstone and his buddy Barney Rubble – along with the whole gang from the prehistoric town of Bedrock.

Our tour guides drove us to a secluded field where we could hear the sound of propane gas ripping into the darkness while our getaway balloons were prepared for flight.

"Whooosh!" came the cry of the propane into the pre-dawn South Dakota sky.

As Matt and I jumped into the basket, we noticed there was no enclosure to keep us on board.

"How do we stay in the balloon?" Matt demanded.

"Don't lean over."

I quickly realized that stretching over the balloon to get a great picture might be the last photo I would ever take. Finally, as the red rays of daylight split the sky, our balloon took flight into the air with 10 of us on board. The winds were calm but we quickly found an updraft that took us high above the Black Hills.

We floated hundreds of feet into the air in our rainbow-colored balloon, soaring majestically like a cloud. I was struck by the silence of the moment and how magical it was to fly like the birds, gliding effortlessly across South Dakota at sunrise. Matt and I could see dozens of bison below us. They were fanning out across Custer State Park, running as a herd toward the horizon, while the wind carried us westward for a bird's-eye view of Crazy Horse Monument, the site of what is considered to be the world's largest active mountain carving.

Sculptor Korczak Ziolkowski started the structure in 1948 with Lakota Chief Henry Standing Bear. Their living tribute to Crazy Horse, the legendary Native American leader, honors his courage in battle defending his people from near extinction by the white man.

The Crazy Horse Memorial is a work in progress but upon completion, will be 641 feet long and 563 feet wide. It is funded entirely by public donations because Korczak Ziolkowski believed in the power of individual enterprise over government subsidies. Ziolkowki's descendants are still carving the Crazy Horse monument, which is now one of the top tourist attractions in South Dakota.

Our living history lesson was interrupted by a downdraft that took us closer to the South Dakota prairie. We were making a quick descent toward Earth and our tour guides warned us to squeeze down low and brace for impact.

Our hot air balloon had no landing gear and the only way to stop was for the basket to hit the ground at a right angle, using friction as a natural braking system. We kicked up a cloud of dust as we scraped the dirt, until finally the basket sputtered to a halt.

We landed with a thud in the middle of an alfalfa field. Far from being angry, though, the farmer invited us to join him for breakfast outside his home. His wife offered us juice and coffee, while our tour guides handed out blueberry muffins and poured glasses of champagne to celebrate our safe landing.

Matt and I were amazed by the homespun hospitality of the people in South Dakota, where a crash landing into a farmer's field could produce a spontaneous, friendly feast. In California, an incident like that would likely result in a personal injury claim and a nasty lawsuit, even if no one got hurt. By contrast, South Dakota still clings to the innocence of its pioneer past, with an emphasis on helping, not suing, your neighbors.

Early the next morning, I could hear snoring in our Rapid City motel room. Startled by the noise, I woke up only to discover the culprit making the sawing sounds was me. I decided to let Matt sleep in for a change; the kid was tired and deserved a break.

After a lazy morning, we headed to Hot Springs, South Dakota, home of the Wooly Mammoth site, a living research facility where you can actually visit an active paleontological dig.

Approximately 26,000 years ago, thirsty mammoths drowned by the dozens after losing their footing in a 60-foot-deep sinkhole. The limestone mud had buried the mammoths, but preserved their bones. At the archeologists' dig, we learned the fossils consisted of mostly teenaged male mammoths that had drowned in the muddy mix. Of the 53 sets of remains at the site, all of them were males, kicked out of the tribe by the adult males and forced to go out on their own.

"See what happens when you try to assert your independence too soon?" I said to Matt.

"Not funny, Dad," he snorted. "Just remember who made history here! I'll give you a hint: It wasn't the middle-aged mammoths who stayed home and played it safe."

"Yes, but the young whippersnappers were the ones who became fossils."

"Which is exactly why we're here," said Matt.

Ouch.

I felt like a chess piece in a giant game of "Teens rule, parents drool."

Neither one of us was willing to budge. So we decided to hit the road again, this time heading south on Route 385 to enter the Cornhusker State of Nebraska, our ninth state on the road trip. I wanted to give Matt the opportunity to enter a new state – even if it was just for dinner. We found a roadside diner in Chadron, Nebraska, the first town over the border, to chow down a high-calorie meal of deep fried chicken and country biscuits drowned in butter.

After dinner, we witnessed another beautiful sunset while heading back to Rapid City. That night, we watched Brad Pitt and Angelina Jolie star in the movie *Mr. and Mrs. Smith,* a liaison that proved to be the undoing of the lovely Jennifer Aniston.

My son may consider me ancient, but dinosaurs are the true natives of South Dakota, dating back some 200 million years, as Matt and I learned the next day when we visited the Black Hills Museum of Natural History in Hill City. The museum is home to Stan the Dinosaur, a giant Tyrannosaurus Rex that is one of the largest and best-preserved dinosaur skeletons anywhere.

Our living ancient history course took us next to Rushmore Cave, where the stalactites and stalagmites date back some 60 million years.

"Almost as old as you are, Dad," Matt reminded me.

"Thanks, Matt, but I'm only half that old."

As it turns out, the Black Hills are home to the second largest cave system in the United States, according to the Museum of Natural History. That was as much studying as Matt could take, so we decided to head back to the hotel to watch a ball game on TV. As a soon-to-be old fart, I needed my rest for the flight home to California in the morning. It would be the official end of our summer road trip – but just the beginning of more good times at the ballpark.

Dodger Stadium, Los Angeles Dodgers

Saturday, July 2, 2005

"I'm grateful for where I am today."
MAURY WILLS

Sarah would play a major role in picking our next ballpark. After being accepted to more than half a dozen colleges, she decided to enroll at the University of Southern California, her first choice. Luckily for me, the school campus is located just a few miles from Dodger Stadium. So after a campus visit to get her ready for her sophomore year, the Luery family headed for the ballpark, where the Dodgers were hosting the Arizona Diamondbacks.

It was a good crowd of 44,457 and the fans were treated to an arsenal of home runs. Chad Tracy, Jose Cruz, Alex Cintron and Shawn Green went deep for the D'backs, who won the game 7-5, even though J.D. Drew slugged two four-baggers for the Dodgers. The L.A. fans were merciless on Shawn Green, booing him every time he stepped to the plate, for the sin of bolting from the Dodgers to become a free agent and ultimately sign with Arizona.

In reality, most Dodger fans wished they had him back. Green, a former Toronto Blue Jay, was just the fifth player in the Majors to hit 40 home runs in a season in both leagues. Green was an All Star in 1999 for Toronto and again in 2002 for the Dodgers, but tonight, he was just the enemy who hit one out for the wrong team.

Meanwhile, Jeff Kent was having a banner year for the Dodgers. He was leading the Majors with a .424 batting average with runners in scoring position. In 1998, as a member of the San Francisco Giants, he had become the first second baseman to post 120 RBI since Jackie Robinson did it in 1949. The Giants should have kept Kent after the 2005 season, but instead he wore out his welcome with Barry Bonds and the rest of his teammates. Kent ended up signing as a free agent with the Houston Astros before eventually landing with the hated archrivals, the Dodgers.

We munched on some delicious Dodger Dogs – considered by many baseball fans to be the best franks at any ballpark – although Fenway partisans in Boston would definitely disagree. But the Dodger Dog is a classic at $10^3/_4$ inches long, sitting plush on a steamed bun. Fans can get them either steamed or grilled "the classic" way, which is my personal favorite, loaded with mustard and chopped onions.

Matt and I were savoring the flavor of our dogs, only to notice that Sarah was meatless.

"What's the matter, babe," I asked, "aren't you hungry?"

"Dad, I'm a vegetarian. I don't eat meat."

"Really, how long has that been going on?"

"About three weeks now, Dad. Haven't you noticed?"

"I guess I missed that," I said sheepishly.

To me, the only thing tastier than a Dodger Dog is the sweet sounds of Vin Scully describing a ball game on the radio. The veteran Dodger broadcaster has been with the club since 1950 – when the team was still playing in Brooklyn. Over the years he's painted the perfect picture of life at the ballpark by weaving stories and archival anecdotes that take you through the annals of yesteryear – from Jackie Robinson to Sandy Koufax, up to the modern era with Matt Kemp.

Dodger Stadium is one of baseball's most beautiful parks. Built in 1962, it was the second home to the Dodgers after they moved west from Brooklyn following the 1957 season. For their first four years, the Dodgers played in the Los Angeles Coliseum, a football stadium much friendlier to USC tailbacks than Dodger hitters. But the Dodgers did win the 1959 World Series in the Coliseum against the "Go Go" Chicago White Sox.

Dodger Stadium, on a clear day, offers spectacular views of downtown Los Angeles and the nearby San Gabriel Mountains, sometimes capped with snow. It seats 56,000 and is beautifully landscaped with 3,400 trees that are maintained by full-time gardeners. It is one of the garden jewels of baseball, with a rich sense of history.

Tradition runs deep in Dodger Stadium, where the team has retired the number 1 jersey for shortstop Pee Wee Reese and number 2 for long-time manager Tommy Lasorda. Duke Snider's number 4 jersey is also retired, honoring the "Duke of Flatbush," who played in six World Series for the Dodgers.

Jim Gilliam played his entire 14-year career with the Dodgers and his number 19 is also retired, even though he was never selected into the Hall of Fame. But Gilliam died at age 49, just before the 1978 World Series and the Dodgers honored him by putting his number on their wall of fame.

And of course, Don Sutton's number 20 is also on the wall, celebrating the pitcher who tops the Dodgers in wins, strikeouts and shutouts, along with games pitched. Legendary manager Walter Alston's number 24 is retired and of course so is number 32, the jersey worn by Sandy Koufax, who was the World Series Most Valuable Player in 1963 and 1965.

Koufax was absolutely dominant as a pitcher, hurling four no-hitters in his career, including a perfect game in 1965 – when not a single runner reached base by hit, walk or error.

Star-crossed Dodger catcher Roy Campanella was paralyzed in a 1958 car accident, but not before playing on five pennant-winning clubs and earning Most Valuable Player accolades in 1951 and 1953. His number 39 is retired, as is Jackie Robinson's number 42. Jackie broke baseball's color barrier, becoming the first black player in the Major Leagues in 1947. He went on to win six pennants for the Brooklyn Dodgers and was the National League's top batter in 1949, with a .342 batting average. Today, his legendary jersey is "retired" by every Major League team, except for the Yankees, where Mariano Rivera is still wearing the hallowed number 42.

The Dodgers have also retired Don Drysdale's jersey number 53. Drysdale won three World Series championships and set the record for six straight shutouts in 1968. But as noted earlier, Maury Wills' number 30 jersey is sadly missing from the Dodgers outfield wall. In fact, at our game, number 30 was imprinted on the back of Dodger first base coach John Shelby. I asked several Dodger fans why they believed the club had not retired Maury Wills' number. No one seemed to know, although everyone agreed it was an insult to the great Dodger shortstop and that by all rights, his jersey should be retired.

"Hey, but Ron Cey and Steve Garvey did not have their jerseys retired either," one Dodger fan pointed out to me. "Nor Davey Lopes," he added.

"But those guys only won just one championship, in 1981," I noted, "whereas Maury Wills won three, the first in 1959, then 1963 and 1965."

"Maury Wills should be honored here in Dodger Stadium," Matt stated. "I really enjoyed meeting him, and I admire his passion for the game. He made the Dodgers go in the '60s – and his number should definitely be retired here at his home park."

I nodded at the budding wisdom of my now baseball-savvy son.

"Remember what Maury Wills told us," I reminded Matt. "He explained that only Hall of Famers get their jerseys retired by the Dodgers – and that Jim Gilliam was the lone exception to that rule."

During our visit with him in the Midwest, Maury had confided to me, "I'm grateful for where I am today."

"Well, if the Dodgers could bend the rule once," Matt said, "then perhaps they could do it again for Maury Wills."

"Yes," I quickly agreed.

And perhaps one day the Dodgers will consider honoring the man who created more excitement on the base paths than any other Dodger player, second only to the great Jackie Robinson.

Rangers Ballpark in Arlington, Texas Rangers

Saturday, April 8, 2006

"It gets late early out there."
YOGI BERRA

It was five in the morning and pitch dark, but one thing was very clear: Matt was in no hurry to race to the airport. The Stinkbug would much rather be sleeping late on a Saturday. However, our flight from Sacramento was scheduled to depart at 6:05 a.m. – whether Matt was on board or not.

Matt didn't want to budge from bed, but I was on a mission: to arrive on time for our game at Ameriquest – now Rangers Ballpark in Arlington, Texas, where the Rangers were hosting the Detroit Tigers. It's a three-hour-and-twenty-minute flight to Dallas, which is two hours ahead of Pacific Time, so even if you arrive early, it's still late. Or as baseball scholar Yogi Berra might say, "It gets late early out there."

Of course Yogi was referring to the shadows that would descend upon Yankee Stadium during World Series games in October, but Matt was definitely not happy about leaving before sunrise.

"Why do we have to take such an early flight?" he demanded.

"Because I don't want to miss the first pitch of our second road trip together," I said optimistically.

All Matt could do was groan.

"There you go again with your romantic ruminations about baseball," he said bitterly.

"But you know the game is..." I started to say before Matt cut me off.

"I know, perfect before the first pitch is thrown," he stated. "I've heard it all before. Why don't you get a life?" he sneered.

"Why don't you get on the plane?"

On the flight, Matt pretended not to know me, as he donned his stereo headphones and cranked up the music from his iPod.

My teenage son was still giving me the silent treatment when we finally arrived at the Dallas/Ft. Worth airport. We hopped into a shuttle van and headed straight to the Crown Plaza Suites, just opposite the ballpark in Arlington. We arrived in the lobby a full five hours before game time and Matt was giving me "the glare."

"A penny for your thoughts," I laughed, trying to break the ice.

"You're taking all the fun out of this trip."

"Not exactly what I had in mind," I responded, "but at least you're talking to me."

"No. You really need to take a refresher course in good parenting," said the teenaged monster I no longer recognized.

"You make me get up early, then you drag me half way across the country, when I could be sleeping in."

"Come on, Matt, let's go for a train ride," I said, trying to break the tension.

Reluctantly, he agreed to follow me to the Trinity Railway Express, which is part of DART – the Dallas Area Rapid Transit system, linking Ft. Worth and Dallas. We hopped on board an eastbound train and arrived in just a matter of minutes in downtown Dallas, where we ate lunch in a park before briefly exploring the Big D.

But time was running short, so we boarded a train back to

Arlington, and that's when Matt finally decided to actually talk to me.

"Dad, I'm thinking about taking a girl to the junior prom, but I have to come up with a clever way to invite her," he confided.

"What's her name?"

"There you go again!" Matt shouted. "Why are you always trying to pry information out of me?"

"She sounds exotic with no name. Now tell me what you like about Mystery Girl."

"She's cute, Dad, and she's a softball player."

"Well, since we're on a baseball road trip, let's come up with some sports metaphors for her," I suggested. "How about if you write her a note and say: 'Matt and Mystery Girl, a big hit together'."

"That's kind of lame," Matt said.

"OK. Well, what position does she play?"

"She's a shortstop."

"I got it then. How about this: Mystery Girl, let's turn two. And we can double play together," I laughed.

"Uggh," Matt groaned.

"Or you could call her 'Diamond Girl,' a play on words from the song by Seals and Crofts."

Matt practically choked from embarrassment.

"Dad, that's why I don't tell you anything," he laughed. "Never mind, I'll come up with something better on my own."

I had gone down swinging on three pitches.

But a strikeout in life is not permanent – for a father and son can always speak the language of baseball.

"I hear Justin Verlander is pitching tonight for the Detroit Tigers," I said.

"I've always wanted to see him. He's one of the best pitchers in the American League."

"Well, tonight you'll get your chance. Verlander is pitching against Kevin Millwood from the Rangers."

Our conversation was cut short by the buzz of batting practice. Rangers Ballpark is a retro ballpark with natural grass and terrific sight lines that put you right on top of the action. In fact, the closest seats on both the first and third base sides are just 56 feet from home plate, shorter than the distance from the pitcher's mound to the catcher.

The park has a façade of granite and brick, with a home run porch in right field. There's also a hill made of grass over the center field fence, providing a natural green backdrop for hitters at the plate. The grassy knoll slopes gently upward to the foot of a four-story office building in deep center, which serves as the Rangers executive offices.

The hitting highlights of the game went to Chris Shelton of the Tigers, who smacked a triple off the wall, for his second three-bagger of the day, leading Detroit to an impressive 7-0 shutout over the home team.

During this game, the Rangers welcomed 1,000 baseball architects who had helped design stadiums around the country.

"Maybe one day the Rangers will honor you as an architect," I told Matt.

His response was to roll his eyes and grab the bag of Crackerjack out of my hands.

"Dad, why are you always embarrassing me with stupid comments like that?" he said spitefully.

"I just want you to know I support you. And I have faith in your abilities. I want you to believe in yourself, just like I believe in you," I said from the heart.

With that, Matt's scowl seemed to melt into a half-smile. "Thanks, Dad. You're alright, even though sometimes you drive me crazy."

That sounded like a backhanded compliment, but I was willing to take anything I could get in the way of goodwill. "How do I drive you crazy?"

"By pressuring me with your high expectations," Matt said

slyly. "You don't need to push me so hard – you underestimate my ability to make things happen on my own."

"Like getting up in the morning?"

"You see, that's what I mean," Matt interjected. "Just leave me alone," he said defiantly.

It seemed our baseball road trip was off to a great start.

Minute Maid Park, Houston Astros

Sunday, April 9, 2006

"That's lame, Dad."
MATT LUERY

Much to Matt's dismay, we were up early again, this time to fly to Houston. Upon arriving at George Bush Intercontinental Airport, we rented a car and drove 20 miles downtown to take in the city sights. The jewel of the skyline is the 75-story JP Morgan Chase Tower building. It spans 1,002 feet above Houston and is the tallest building in Texas. The Chase Tower is an architectural triumph designed by I.M. Pei.

"That building," I pointed out to Matt, "is why Houston has an edifice complex."

"That's lame, Dad."

"Maybe one day you'll design buildings like that," I said, then added hopefully, "or perhaps you can work on a baseball stadium like Minute Maid Park." Matt just stared silently, as if to say, 'Don't put any more pressure on me.' I took the hint and kept my mouth shut.

The downtown Houston skyline towers over the stadium. Minute Maid Park features natural grass and an actual train that runs on 800 feet of track behind the left field seats. In keeping with the name of the ballpark, the train carries Minute Maid oranges. The transit theme is a testament to Houston's past, when Union Station served as the city's central rail terminal in the early 20th century. The icon is ironic now in a city that is dominated by a never-ending sea of cars and chrome bumpers on clogged freeways.

Minute Maid Park is unique for having a flagpole located on the playing field – and an uphill slope in deep center that rises 30 degrees, creating havoc for visiting center fielders.

But the coolest feature is the retractable roof, designed to beat the Houston heat and humidity. Luckily for us, the day was sunny and dry with blue skies overhead.

But when the air is moist and hot, the roof closes with 50,000 square feet of glass, affording a great view of the downtown Houston skyline.

Outside the stadium, there's a statue of Astro legend Jeff Bagwell playing catch with Craig Biggio's statue. Inside the ballpark, Houston's Andy Pettitte gave up a lead-off home run to Marlon Byrd of the Nationals, but the Astros eventually prevailed in a 7-3 victory over Washington.

"For a football-crazy state," I told Matt, "Texas has two top-notch baseball parks."

Matt munched silently on his hot dog and nodded. He was still speechless as we headed back to the hotel. Within minutes, my son was back in dreamland.

⚾ ⚾ ⚾

We woke the next morning and drove to Rice University, a lovely campus surrounded by majestic oak trees that provide a canopy of shade and welcome relief from the hot Houston summers. The school is small, with 2,900 students and of those, just 100 of them are enrolled in the highly competitive architecture program, where Matt would later apply for admission.

We toured the architecture studios and Matt talked to students about the rigorous demands of the program. While academics are intense at Rice, the sports program is also very rich in tradition – especially the baseball program. In fact, Rice won the 2003 NCAA baseball championship, and at least two dozen Owls have made it to the Major Leagues – a tremendous accomplishment for a small, academic powerhouse.

After our campus tour, we headed west on Highway 290, only to find that Houston seemed to extend forever.

"Wow!" Matt exclaimed. "This is the biggest urban sprawl I've ever seen. It's mile after mile of shopping centers and car dealerships. People here must spend their whole life commuting," he continued. "I'd much rather live in a loft in the urban core of a city and walk to work."

"Many cities are developing their inner core," I said, "which is attracting young, urban professionals. But I think you're really going to like our next destination."

After a two-hour drive, we arrived in Austin – which dazzled us with an array of 10 foot-tall guitar figurines, welcoming us to "Guitar Town." We made a beeline for 6th Street to take in the city's legendary music scene. The street was jammed with music clubs and bars that filled the air with the country sounds of steel guitars and the booming bass vibes of rock music.

Matt was instantly smitten.

"I could see myself being here," he said.

"Yes," I quickly agreed. "This is a great town with lots of music and cultural attractions."

"And the girls are gorgeous here," Matt observed.

It was hard to argue with that.

We drove up Guadalupe Street and had a delicious rib dinner at Ruby's Barbeque, located just a few blocks from campus and then checked in to the Doubletree Hotel. In the lobby we could smell the irresistible aroma of freshly baked chocolate chip cookies – a treat for every guest – and the perfect sendoff to a good night's sleep.

⊘ ⊖ ⊘

By the next morning, the Stinkbug was refreshed and needed no prompting to explore the campus of the University of Texas. The school is world renowned for having one of the top architecture programs in the country.

Matt also had an interview with the assistant dean of the School of Architecture and then took a tour of the studios with one of the students. UT has an incredible building materials library, featuring 16,000 design samples including wood, stone, glass and concrete components where students can have an entire field trip inside just one building.

"Dad, this is awesome!" Matt gushed with enthusiasm.

"Yes it is. But before you go shouting, 'Hook 'em, Horns!' just remember: it's extremely competitive here and very tough to get in – especially from out of state."

Our tour guide told us UT enrolls just 63 architecture students in the freshman class and of those, 90 percent are from Texas.

Despite the overwhelming odds of not getting accepted, Matt liked UT's admission application: it is focused on student essays rather than portfolios. What's more, the school really encourages kids to be proficient in AP physics and calculus, brutal subjects for anyone. For me, a math moron, it would be impossible to give my son any sort of help on those topics – and I supposed that's the way the school designed it.

By contrast, writing a snappy story is something I can do in a matter of minutes, but when it comes to calculations or figures, I am totally lost. Matt, however, developed a proclivity for numbers, but I know he didn't get it from me. The only numbers I can really appreciate are baseball statistics. I love diving into discussions about Runs Batted In or Earned Run Averages, just don't ask me to explain geometric formulas.

One stat I can always figure out is the score and on this evening, Matt and I watched the Longhorns lose 6-3 to their UT rivals from Arlington. But Disch-Falk Field is a beautiful college ballpark and that's where we met our Texas friends Cheryl and Gale Hasselmeier. Their daughter Kristen went to USC with Sarah and the two girls had become very good friends. Cheryl and Gale treated us to hot dogs on a beautiful spring evening at the ballpark, where the entire crowd sang in unison to the Texas anthem, "The Eyes of Texas are Upon You."

I just love the Texas spirit, and I could see that Matt was definitely hooked on the Longhorns.

Robert and Mike Luery, 1977

Comerica Park, home of the Detroit Tigers

Statue of Hank Aaron, at Miller Park,
home of the Milwaukee Brewers

Dodger Stadium, home of the Los Angeles Dodgers.

Wes Parker,
Dodger legend

Atlanta skyline from Turner Field, home of the Atlanta Braves.

Petco Park, home of the San Diego Padres

North Dakota sunset

Yankee Stadium original seats
at Roger Maris Museum,
Fargo, North Dakota

Roger Maris gravesite,
Fargo, North Dakota

Maury Wills Museum, Fargo, North Dakota

Matt meets Maury Wills in Fargo

World's biggest buffalo, Jamestown, North Dakota

We have no landing gear

Crash landing in South Dakota

Rangers Ballpark in Arlington, home of the Texas Rangers

Minute Maid Park, home of the Houston Astros

Peter Golenbock, Matt and Mike at Tropicana Field, home of the Tampa Bay Rays

Barry Bonds on the brink of history, AT&T Park, home of the San Francisco Giants

Barry Bonds hits home run #715, May 28, 2006

A Giant celebration in San Francisco

Tarps cover the upper deck of (O.co) Oakland-Alameda County Coliseum, home of the Oakland A's

Kauffman Stadium, home of the Kansas City Royals

Busch Stadium, home of the St. Louis Cardinals

Matt, Mike and Marty Gonzalez in St. Louis

St. Louis Arch

Corny picture in Indiana

On the waterfront outside Great American Ballpark, home of the Cincinnati Reds

Rock Hall of Fame, Cleveland

High above downtown Pittsburgh

PNC Park, home of the Pittsburgh Pirates

Luery Boys:
Russ, Shane, Matt and Mike
in Boston

Fenway Park,
home of the Boston Red Sox

Duck Tours on the Charles River, Boston

Canoeing at
Camp Androscoggin,
Wayne, Maine

Basketball Hall of Fame,
Springfield, Massachusetts

My sister Roberta
(1967 – 1988)

My vandalized boyhood home, Stamford, Connecticut

Tropicana Field, Tampa Bay Rays

Wednesday, April 12, 2006

"This guy hits moon shots."
PETER GOLENBOCK

Matt wasn't happy about the early-morning departure from Austin. But the Luery boys were heading east to Florida, where the day was already an hour ahead of us. I was excited about seeing my lifelong friend Peter Golenbock, who had been my counselor at Camp Androscoggin in Maine more than four decades earlier.

Peter was the baseball coach at Androscoggin, where he guided a group of semi-talented 11-and 12-year-old kids to a terrific season in 1967, winning eight games and losing only two.

Peter is now a sports journalist and prolific author living in St. Petersburg, where we visited the pier and enjoyed a seafood lunch high above Tampa Bay. Peter gave us a tour of the city, then took us to Tropicana Field, home of the Tampa Bay Devil Rays, a team that two years later would re-brand itself as the Tampa Bay Rays, dropping the name "Devil" altogether.

The team owners would say the change simply highlighted the rays of sunshine over Tampa Bay, but skeptics were convinced the club was trying to appease religious conservatives by dropping the name "Devil."

For most baseball fans, there was no conspiracy, just a gnawing need for new luck, for a team that always had a devil of a time escaping the basement of the American League standings. From their inception in 1998 through 2005, the Devil Rays had finished in last place every year except for three times, an incredible record of ineptitude that required something – anything – to change. The plan may actually have worked because in 2008, the newly named Tampa Bay Rays miraculously made it to the World Series for the first time in team history.

Tropicana Field is an enclosed stadium with a domed roof comprised of Teflon-coated fiberglass. It's the only Major League stadium with artificial turf and an all-dirt base path.

"The Rays consider this a state-of-the-art stadium," Peter told me.

"Well, as a baseball purist, I call it ugly," I said in protest. "There's no natural grass and ironically, you can't see the sky in a place that calls itself The Sunshine State."

Matt chimed in. "I agree," he said. "I'm just not a big fan of domed stadiums."

In the absence of natural elements like wind and sun, the atmosphere at Tropicana Field is antiseptic and devoid of any character. However, on the plus side, there's never been a rainout there.

Our game would turn out to be an exciting one. In the bottom of the eighth inning, the Rays loaded the bases as slugger Jonny Gomes stepped up to the plate. Gomes dug his spikes into the dirt and Peter declared, "I hope you get a chance to see this guy smack it, because he hits moon shots."

Baltimore pitcher Sendy Rleal then hung a curveball that Gomes smacked high and deep – a moon shot deep into the left field seats for a grand slam home run, sending the crowd into a frenzy. Matt and I slapped high-fives with Peter, who had successfully called the shot that rocked the Rays to a 7-4 win over the Orioles.

To me there's nothing more exciting in baseball than witnessing a game-winning home run – especially one with the bases loaded. I could only imagine what Gomes was thinking as he rounded third base. Four years later, I would have a chance to interview a player who knew firsthand what it's like to be the hero of the game.

As a member of the Toronto Blue Jays, Ed Sprague Jr. hit a game-winning home run in Game Two of the 1992 World Series against Jeff Riordan, one of the top relievers at that time. Ed's homer made the difference in launching the Jays to their first World Championship ever, in a win over the Atlanta Braves.

In 2010, I chatted with Ed in Stockton, California, where he's now the head baseball coach for the University of the Pacific Tigers. While on campus, I asked him about the pressure of pinch-hitting against Riordan in a pivotal game.

"Well, I had pinch hit in the playoffs a little bit," Sprague told me. "I got an opportunity. I was actually in the dugout and happened to have my bat in my hand, in Game One in the American League Championship Series against the A's, and they were beating us pretty good. And Cito [manager Cito Gaston] actually came in. Cito looked out and saw I had my bat and said I'd pinch hit for Manny Lee or somebody. I got a base hit in that game," Sprague explained.

"So I think he thought maybe this kid can pinch hit. I got an opportunity to pinch hit in Oakland against Eckersly and he punched me out. But we rallied and Alomar hit the big home run that sent us on. That was kind of my role in Game Two. He gave me plenty of warning, I was going to hit for Duane Ward in the bottom of the inning, so I went back and got loose."

Sprague sought advice from Blue Jays Designated Hitter Rance Mulliniks, asking what approach he should take at the plate.

Mulliniks told him, "Ed, he's a high fastball pitcher; he's going to try to get you to elevate the fastball. Just make sure he gets it down."

Sprague was thinking about taking the first pitch from Riordan, but he decided instead to be aggressive at the plate. "Most of the time you want to come off the bench and come up swinging," he explained. "So that was it."

"And it was on the first pitch that you hit it out? " I asked.

"First pitch fastball, yup," Sprague confirmed.

"And he got it right in your power zone?"

"Exactly."

"What was it like when you saw that ball go over the fence for a two-run homer that turned out to be the game-winning hit?"

"Well, I was excited, obviously," the World Series hero said. "I think probably the most exciting thing was looking in our dugout as I was rounding the bases and seeing everybody jump up and down...This is, essentially, you know, my second year, but I was still in my rookie campaign. I had a partial year in '91 and a partial year in '92 and so when you get back to the bench and Dave Winfield's giving you a big chest bump and everything else, it was pretty special."

Throughout his baseball career, Ed Sprague Jr. made a mark of winning big games, including back-to-back college World Series championships for the Stanford Cardinal in 1987 and 1988—the same year he won an Olympic Gold Medal with the U.S. Men's baseball team. Sprague would later go on to win back-to-back World Series titles with the Toronto Blue Jays, making him the only player ever to earn consecutive championships in both college and Major League Baseball on top of earning an Olympic Gold Medal.

I wondered how the grandeur of hitting a game-winning World Series home run compared with his past accolades from college.

"I think it's just different," he said. "Winning the College World Series in '87 was the pinnacle of where we could be. I mean, you couldn't be any higher than that, so that was very special. I'd still say, above everything, that was probably the most special because that was our first championship that I'd experienced. It was the first one for Stanford. You know, you live with guys, it's different – you're with these guys 24/7; it's just a different atmosphere. And then to repeat that was amazing as well.

But you know, winning the World Series," Sprague continued, "you're at the ultimate peak of what you can do as a professional ballplayer. To be a part of it was really something special and to do it for a Canadian team, and really you don't just have one city or one state rooting for you, you have an entire country that was rooting for you. It was quite a different experience."

I was elated that Matt had the chance to experience the joy and exhilaration of witnessing a game-winning home run – a dramatic ending to a terrific evening in Tampa Bay.

Sun Life (Dolphins) Stadium, Florida Marlins

Friday, April 14, 2006

*"If you don't know where you are going,
you might not get there."*
YOGI BERRA

Matt was grumpy and I can't say I blamed him. Who could be enthused about a 4:30 a.m. wake-up call? Certainly not the Stinkbug, who dragged his little carcass around so slowly, we barely made the 6:30 flight from Tampa to Miami.

By 8 o'clock we were on the ground in Miami and cruising along in our rental car, when I realized something was wrong. The coffee hadn't kicked in yet, so it took me several miles to figure out I was traveling north instead of south on La Jeune Road.

Wrong Way Mike had done it again.

"Dad, why did you get me up so early only to go the wrong direction?" Matt asked with biting sarcasm. "I could have slept in longer if I knew you were going to waste all this time by going the wrong way."

Some people have an internal compass that guides them, but my instincts always seem to get me lost. And Matt was not about to let me forget it.

"Dad, do you know where you're going?" he yelled.

"Of course I do, Matt," I said with false bravado.

"Yeah, I think you're going nowhere – fast," he said in his most insulting tone. "Why don't you pull over and ask directions?"

He was right. I was lost. So I pulled into a gas station and asked for directions to the University of Miami campus. Upon finally arriving, I parked the car carefully, while Matt bolted and did his best to avoid me. I found him moments later on a student-led tour of the School of Engineering.

Next, a staff member guided us through the School of Architecture, where the studios were filled with students working on projects.

Matt was most impressed by the tropical palm trees and manmade lakes on campus. "This school looks like a resort," he said.

But in talking to students on campus, we quickly learned just how challenging the academic workload could be for architecture students. Architecture majors, we were told, typically did not join fraternities – there simply was no time to be studs with suds when there was so much studio work to do.

The University of Miami has strong credentials in urban design and is very selective in the admissions process. Only 55 freshmen enroll every year in the architecture program, from a campus of 9,000 students, with about 60 percent of them female. I could tell Matt was very impressed by the campus sights, but we were both tired and anxious to find the car.

As we headed back to the parking lot, I slowly began to realize that nothing looked familiar. We walked aimlessly for half an hour until Matt broke the silence.

"Dad, do you know we're walking in circles?" he said acrimoniously.

"No we're not," I said with bluster, knowing I was about to be busted.

Wrong Way Mike had done it again, getting us lost twice in

one day. I tried valiantly to find humor in the situation.

"It's like Yogi says – if you don't know where you are going, you might not get there."

"That's it, you're fired as trip director," said Matt as he took off in the other direction to search for the car.

I stood my ground and intensified my search, right where I was, somewhere between hopelessly lost and desperate.

"Call me on your cell phone if you find the car," I said hopefully.

"You're on your own!"

Twenty minutes later, I was still circling my shadow in the parking lot when the ring of my cell phone broke the silence that surrounded me.

"I found the car, Sherlock Holmes," said the Terrible Teen.

"Where are you?" I demanded.

"I'm not telling," he snorted. "Not until you promise I can sleep in tomorrow."

"Deal!"

✽ ✽ ✽

I kept my word and Matt slept until noon the next day. After a quick brunch, we toured Vizcaya Museum and gardens – the beautiful home of a former industrialist located on the waterfront. Next we drove down to Miami Beach and strolled along the white sands surrounding the Art Deco District – which is considered to be the largest concentration of architecture from the 1920s and '30s in the world. We stopped briefly to watch a polo match on the beach, featuring horses running at full throttle in the midst of luxury condominiums.

Miami's waterfront was impressive as we drove on to Dolphins Stadium (as it was then known) located some 25 miles north of downtown, taking you nearly all the way to Ft. Lauderdale. The suburban stadium was the home venue for the Florida Marlins from 1993–2011. However, the Marlins were merely visitors there, simply occupying space in the summer until the Dolphins arrive in the fall. Dolphins Stadium, as the name implies, is built for football.

Multi-use stadiums never really work as baseball parks because fans are so far away from the action and there is no level of intimacy – and in Miami, the empty seats often outnumber the paying visitors.

But on this warm Florida night, it was great to be at a ball game, especially with the hometown Marlins victorious 5-3 over the Washington Nationals. Dontrelle Willis got his first victory of the season despite giving up two runs in the first inning.

Dolphins Stadium would be renamed Sun Life Stadium in 2009 – but the Marlins plan to open a new baseball-only ballpark in 2012. It will be built on the site of the old Orange Bowl in the Little Havana section of Miami, less than two miles from downtown. Best of all, it will have natural grass and a retractable roof – to help ward off the rain and high humidity. The new ballpark will have 37,000 seats, and Matt and I plan to be there in 2012 to keep alive our streak of visiting every Major League stadium.

Turner Field, Atlanta Braves

Saturday, April 15, 2006

*"Sometimes the best plans
are no plans at all."*
MATT LUERY

Our day began with another early flight and of course, another fight with Matt over getting out of bed.

"Dad, why are you dragging me out of bed so early on a Saturday?" the Stinkbug wanted to know.

"It's time to fly to Atlanta. We have big plans."

"Sometimes the best plans are no plans at all," he countered.

Yes, I admit, I did have an agenda. First, to check out the Georgia Tech campus, where the Yellow Jackets were battling the Clemson Tigers in a college baseball game. We sampled the action for a couple of innings; long enough to see the Yellow Jackets take a 5-3 lead on a two-run double.

Georgia Tech has some great athletic teams, but it is also an academic pressure cooker, as Matt discovered by talking with one of the students.

"What's the life here on campus like?" Matt asked.

"Well," said the student, "there are three basic activities: You can study. You can have a social life. Or you can sleep. And at Georgia Tech, you get to pick which two you want."

Matt laughed, but deep inside I think he realized he might be in over his head at Georgia Tech.

"Matt," I said, "it may be an intense, competitive environment, but students at Georgia Tech say they graduate with instant job offers. And that's a good thing."

He shrugged his shoulders and headed for the car. We took a spin across Atlanta to Tech's crosstown rival, Emory College, then made a brief detour to see the outside of the Georgia State Capitol.

But it was Turner Field that proved to be the gem of Atlanta. From high up above the backstop, you can see the entire Atlanta skyline, including the red neon bottle marking the Coca-Cola headquarters building. The skyscrapers glistened as Atlanta's downtown turned from day to night.

The field is built for baseball and includes all-natural grass and two huge vision boards to provide game highlights. There's even a 27-foot-long neon tomahawk to help fans do the "Tomahawk Chop" in the middle of a Braves rally. Even on televised games, you can hear the fans chanting, "Ooooooh, ah – oooooooah!"

Turner Field pays tribute to the storied history of the Atlanta Braves, with giant baseballs on the outfield wall, honoring retired numbers 3, 35 and 44 – along with 21, 41 and 42. Number 3 represents Dale Murphy, who holds the Atlanta franchise record for most home runs (371), RBIs (1,143), hits (1,901), runs (1,103) and games played (1,926).

Henry Aaron, number 44, played his entire career with the Braves, hitting 755 home runs, but many of those dingers occurred when Aaron wore a Milwaukee uniform; well before the team moved to Atlanta in 1966. Hammerin' Hank dominated baseball for two decades – hitting 20 or more home runs for 20 seasons in a row. He hit 245 of his homers after turning 35 – an age at which most sluggers are well past their prime.

Aaron had a batting average of at least .300 for 14 seasons and was the model of consistency as a player. He began his career in 1954 and played for 23 years, finishing with the most runs batted in (2,297) and the most extra-base hits lifetime, with 1,477. His home run total is second only to Barry Bonds (762), but Aaron did it naturally, without any performance-enhancing drugs. Most baseball fans believe Barry Bonds used steroids to inflate his stats (I'll have plenty to say on that topic in the next chapter).

The other retired numbers at Turner Field include several pitchers: Warren Spahn (21), Greg Maddux (31) and Phil Niekro (35). Number 41 belongs to Eddie Mathews, a third baseman and nine-time All Star who played for the Braves in Atlanta, Milwaukee and even Boston – where the franchise first began. And of course, 42 is the retired number for Jackie Robinson, the Brooklyn Dodger who first integrated baseball in 1947.

The Braves have done a great job of highlighting their history, but on this night the story was John Smoltz, who shut out the Padres 2-0 on a four-hitter.

After the game, Matt and I took a 10-minute walk from Turner Field to our hotel room at the Comfort Inn – literally across the street from the park. In the morning, we flew back to California, wrapping up a Southern road trip to five Major League parks and two college baseball stadiums. But our baseball journey was not over – in fact the year's most important chapter was about to unfold.

Barry Bonds Hits His 715th Home Run

Sunday, May 28, 2006

AT&T Park, San Francisco Giants

"He was going after the Babe because he felt black ballplayers didn't get their shot."
RON HYDE

Giants slugger Barry Bonds was on the brink of history, tied with Babe Ruth at 714 lifetime home runs. Like every baseball fan in America, I wanted to be in the stands to see Barry Bonds hit the next shot that would be seen and heard around the world. Unlike every baseball fan though, Matt and I had miraculously scored tickets to see San Francisco host the Colorado Rockies on the last day of a home stand before the Giants hit the road.

It was really luck more than anything else, but by looking at the baseball schedule early in the season, I tried to anticipate what might be Bond's date with history. The Giants slugger needed only seven dingers to eclipse the Babe when the 2006 season began, so I figured Bonds might be close by mid-May. But I also suspected that Bonds would stall at 714 and buckle under the pressure, as any human would likely do. So I picked out two seats for Sunday, May 28, and hoped my hunch would be right.

Bonds smacked number 714 against the Oakland A's on May 20 – and on that day I figured I had overestimated the pressure quotient. But Bonds went homerless for 17 official at bats spanning over five games, and now the schedule dictated that our game would be the last chance for Barry to hit one out before hitting the road. And with the Florida Marlins next on the schedule, I believed the baseball gods would not want Bonds to break the record in a near-empty stadium.

Of course, baseball purists were actively rooting against Bonds, calling him a steroid abuser whose accomplishments only tainted the game through the use of performance-enhancing drugs. Fans in visiting ballparks would throw toy syringes onto the field and chant, "Stair- ROIDS, Stair-ROIDS!" whenever he stepped up to the plate.

But even the most hardened cynics could not negate the electric atmosphere in San Francisco on this sunny spring day. AT&T Park (previously Pacific Bell Park) was filled to capacity with fans in every one of the 41,503 seats. Built in 2000 as the first privately financed baseball venue since Dodger Stadium in 1962, the Giants had presciently planned their diamond with number 25, Barry Bonds, in mind. The right field pole is just 309 feet from home plate, giving Bonds a shot at jacking one into the Splash Zone of McCovey Cove even on a check swing. This ballpark is in fact dripping with history, from Willie McCovey's tribute to the nine-foot statue in the front of the stadium depicting Willie Mays. It had been the Say Hey Kid who electrified Giants fans from New York to San Francisco as one of the greatest center fielders ever to play the game.

The park also features a giant, 80-foot Coca-Cola bottle with playground slides for the kids and tasty shrimp gumbo at a snack stand named after former first baseman Orlando Cepeda (in the stands behind center field). Fans lucky enough to sit in the first row of seats are just 48 feet from home plate, placing them closer to the batter than even the pitcher.

AT&T is the only stadium in Major League Baseball offering a built-in section for fans to see the game for free. The "knothole" is an arched opening perched inside the right field wall, where up to 100 people can walk up and watch the game from just outside the park without having to pay for a ticket. The "knothole" provides a close-up view of the right fielder, who is stationed only a few feet away. The "knothole gang" of diehard fans have their own clubby culture with a strict set of rules, which means no dogs, no drinking and a mandatory rotation of new "knotholers" every three innings.

But no matter where you sit or stand you're likely to see a panoramic view of San Francisco Bay and the marina surrounding you in a sea of blue water and cobalt skies. AT&T is absolutely my favorite place to watch a baseball game: a classic retro ballpark with natural grass, brick walls and an old-time feel inside of a thoroughly modern park—it even features universal wireless access!

My favorite feature though, is the compilation of quotes from Yankee legend Yogi Berra, which adorns a wall near the left field side of the park. Yogi's pearls of wisdom include "I always thought that record would stand until it was broken," and "You can observe a lot by watching." And anyone with an appetite can understand the intrinsic, but twisted logic of this Yogi-ism: "You better cut the pizza into four pieces, because I'm not hungry enough to eat six." In San Francisco there is no obvious connection to Yogi Berra, but he is a baseball icon universally loved by fans and his witty words are perfectly placed inside the most majestic park in the land.

On this day, the stands were rocking as Barry Bonds stepped to the plate in the fourth inning. Byung-Hyun Kim was pitching for the Rockies and on a full count, he delivered a 90-mph fastball right down the center of the plate. Bonds swung and crushed it deep to center field for a two-run homer, sending the San Francisco faithful into a frenzy with fireworks cascading overhead while orange and black streamers fell from the sky.

Matt and I were delirious, slapping our palms with high-fives as Barry Bonds raised his arms and began trotting around the diamond in triumph.

"Wow, Matt, this is a great moment in baseball history!"

"I know, Dad. And I'm really glad we could see it together."

I wondered what Bonds was thinking as he rounded third and jumped onto home plate with a sea of Giants surrounding him.

"I know exactly what he was thinking," my friend Ron Hyde would tell me years later. Ron and I were newsroom veterans who shared a passion for baseball. But Ron also had a special history with Barry Bonds, having served as his unofficial babysitter when the young slugger was just 12.

Ron was about 16 at the time, and spent that summer attending every single Angels game in Anaheim as a special guest of Don Kirkwood, an Angels pitcher who just happened to be the cousin of Ron's best friend. It was at "the Big A," as Anaheim Stadium was then known, that Barry's mom, Pat Bonds, enlisted Ron and his friend to "watch" young Barry for the princely sum of $50 a game. Barry's dad, Bobby Bonds, played outfield for the team, then known as the California Angels.

So Ron and Barry hung out together in the summers of 1976 and 1977, going to Disneyland and playing a lot of ball. After the Angels games, Ron and Barry would go back to the Bonds' house to hang out.

"His father, Bobby, would be in the middle of the living room, with sparse furniture. He would be with the other Angel players, smoking cigarettes, drinking beer and playing cards," Ron told me. "We were not to disturb them. We had to go our separate ways."

"There was a stretch when Bobby Bonds hit home runs in nine out of 10 games," Ron said. "We knew he was special. And Barry said, 'Hey, he's just my dad out there playing baseball. I love baseball too.'"

"So what was Barry Bonds thinking when he hit number 715?" I demanded to know.

"I'll tell you what was going through his mind," Ron said. "It wasn't the 755 Hank Aaron record. Barry Bonds always pointed out that the record he was targeting was the 714 home runs that were set by Babe Ruth. Barry thought Babe Ruth garnered a lot of attention fairly or unfairly, in an era when black ballplayers weren't allowed to play the game. He cites a lot of heroes in his lifetime, but he always pointed out, he was going after the Babe because he felt that black ballplayers didn't get their shot.

A lot of the ballplayers never got their shot back in the 1920s and '30s and had to play in the Negro Leagues, separate leagues. Barry always recited the tales of the traveling caravans of pro ball players who did play, that would lose to the Negro League teams. So he wanted to play homage to a lot of those players who never got an opportunity, by bringing the Babe down. And that 715 was a special moment for him. And then of course, he set his sights on Hank Aaron's 755," said Ron.

And while Barry Bonds is now known as the greatest home run hitter in the game, and certainly the best lefty slugger ever, the truth is that Bonds started off as a righty hitter.

"So during the day on these home stands we would go over to their house in Tustin," Ron explained. "They had a nice condo and we'd go to the park across the street and play ball and goof around."

"I was a varsity baseball player and my buddy played baseball as well. I was a left-handed hitter and we'd be out there doing our thing and Barry Bonds would come up and we'd throw the ball and he was batting right-handed, like his dad, Bobby," Ron told me.

"He hit some pretty decent shots out there and then he'd kind of goof off and he says, 'Well, I can hit like you too, Ron; I'll go left handed.'"

"And here's this 12-year-old boy hitting the ball about 320, 330 feet – left-handed. And I remember looking at him and saying, 'Barry, why don't you hit left-handed all the time? You play Little League. Why aren't you hitting left handed?'"

"He said, 'I want to be like my dad. I want to hit right-handed.'"

"I said, 'But you're much better left-handed; you ought to think about it.'"

"And he said basically, as a 12-year-old might, 'Well, I'll think about it. But I like hitting right-handed; I want to be like Dad.'"

"But somehow that idea you planted in him germinated," I said to Ron. "And Bonds did in fact become a left-handed hitter. Did you ever remind him that you proved to be a spark in his success?"

Ron said, "I have reminded him of that."

"Let's fast forward down the road," he added. "I was going down to cover spring training and specifically the Giants. I brought it up right before a spring training game with the cameras rolling and the field pretty much barren as the final sprinkles were being administered by the hose and the umpires coming to home plate to confer with the managers and get the lineup card. Barry summons me from just off the dugout and says, 'Let's go for a walk and talk.' And so we start maybe halfway out to right field, down the right field line and we're walking in the direction of home plate, slowly and we're doing this interview."

"How ya doin', Barry, how's the season?" Ron asked the Giants slugger. "You know we go way back. Do you ever think about the old days at the Big A in Anaheim?"

"He said, 'I often think about that. It's kind of how my baseball career started. I really fell in love with the game at that point in time.'"

Ron said to Barry, "Do you remember us playing ball, out in the park, and having a good time?"

Bonds responded, "Oh, I remember. And he says, 'Ron, you were a heckuva ballplayer.'"

Ron said he was dying to ask Barry this question: "Do you remember who made you become a left-handed hitter?"

Bonds responded, "Well, I don't know if I should give you all the credit. But you did indeed suggest to me that I start batting left-handed. And then after my dad saw me hit, he said, 'Son, you're a lefty, hit left-handed.'"

And then Ron added, "And the rest, as they say, is history."

But how will Bonds be remembered in the history books of baseball? Will he be enshrined in Cooperstown as a legend of the game, or will he be a phantom, hidden from sight like Pete Rose?

"The stain of his era will always be with him," Ron opined. "Many of us just remember the courtroom with Rafael Palmeiro pointing his finger at Congress; Mark McGwire refusing to talk about the past."

Ron was on a roll.

"Many people have suggested they should have a separate wing in the Hall of Fame. Still, in that era, which is loosely 1990 to 2005, steroids or not, pitcher, position player or not, he was indisputably the best player of his era."

"And as time passes, people will be a little more forgiving as they look at Barry Bonds as one of the greatest players of all time."

"And let's face it," Ron said, "those years we were watching him, no matter whether you were a Giants fan or not, when you heard the name Barry Bonds step up to the plate, you dropped what you were doing to watch him bat. And few players could ever exceed what Barry Bonds did as a player, no question about it."

While Bonds suffers from having a surly reputation, there is another side of him that few people ever get to see.

"Well, he is a volatile personality," Ron readily admitted. "He very much keeps to himself, but he can be very charming at times," said Ron as he fondly remembered the Barry Bonds of his youth. "But that childhood innocence and love for the game was quickly shattered by the stench of steroids and super-human expectations placed upon him by the fans and the media," he added. "I've always thought Barry was abrasive to the media," Ron continued. "Barry kept to himself, he didn't understand how the game was played, especially with the proliferation of mass media, you know, in his later years: the Internet, the cable networks, the sports channels. He never really got it. And the media were scared to come to his locker after a game, be it a win or a loss."

If Bonds had been more gracious to the baseball writers who followed him day in and day out, he might have evoked more sympathy. Ron told me the story of meeting a crestfallen Barry Bonds, following the Giants' disastrous defeat to the Anaheim Angels in Game 7 of the 2002 World Series.

"And here are the media members from all over the country, scared to approach his locker after the devastating, earth-shattering loss," Ron said. "All Barry ever wanted was a World Series ring, never mind breaking the single season home run record, the Hank Aaron career home run record. Everybody was timid, intimidated to go over and talk to him."

But then, "Our eyes met," Ron confided. "We made eye contact. And I kind of got the look from him: 'OK, let's go over and do this interview.' I walked over with my cameraman, we sat down, and I said to him, 'Sorry, Barry.' And he said, 'I know, Ron. It hurts so much I can't tell you.'"

Ron continued, "We have a lot of good memories in this ballpark."

Bonds responded, 'Yes we do. A lot of great memories.'"

"So we proceeded to do the interview," Ron said. "And I think a media member from the *New York Times* started to walk over, assuming that it was OK to participate in this interview. And Barry looked in his direction with those piercing eyes and in no uncertain terms said, 'I'm talking to my friend.'"

"So the *New York Times* reporter retreated," Ron explained. "And with everybody waiting their turn, Barry gave me a man hug and we went on our way."

"You know, he's a very introspective person," Ron said. "There is a side of him that is very soft and genteel, if you will; I don't know if I should use that terminology but he's very soft spoken and reflective. He realizes he's been blessed in many respects."

"What about the dark cloud of steroids over Bonds' head?" I inquired.

"Well," said Ron, "he would have been a Hall of Famer without steroids; he's certainly a Hall of Famer in my book. At times not the greatest human being and he's certainly not going to extend his reputation as a nice guy no matter what he does in his post-baseball career. But I got to definitely see a different side of Barry Bonds as a child and then in later years as an adult."

I think Ron is right. Barry Bonds was his own worst enemy. But I do know from personal experience that Bonds was without a doubt, the most exciting player I've ever watched at the plate. Whenever he was up, everything else stood still as fans watched and waited for the crack of the bat that could produce bedlam in any ballpark.

But will Barry Bonds be inducted into the Hall of Fame? I asked that question to Dodger legend, Wes Parker, who has been a close observer of the game of baseball for decades. Parker pulled no punches.

"I doubt it," he said, "But I will tell you this – when Barry

Bonds was on a roll, when he was hitting all those home runs and hitting for average –he's the best hitter I've ever seen in my life!

I talked to (Hall of Famer) Orlando Cepeda about it. He said the same thing. I talked to (Hall of Famer) Willie McCovey about it. He said, 'Barry Bonds was the best hitter ever – during that stretch.'"

Watching Barry Bonds hit number 715 with Matt by my side was the thrill of a lifetime. It's a memory we will cherish forever, a moment locked in time where we can always connect and remember where we were on that historic day. And of the 41,000 plus in the ballpark with me that day in San Francisco, few will ever remember who won the game – it was actually the Rockies, by a score of 6-3.

And who was the winning pitcher that day? It was Byung-Hyun Kim, the same guy who gave up the historic homer to Barry Bonds in the fourth inning. I'm guessing Kim will hold his grandson on his knee one day and describe how he beat Barry Bonds and the Giants on a beautiful spring afternoon in San Francisco. And somehow he just might forget to mention giving up that hallowed home run – a hit that will put Kim in the record books forever.

(O.co) Oakland-Alameda County Coliseum, Oakland Athletics

Sunday, August 5, 2007

*"I like playing for Oakland,
they have a very colorful uniform."*
RICKEY HENDERSON

To this baseball fan, San Francisco is home to baseball's most beautiful park, while Oakland without a doubt, harbors one of the ugliest. The two parks are just 16 miles apart, putting them closer in proximity than any other stadiums in the Majors, but they are truly worlds apart.

While AT&T is world class and considered by many to be baseball's crown jewel, the Oakland Coliseum (also previously known as Network Associates and later McAfee Coliseum) is a diamond in the rough; it is truly a football stadium. The Coliseum has a gritty, industrial feel to it, with its monstrous slabs of cavernous concrete that harbor more empty seats than fans.

The biggest eyesore is in dead center field, home to "Mt. Davis," built in 1996 as a (mocking) tribute to Oakland Raiders owner Al Davis, who insisted on converting a decent baseball park into a football mausoleum, replete with 10,000 nosebleed seats so high above the clouds that Raiders fans must use powerful binoculars to see the action.

By converting the Coliseum to a multi-purpose (football) stadium to accommodate his rowdy Raiders, Davis ripped out the baseball bleachers overlooking the scenic Oakland hills. In so doing, he eliminated any semblance of baseball ambience, creating instead a freaky football circus tent-like atmosphere, replete with an ugly green tarp that covers the entire upper deck – to hide the fact that virtually no one is there to watch. Baseball fans, of course, are not so easily fooled; they just stay away from the Coliseum in droves.

Oakland has historically been plagued by poor attendance. Even when the A's won consecutive World Series in 1972, 1973 and 1974, the team averaged fewer than 13,000 fans a game. And in 1968, the team's first year in Oakland, only 6,298 souls were in the ballpark when Catfish Hunter threw a perfect game on May 8 against the Twins.

Attendance improved in the "Bash Brothers" era, when Mark McGwire and Jose Canseco led the A's to three consecutive American League pennants from 1988 – 1990. But the team has never drawn 3 million fans in any season, something the Yankees, Dodgers and Cardinals do consistently.

The Oakland Coliseum is also doomed by poor design, including what seems like miles of foul territory on the first and third base sides, shattering any sense of intimacy that fans crave from the ballpark. Pitchers generally love the park for its immense foul territory, creating extra outs from hitters who curse the beastly stadium for their depleted batting averages, which are said be 5 to 7 points lower in Oakland than anywhere else. Fans don't like it because they catch fewer foul balls and are farther from the action.

But every road trip has to start somewhere and the Coliseum does field a Major League team, although many fans refer to the homeboys as the Oakland Triple A's, because of their minor league talent and subordinate salaries. And so on a hot summer day, my daughter, Sarah, joined Matt and me in the car to leave Sacramento's sweltering heat for a 90-minute drive to Oakland, where winter was in full force.

The Coliseum was shrouded in a soupy swarm of drizzle and clouds. The game time temperature was just 61 degrees as we entered the seemingly frozen field, donning sweatshirts to keep the fog at bay.

"It's like a different season here," Sarah said.

"Yes," I agreed. "It's like that old Mark Twain saying: 'The coldest winter I ever spent was a summer in San Francisco.'"

"But, Dad, we're in Oakland," Matt insisted.

"Yeah, I know, but just imagine how much colder it must be on the other side of the Bay."

Matt just shrugged his shoulders. "This is not a good start to our road trip."

"No, this is just a warm-up for all the games we'll catch next week."

"But, Dad, it's not very warm," Matt declared.

"Oh, by the way, Dad," Sarah said. "I'm meeting an old boyfriend here at the game. I hope you don't mind if I sit with him."

"Who is this guy?"

"Just some guy from college. You don't know him," she said mysteriously.

"Well, how can I get to know him if you won't tell me anything about him?"

"Dad!" Matt shouted. "All you need to know is that Sarah wants to be alone so she can spend a little face time with him."

"She can go on Facebook anytime."

Matt and Sarah seemed amused by my parental dilemma.

"Dad, I'll sit with you and Matt for one inning, then I'll leave to visit him."

"Why can't he come and sit with us?"

"Because, Dad, he's intimidated by you."

"How could he be intimidated; I haven't even met him yet?"

"Well, this whole line of questioning is intimidating," Sarah said. "Besides, your reputation precedes you."

"What does that mean?"

"Well, you're kind of a ballbuster, Dad," Sarah said. "Like the time you told my high school boyfriend to have me home by 11 sharp or you'd call the California Highway Patrol at 11:01."

"And it worked. He brought you home 10 minutes early."

"Exactly," Sarah said.

And with that she darted off to meet Romeo in the upper deck.

"Well, Matt, I guess it's just you and me."

He said nothing as the Los Angeles Angels (of Anaheim) scored a run in the first inning on a triple to deep right center field by Garrett Anderson. The A's tied the score in the bottom of the second on a double by Mark Ellis, but the Angels went on to win the game 4-3 on a strong performance by their ace, John Lackey, who struck out 5 batters to win his 14th game of the season against only 6 losses.

Afterward, I hunted for Sarah, who was busy talking to the boy from college.

"Hello, Mr. Luery," he said. "It's nice to meet you."

"Hmmm," I thought to myself, "maybe this kid isn't so bad."

As we walked out of the Coliseum, he asked, "Would you like me to take a picture of you and Sarah and Matt?"

"Sure," I said. "That would be nice."

I think I was beginning to like the kid.

Click.

And with that, he took off. And the Luerys headed back to Sacramento, where it was warm, sunny and summer all over again.

Three years later – almost exactly to the day – I would return to the Coliseum for a memorable day at the ballpark with my 13-year-old nephew, Jacob Fenton. He was lucky enough to get his A's hat autographed by relief pitcher Jerry Blevins, then moments later he caught a batting practice foul ball with his nose. A little blood, a visit to First Aid, a little ice and all was good. The A's ground crew was nice enough to retrieve the ball and then present it to my nephew, whose mood turned instantly from tears to triumph. He would bring home a souvenir – and a shiner my sister will never let me forget!

Kauffman Stadium, Kansas City Royals

Wednesday, August 8, 2007

"Dad, you used to be cool.
What happened?"
MATT LUERY

Kansas City is home to more than 100 barbecue restaurants, offering diners the delectable delights of pork ribs, smoked chicken or beef brisket with sweet and tangy sauces. Shortly after landing, Matt and I drove to Gates Bar-B-Q, famous for its sauce bottles, which depict a man in a full tuxedo and top hat. Gates is a Kansas City original, dating back to 1946.

The local legend is that staffers are trained at "Rib Tech," where they learn everything from cooking ribs to greeting customers with a friendly "Hi, may I help you?" as soon as you walk through the door.

I ordered a slab of ribs and devoured them; Matt, however, was a bit more tentative, not quite sure what to do with the white bread that came with the meal. White bread was a totally foreign concept for Matt, who had been raised on a constant diet of whole wheat bread, thanks to my health-conscious wife.

"How do you like it?" I inquired.

"It's OK," Matt said as he reached for the fries.

"So much for variety."

After lunch, I was eager to explore Kansas City before taking in our first event – a night game at Kauffman Stadium.

"Let's drive around town, Matt, and then cross over the border to Kansas, so you can experience a new state," I said encouragingly.

But instead Matt was prone on the bed, engrossed in VH-1 on the hotel TV.

"No, Dad, I'm watching the Top 100 hits of the '80s."

"Guess what? The '80s are over. Let's enjoy 2007 before it becomes a retro show on TV."

"No, I'm enjoying Domo Arregato, Mr. Roboto."

"Yeah, I like Styx," I told Matt. "Actually I interviewed them in San Antonio for a story I did on rock music."

"You met these guys?"

"Yeah. Come on, I'll tell you all about it in the car," I said with a smile, realizing my little scheme was about to work.

We talked about rock bands as we crossed from Missouri into Kansas.

"Who are your favorite '80s artists?" Matt wanted to know.

"Well, I like Blondie, Prince and Michael Jackson. Also, there's Hall and Oates, Tom Petty and the Heartbreakers, Cyndi Lauper and Pat Benatar. And U2 is definitely one of my favorite '80s bands, along with ZZ Top."

"Dad, you used to be cool. What happened?"

"Rap happened," I said. "After that, you and I went in different directions."

"Oh yeah, then you lost your mojo."

"Well, my mojo just got us back to Kansas City. And now we're here at the ballpark."

For once, Wrong Way Mike had gotten it right.

Outside the stadium, a life-size statue of Frank White, a five-time All Star who played second base for the Royals for 18 seasons, greets the fans. Legendary third baseman George

Brett is also memorialized in bronze, along with Royals' founders Ewing and Muriel Kauffman.

Kauffman Stadium has hosted more than 63 million fans since it opened in 1973. It blooms with natural landscaping and is considered to be one of the most spacious parks anywhere, with easy access from Interstate 70. Its signature feature is a 322-foot-wide water wonder in the outfield, which the Royals say is the largest privately funded fountain in the world. It's a spectacular sight when the fountains flow with cascading water after a Kansas City home run.

In the stadium parking lot we noticed dozens of cars with Minnesota plates, carrying rabid rooters to cheer on the visiting Twins against the hometown Royals. On the inside, it appeared half the 21,503 people in attendance were Twins fans. They sported the distinctive TC baseball hats (for Twin Cities) and came decked in blue T-shirts with bright red letters screaming out "Twins." They came from towns like Cedar, Minnesota, and drove eight hours to support their team on the road.

These Twins fans were very talkative, especially the guy next to me.

"We drove down to see the Twins, don't ya know," stated the Man from Minnesota.

"Alrighty now," said his son.

The dad then held up a handmade sign declaring, "Drove 460 miles to attend a game with my son. No mom, no sister, priceless."

"You guys came a long way to see a baseball game," I said.

"Ya, sure, you betcha," said the Man from Minnesota.

The Twins were on fire for this game, with Michael Cuddyer and Torii Hunter going deep to lead the visitors to an 11-4 victory over the hapless Royals. Johan Santana was masterful for Minnesota, striking out six en route to the victory. Talk about total dominance: Santana's Twins had beaten the

Royals in every one of his last 12 starts, the stadium scoreboard informed us.

Our baseball trip was off to a good start and as we left the park, we learned the Royals planned to refurbish the stadium for the 2009 season. Matt and I looked at each other and sighed.

"One day," I said, "we will have to return to Kansas City to see the refurbished ballpark."

"Absolutely."

Father and son were in rare agreement.

Busch Stadium, St. Louis Cardinals

Thursday, August 9, 2007

"Hey, we're not that old."
MARTY GONZALEZ

The screaming alarm shattered the silence in the room.

Somebody had programmed the clock radio for loud rock, and the sounds of Led Zeppelin's "Stairway to Heaven" filled the air. Our 9 o'clock wakeup call had arrived.

I dove into the bathroom and soaked myself in the hot shower, energizing me for the day.

Matt the Stinkbug was still in bed. Of course.

"Come on, Matt," I said, "we're driving across Missouri today. It's the Show Me State. Show me you can actually get out of bed."

"I'm up," came the response from under the sheets.

"Really? You don't look up."

"I'm just trying to get out of bed," came the muffled reply from the pillow.

"I'm not seeing any signs of progress."

"Dad, if you just leave me alone, I'll get up."

Taking the hint, I left the room to find some coffee downstairs. I browsed the sports section of the *Kansas City Star* and grabbed some pastries for Matt, then headed back upstairs.

Matt's diversion plan worked to perfection. By the time I returned, he was showered and ready to go. I tried my best to act nonchalant.

"Here's some breakfast for you," I said. "You can eat the pastries in the car."

We headed east along Interstate 70, where we noticed signs for Independence, Missouri.

"Matt, Independence is the hometown of Harry Truman, one of our great presidents. He integrated the armed forces and effectively ended World War II by dropping an atomic bomb on Hiroshima and Nagasaki, Japan," I informed my son.

"How many people died in Japan from those bombs?" Matt wanted to know.

"More than 100,000 people lost their lives."

"And you consider Truman a great president?" he challenged.

"Well, it was strategic to bomb Japan," I said. "If not for those atomic bombs, the war in the Pacific would have continued for months or maybe years, and thousands of American troops would have died."

"So, what are you saying, Dad, better them than us?"

"Well, Truman was the president of the United States. As Commander in Chief, he was responsible for preserving American lives and so he did what he had to do to win the war and bring our troops home."

"So the end justifies the means, is that what you're saying?"

There are no easy answers to a question like that. How do you handle a teenage son who was beginning to challenge everything?

I decided to take the easy way out. I changed the subject.

"Hey are you hungry?" I asked.

Without waiting for an answer, I parked right in front of Shakespeare's Pizza in Columbia, home of the University of Missouri Tigers. Mizzou has one of the top journalism schools in the country, and one of the Missouri grads from my newsroom had recommended Shakespeare's as being top-notch. The pizza was in fact, delicious and served as a welcome diversion from our heavy conversation about war and peace.

$$\otimes \otimes \otimes$$

After lunch, we continued our journey eastward, arriving in St. Louis just in time to see the Cardinals host the San Diego Padres at the brand new Busch Stadium. The Cardinals opened their 46,000-seat stadium in 2006. It is a retro-style ballpark with natural grass and a panoramic view of the downtown skyline, highlighted by the magnificent St. Louis Arch, which towers some 630 feet above the Mississippi River.

Outside the ballpark there are statues of Cardinal greats Bob Gibson and Stan Musial. Gibson, the Cardinal leader in career victories with 251, was one of the most intimidating pitchers of his era, knocking down any batter who dared to dig in at the plate. During the 1968 season, Gibson's Earned Run Average was just 1.12, fourth best of any pitcher in Major League history. Stan Musial was a fan favorite, making the National League All-Star Team every year from 1946 to 1963, ending his career with 3,630 hits (fourth highest total in baseball history) and a lifetime batting average of .331.

As for tonight's game, St. Louis was a sultry city baking in 93-degree heat as Joel Peneiro delivered the first pitch. The ballpark was bathed in a sea of Cardinal red, with 42,848 fans (nearly all of them, it appeared, sporting the home team colors). Among them was my best friend, Marty Gonzalez, who had flown in from California. Marty was traveling on business, and we had had arranged to meet at the ballpark.

"Meet me in St. Louis," Marty said.

"Reminds me of the famous movie of the same name, with Judy Garland," I said.

"What movie is that?" Matt wanted to know.

"Well, it came out in 1944. It's the story of four women living in St. Louis who were celebrating the World's Fair of 1904."

"Nineteen-oh-four. Isn't that the year you and Marty were born?" teased the Stinkbug, who now resembled a Smart Ass.

"Hey, we're not that old. That would make us over a century today," Marty responded.

"Yeah, exactly," said my son, the know-it-all. "You guys are like the redwoods – ancient."

"I prefer to call it vintage," said Marty. "And remember, the redwoods are one of the most majestic things on Earth."

The game was a laugher for the Cardinals, who shut out the Padres 5-0. Rick Ankiel hit a three-run homer in the seventh inning to seal the win. Ankiel is a former pitcher who decided to switch to the outfield, where he could play every day and take advantage of his hitting prowess. After lighting up the Padres, the Cardinals lit up the sky with fireworks for a postgame celebration of their victory.

$$\otimes \ominus \oslash$$

The next morning, I checked out the free hot breakfast at the Drury Inn, located just a few steps from Busch Stadium and the St. Louis Arch. Of course Matt was nowhere near the hotel lobby to enjoy it because he was sleeping in. Again. So I decided to do what any dad would to motivate his son. I called the room to wake him up.

"Matt, this is your father speaking," I said in my best broadcast voice.

"I know who you are."

"Well, get your buns down here to enjoy your free breakfast. The restaurant closes in 10 minutes."

For some reason, my plea seemed to work. Matt made it down just as the kitchen staff began wheeling away the waffles and scrambled eggs. I could see the disappointment in his eyes. He could feel the pangs of hunger screaming inside his stomach. Fortunately, I had planned ahead.

"Matt, I saved you a plate of pancakes and some blueberry muffins."

"Thanks, Dad," he said while wolfing down his breakfast. "I really appreciate it."

"Well, I thought you might be hungry. And besides, today we're going to visit the St. Louis Arch."

Matt's eyes lit up. As an aspiring architect, he was fascinated by the Gateway Dream, built by architect Eero Saarinen between 1963 and 1965. Standing 630 feet, it is America's tallest national monument, with 1 million people riding the trams to the top each year.

Matt and I enjoyed the majestic view from the summit. We could see the mighty Mississippi River below, with the buildings of downtown St. Louis shimmering in the morning sun. To the east, the flatlands of Illinois beckoned.

The history of the region comes alive in the museum downstairs, which chronicles the adventures of Lewis and Clark. The Museum of National Expansion retraces the steps of the 19th-century pioneers who followed the Missouri River to explore the Wild West, ending up eventually at the Pacific Ocean along the Oregon coast. The museum is a fantastic way to make American history come alive and Matt truly enjoyed it.

In the museum gift shop, I bought a book for Matt that describes the building of the Arch. He devoured it from cover to cover as we drove across the plains of Illinois and Indiana.

"So what did you learn about the building of the Arch?"

But I would quickly learn what a big mistake that was.

"I don't want you to quiz me!" he shot back. "It's summer and I'm on vacation."

I was stunned momentarily, but quickly realized the best way to teach a kid something is to make it fun; not give him a verbal test with questions. We got along much better, I discovered, when I let Matt determine his own pace, just as he did by guiding himself through the museum in St. Louis. That approach seemed to work better than drilling something down his throat. Don't force it, I told myself, just let it come naturally.

After about four hours of driving along Interstate 70 through the cornfields of the Midwest, I wanted to get out and stretch my legs. Somewhere in Indiana, the Crossroads of America, I spotted a convenience store and pulled over. We loaded the car with chips, munchies and a few soft drinks. Before getting back in the car, I directed Matt to a nearby field of corn.

"Stand here," I said, "so I can take your picture."

"Why?"

"Because this cornfield has symbolism."

"Really?" he said with sarcasm.

"Yes," I said. "You know the movie *Field of Dreams* with Kevin Costner? Remember when Shoeless Joe Jackson and the legendary players emerge from the cornfields like a mirage to play a game of baseball?"

"Yeah, what about it?"

"Well, this could be our Field of Dreams, symbolizing our cross-country journey to discover America's pastime and in the process, we find each other."

"Dad, that's so corny," Matt sneered.

"You just said that in a cornfield."

We both laughed at the irony, breaking the tension of the summertime heat.

"So, we're in this together? Is that what you're trying to say, Dad?"

"Yeah, something like that." I turned the ignition.

The radio was playing "Born to Run," so I cranked up the song to full-throttle volume, shouting out the lyrics at the top of my lungs. Bruce Springsteen guided us all the way to Ohio.

Great American Ballpark, Cincinnati Reds

Friday, August 10, 2007

"Are you challenging us to a fight?"
ANONYMOUS CINCINNATI REDS FAN

Cincinnati is a beautiful city of hills with tree-lined streets overlooking the Ohio River. Matt and I checked into the Hilton Netherland, located inside the Carew Tower, which at 574 feet is Cincinnati's second-tallest building. We explored the city's downtown by walking along the riverfront and then hopped on a bus, which took us over one of the five bridges lining the river, to Newport, Kentucky.

"Welcome to the Bluegrass State."

"Why do you do that?" Matt inquired angrily.

"Do what?"

"Why do you pretend you're on TV doing the play-by-play for our trip? Can't you just enjoy the moment instead of always trying to capture it on tape?"

"I can't help it. I'm a broadcaster so it comes naturally to me. Plus, this is your first trip to Kentucky, so I wanted to make sure you add it to your growing list of states. How many do you have now?"

"I think it's close to 40," said Matt. "And why do they call Kentucky 'the Bluegrass State'?"

"I thought you'd never ask. This is horse country. And 'bluegrass' refers to the beautiful fields and bucolic pastures where you might find horses. Of course, the grass is really green, but folks here say the purple stems of bluegrass have a bluish tint when seen from a distance – especially in the springtime."

"Where do you come up with this stuff?"

"I do a lot of reading."

"Yeah, on Wikipedia, I bet."

"A good reporter never reveals his sources."

We entered the city of Newport, Kentucky, which as it turns out, has a rather checkered past. Newport was once known as "Sin City" for its rampant prostitution. It's also the home of native son John Thompson, who invented the Thompson Machine Gun (or Tommy Gun), made popular by gangsters in the 1920s. But modern-day Newport is an up-and-coming city with high-rise condos lining the Ohio River and offering a gorgeous view of the Cincinnati skyline. From Newport you can get a terrific look at Great American Ballpark, which was named after an insurance company and is the place the Reds have called home since 2003.

The natural ryegrass of the stadium is grown right at the park, which follows the curves of the Ohio River and has a seating capacity of 42,271.

Four toothbrush-shaped light stands tower over the outfield bleachers, which on this day were filled with the jubilant sounds of the Ohio State University marching band. Of course, being fervent USC fans, Matt and I tried not to show too much enthusiasm for the Buckeyes, but the band was truly talented and got the crowd fired up with the Ohio State fight song. Instantly, thousands of people in the ballpark began singing in unison about fighting for Ohio. Matt and I slunk down low in our seats and prayed for anonymity, but it didn't last long.

We sat in the stands behind first base, where we met a group of guys from Chicago. As it turns out, they were starting their own baseball road trip, which mirrored our journey, only in reverse.

"We're starting here in Cincinnati," said the fan sporting a Cubs cap. "Then we're heading west to see the Cardinals play in St. Louis and the Royals in Kansas City. Where are you guys from?" he asked.

"We're from California," I said. "My son, Matt, is a student at USC."

Instantly, half the heads in our row turned around to stare at the enemy; Ohio State and USC are historic rivals.

"That's alright, we won't hold that against you," said a Cincinnati partisan sitting right behind me. "Tonight we're all baseball fans," he said with a laugh, "and anybody making a baseball road trip like you can't be half bad – even if they do root for the Trojans."

"Fight On," said Matt.

"Are you challenging us to a fight?" asked the Reds fan.

"No, 'Fight On' is the USC motto," Matt explained. "We're just here to have fun."

At Great American Park, the fans were all bathed in a sea of red, showing solidarity with their hometown team, the oldest franchise in Major League Baseball. The team dates back to 1869, when they were known as the Cincinnati Red Stockings. Great American Park features statues of Reds legends Ted Kluszewski, Ernie Lombardi, Joe Nuxhall and Frank Robinson, but curiously missing is the Reds' greatest player, Pete Rose.

He is baseball's all-time leader in hits with 4,256 in his career. Rose led the Reds to World Series victories in 1975 and 1976, but Matt and I couldn't find any tributes to him at the ballpark. Baseball has blacklisted Rose because of his addiction to gambling on games involving teams he managed later in his career. The only reference to Rose we could see was a rose garden, located near the Reds Hall of Fame museum, adjacent to the ballpark.

But on this day, we got to see another great Cincinnati legend, Ken Griffey Jr., as he pounded his 590th career home run out of the park. Still, the four-bagger was not enough for the hometown Reds, who ended up losing to the San Diego Padres 12-7 in eleven innings. Ironically, Trevor Hoffman, one of the greatest relief pitchers ever to play the game, gave up two doubles in the ninth inning to blow a save for the Padres, sending the game into extra innings, where the Padres scored five runs in the top of the eleventh.

Most of the Cincinnati fans headed to the exits, allowing Matt and me to scoot down near the action, just five rows behind the third base dugout. We were so close, we could hear the home plate umpire shout out the balls and strikes as Griffey hit a shot deep to left field for what we hoped might be his second home run of the day, only to see it caught near the warning track.

At Great American Ballpark, I saw a fan hold up a sign saying a baseball has 108 stitches – more than even open-heart surgery. The implied message: It's easy for baseball to break your heart and on this night, the Cincinnati Reds did just that, to the disappointment of the 21,394 partisans in the park.

"Don't worry, Matt," I said. "Tomorrow is another day, to be followed by another game in a new city. And for once, we'll be rooting for the road team."

Progressive Field,
Cleveland Indians

Sunday, August 12, 2007

"Sleep is underrated. And I can't get enough of it."
MATT LUERY

Matt and I left Cincinnati and rolled onto Interstate 71, weaving our way through Ohio on a northeasterly slant, passing through Columbus and Mansfield with Matt's musical mix cranked to the max.

"What is this?" I inquired.

"It's OK Go."

"I am going," I said, reminding him of the obvious. "I'm going 65 as a matter of fact."

"No, Dad," he chuckled. "It's the band OK Go."

"Who else do you like to listen to?" I asked.

Matt then proceeded to turn me on to the Kaiser Chiefs, The Fratellis, Panic at the Disco, The Strokes and The Kooks. I liked most of the music.

"See, I don't mind being your musical lab rat, but now it's my turn," I said while sliding in a Moody Blues CD. Suddenly it was "Tuesday Afternoon" and we were looking for "Knights in White Satin."

"Hey, Dad, that's pretty good," Matt admitted. "So what was the British Invasion?"

It was the opening I had always hoped for – a chance to walk down memory lane singing the tributes of The Beatles, The Rolling Stones and The Who's On First, uh, I mean The Who. I told him all about the Mersey Beat – representing the sounds and soul of Liverpool – where The Beatles originated, along with The Searchers, Gerry and the Pacemakers and Freddie and the Dreamers.

"I really love the Animals," Matt declared.

"'Don't Let Me Be Misunderstood' is one of my favorite songs," I stated passionately.

"And I'm a big fan of the Kinks," Matt informed me as we launched into a fan-filled tribute to the songwriting brilliance of Ray and Dave Davies. We talked about the origins of British rock all the way to Cleveland, home of the Rock and Roll Hall of Fame, located on the shores of Lake Erie.

Cleveland has changed a lot from the late '60s when an oil slick on the Cuyahoga River caught fire and the city was known as "the Mistake by the Lake." Today, Cleveland is a bustling metropolis undergoing a rebirth, thanks in part to architect I.M. Pei, who designed the iconic Rock and Roll Hall of Fame – a seven-story museum tower highlighted by a glass pyramid. Pete Townshend of The Who was on hand for the groundbreaking in 1993, along with the legendary Chuck Berry. The museum is a living tribute to the past, present and future of rock and roll, with each floor telling a different story of the musicians who changed the world.

On our visit, Matt and I were treated to a newly opened exhibit on The Doors, which featured vintage clothing, album covers and music from one of L.A.'s most influential bands. I served as Matt's musical guide, while he soaked up everything he could about the poetic life and tragic death of Doors lead singer Jim Morrison. We could have stayed at the museum for days, but decided to change course and do something spontaneous – something not on the Luery agenda.

"Matt, how would you like to catch a football game tonight?"

"But we're on a baseball trip. What have you been smoking?"

"Nothing," I said, "but I did catch a whiff of Jim Morrison's jacket and I think I got a contact high."

As luck would have it, the Cleveland Browns were hosting the Kansas City Chiefs in an exhibition game, at their football-only stadium located on the waterfront, just minutes from the Rock and Roll Hall of Fame.

Cleveland Browns Stadium opened in 1999 with an all-grass playing surface and a seating capacity of 73,200. The fans are rabid, but realistic in their expectations, because the Browns are perennially bad. In fact, the Browns are one of four teams that have never played in the Super Bowl.

Nevertheless, the "Dog Pound" fans love to scream "Woo Woo!" for their beloved Brownies and on this night, the Clevelanders were good enough to eke out a 16-12 victory over the Chiefs, without even scoring an offensive touchdown. The Browns' only entry into the land of quick-six came on an 88-yard kickoff return by Chris Barclay, who thrilled the crowd in the fourth quarter to seal the deal for the home team.

By the next morning, for some reason, Matt began pestering me with his new, annoying habit of calling me by my first name.

"Hi, Mike," suddenly became his favorite phrase and he used it frequently – just to bug me.

"Matt, you know I hate it when you call me that!"

"Why?" he asked impishly. "Mike is your name."

"Yes," I admitted, "but I am your dad, not your buddy."

"Well, we can be friends on Facebook."

"No, I mean we are not equals. I'm the father and you are my son. Whatever happened to respecting your elders?"

"It's an old fashioned concept, Mike. Better get used to it."

Matt's attempt to knock me off my pedestal was strategic. He called me "Mike," I discovered, whenever I asked him to be responsible or do something he didn't want to do, like getting up in the morning.

That's when he responded with "OK, Mike" or "Hi, Mike" as part of his psychological game to show defiance and independence at the same time. In his own way, my teenage son was rebelling against me by putting us on equal footing. But even though Matt was old enough to vote, I will always consider him to be my "little boy." After all, dads are supposed to guide their sons forever.

Being a dad is a lifetime deal. It doesn't end when your son turns 18 or even 21. So I told Matt, "Show me a little respect," and then added, "your old man isn't senile and knows a thing or two about life. How about just saying, 'Sure, Dad'?" I asked with a gleam of hope.

"OK, Mike."

Yeah, I guess after taking a kid across the country on a magical journey to every baseball park in America, a little respect is too much to ask. I decided to let it go and hoped that one day it would pass.

It's a good thing we have baseball to bind us together and on this day, two tickets to see the Cleveland Indians host the New York Yankees at Progressive Field. We took a shuttle from our hotel in Independence, Ohio, which was filled with Yankee fans. On board the shuttle we met a family from Buffalo, New York. They were in town to see two games of the series in one of baseball's best stadiums.

Progressive Field is a baseball gem that opened in 1994 in the heart of downtown Cleveland and offers a terrific view of the city's skyline. Matt and I were exhilarated to be there – even though we were parked in the nosebleed seats high up in the upper deck, five stories above the field.

Undaunted by the height, we were awed by the architectural layout of the stadium, offering comfortable seats angled 8 to 12 degrees, so fans perched in the rafters can see the game without hurting their necks.

The highlight inside is Heritage Park, filled with monuments of Tribe legends like Bob Feller, the greatest pitcher in club history with 266 wins and 2,581 strikeouts. Also there is home run slugger Rocky Colavito, one of the most popular players ever to don an Indians uniform. Heritage Park is located behind the center field wall, offering fans a nostalgic link to the club's historic roots, dating back to the 1890s, when the legendary Cy Young pitched for the Cleveland Spiders.

Cleveland's modern ballpark is perched along three downtown streets (Ontario, Carnegie and East 9th Street) with all the ambience of an urban battlefield, especially with the Bronx Bombers in town. Of the 41,612 people in the stands, at least half were Yankee fans, dressed in blue T-shirts with the team's logo on the front, or wearing the famed pinstriped jerseys. The buzz was electric as they screamed out, "Let's Go Yankees!" in the middle of enemy territory, while the Indians faithful responded with a round of boos.

And on this day, the visitors were victorious, pounding out a 5-3 victory, thanks to a Jason Giambi's two-run homer and a solo shot from Melky Cabrera. Andy Pettitte was on the mound again, this time for the Yankees. Just a year earlier, Matt and I had seen him pitch in Houston as a member of the Astros. Pettitte got the win for the Yanks after getting the Indians to hit into two inning-ending double plays. Yankee shortstop Derek Jeter was brilliant, making a great acrobatic leap from deep in the hole to throw out a Cleveland runner. The Indians left eight runners on base, despite a lineup featuring Grady

Sizemore, Casey Blake, Victor Martinez and Ryan Garko. Even the Heritage Hall legends of Larry Doby and Satchel Paige could not turn this day into a Cleveland celebration.

After the game, Matt and I took the shuttle back to our hotel and loaded up the car to travel along Highway 11 through the scenic, rolling hills of eastern Ohio. The bucolic highway is devoid of any billboards and filled with farmhouses that dot the landscape of fertile fields in America's heartland.

While the beauty of the area was intoxicating, I knew I needed to find my bearings.

"Matt, can you check the map and see exactly where we are?" I asked nicely.

"No," was the swift response. "Just enjoy the serendipity of the moment," said the Stinkbug.

"You're fired as a navigator!" I shouted.

"Good. I don't want to be your navigator. What's the difference if we take the wrong road?" Matt snapped. "It's not the destination but the journey that counts."

"I need to know where I'm going."

Suddenly, we were engaged in a heated shouting match. It was a blustery battle between Order and Serendipity; a feud over Controlled vs. Spontaneous. I preferred the Predictable, while Matt relished the Random. Neither side would budge, so I pulled over, reached for the road map and plotted our course.

We crossed the border into West Virginia, a new state for Matt and so naturally, I insisted we had to get out of the car.

"Why are we getting out here?" Matt demanded as we pulled into the parking lot of a small diner in the tiny town of Chester, home to some 3,000 souls along the banks of the Ohio River.

"Because this is the West Virginia panhandle. If we don't stop here, we'll miss the Mountaineer State."

"I'm breathing West Virginia air, right now. Why do I have to get out of the car?"

"Don't even start with me. Besides, I know you're hungry."

I ordered a chicken-fried steak with mashed potatoes and gravy to savor the local flavor of the roadside restaurant. Matt had no desire to go native, so he wolfed down a hamburger.

How boring to have no sense of adventure.

An hour later, we were crossing into Pennsylvania, where I forced Matt into another obligatory picture.

"I want to go with the flow and all you want to do is stop," said Matt.

"Just let me take this picture and we'll be gone."

Click.

Within seconds we were speeding into the coal-black hills of western Pennsylvania. The nighttime solitude of the moonless sky was interrupted by a giant tunnel that took us into more blackness, until suddenly the city lights of Pittsburgh illuminated our way to the Steel City. We arrived at the downtown Doubletree Hotel, where the smell of warm chocolate chip cookies lingered through the lobby, drawing us in helplessly.

Upon devouring our late-night snack, we headed to our room to relax and watch baseball highlights on ESPN.

"Let's get up early tomorrow," I said, "so we can explore Pittsburgh."

"No, I want to sleep in," said the Stinkbug.

"Sleep is overrated."

"No, sleep is underrated. And I can't get enough of it. You're too wound up, Dad. Just take it slow."

"But as a dad, it's my job to show you everything I can – to explore the world."

"The world starts tomorrow, Dad. Good night."

And with that, he flicked off the lights, leaving me alone in a sea of radiation beaming from the television.

I clicked off the remote and plunged the room into darkness.

PNC Park, Pittsburgh Pirates

Monday, August 13, 2007

"Let's play two."
ERNIE BANKS

I woke up with a start. The early-morning light was radiating inside the hotel room, beckoning me to the window. Outside I could see the sun shining over the Pittsburgh skyline on a beautiful summer day. It was 8:53, so I quickly hopped in the shower, put on my clothes and was ready to roll. Matt, however was not.

"It's time to get up," I said gently.

No response.

The Stinkbug was sound asleep.

"Matt, let's make tracks," I stated a little louder.

Silence.

"Matt, it's time to get up and go."

"Mike, let me sleep!"

"Hey, that's 'Dad' to you," I reminded him. "Now come on, let's explore Pittsburgh."

But this time there was no budging the Stinkbug until noon, when Matt's hunger pangs finally forced him to get his little carcass out of bed.

After a quick meal, we raced over to Mt. Washington for a ride up the tram – or as Pittsburghers called it, "the Mon," which is a cable railway that glides up a monstrously steep hill overlooking downtown.

Perched some 367 feet above Pittsburg, Mt. Washington offers a panoramic vista of the city's skyscrapers rising above Pittsburgh's Golden Triangle, where the mighty Monongahela and Allegheny Rivers merge into the Ohio River.

The view was breathtaking. Originally known as "Coal Hill" for the dark deposits below the surface, Mt. Washington is the country's second most beautiful place in America, behind only Arizona's Red Rock Country, according to a 2003 poll conducted by the USA Weekend Annual Travel Report. I took plenty of pictures of the skyline and even convinced Matt to allow the two of us to be photographed together, something that rarely happens.

"People only get in the way of pretty landscapes. They detract from the scenery. But in this case, the view is so spectacular, I'll make an exception."

Click.

And with that, Matt even sported a smile to complement his bushy, blonde hair and black T-shirt that proudly proclaimed, "NorCal," commemorating his Northern California roots.

"You're not from here, are you?" said the waitress at the nearby Hard Rock Café, overlooking the Monongahela River.

"No, we're from California," I said.

"Yeah, you're too sunburned," she said. "No one around here looks that red."

I didn't know whether to feel flattered or reach for the sunscreen.

After lunch, Matt and I boarded a water taxi that took us for a ride along Pittsburgh's riverfront. The craft calmly navigated the Allegheny River and took us right to PNC Park, home of the Pirates.

The Pirates may be perennial doormats in the National League Central, but Pittsburgh has hit a grand slam when it comes to ballparks. Built in 2001 on the shores of the Allegheny, PNC has a riverfront feel to it, with the city's majestic skyline rising over the center field and right field stands. Fans can even walk to the park along the Roberto Clemente Bridge, named after Pittsburgh's legendary right fielder, who played his entire 17-year career with the Pirates. Clemente finished with 3,000 career hits and a .317 lifetime batting average, while winning two World Series championships (in 1960 and 1971).

Clemente died in a plane crash in 1972 on a mercy mission over Nicaragua, where he was trying to provide relief for earthquake victims. His body was never recovered, but he left a lasting mark on the city of Pittsburgh and the game of baseball for his tremendous accomplishments both on and off the field.

In addition to his humanitarian work, Roberto Clemente was also the first Latin American player to win a World Series as a starter (1960), earn a league Most Valuable Player award (1966) and win a World Series MVP award (1971), when he guided the Pirates to a World Championship.

PNC, named after a Pittsburgh-based bank, is in fact the fifth ballpark for the Pirates, who can trace their origins back to 1887, making them one of the oldest clubs in baseball. The architects have crafted the stadium for intimacy – no seat is more than 88 feet above the field. Before the game started, the Luery boys explored every viewpoint of the stadium, including a spectacular perch high above home plate overlooking the downtown skyline. Matt even agreed to have his picture taken with the yellow-colored Roberto Clemente Bridge right over his shoulder. Pittsburgh glistened in the distance with the downtown buildings towering over my teenage son.

It was high up above home plate that we met a local architect named Christine Jackson, who told us the history of the park. We learned that her company, Astorino, helped design PNC

Park. She said the architects wanted the fans to be right on top of the action and in fact, it's just 443 feet from home plate to the Allegheny River.

In my opinion, the Pirates have the second most beautiful stadium in baseball, behind only AT&T Park in San Francisco. Nevertheless, the Pirates haven't had a winning team since 1992 – the longest span of losing seasons in the four major professional sports of baseball, football, basketball or hockey. As a result, the Pirates' fan base is very small, which allowed Matt and me to sit anywhere we wanted. We purposely picked right field, where the outfield wall is just 21 feet above the playing field. The number 21 is significant, honoring legendary right fielder Roberto Clemente's number 21 jersey. On the left field side, the wall is just six feet above the warning track, allowing fans to truly get into the action.

Matt and I had high hopes of catching a Barry Bonds home run, as the San Francisco Giants were in town for a doubleheader with the Pirates.

Even though we were sitting in the deepest reaches of the right field bleachers, we could see every detail of the game below. Barry Bonds did hit a single, but could do little more as the Giants lost the first game 3-1, in a lightning quick one hour and 51 minutes, the shortest game I've ever attended.

The Luery boys didn't leave the park however, because the Pirates and Giants were ready for an encore, or as the legendary Cubs shortstop Ernie Banks once put it, "Let's play two." Matt and I were about to be treated to a rare doubleheader made possible by a previous rainout. Sadly, the word "doubleheader" has virtually disappeared from the baseball lexicon, as bottom-line-driven owners have discovered that getting fans to pay for two games on two nights is more profitable than giving them a twofer on a single date.

The second game of our doubleheader was a San Francisco slugfest, with the Giants pounding out 10 runs in a rout of the

Pirates, who could only score three times. Barry Bonds skipped the night game to rest his burly body, but it didn't matter as we savored the flavor of Pittsburgh's beautiful ballpark.

Altogether on this road trip, Matt and I attended 6 baseball games in 5 ballparks, plus 1 football game, while driving through 8 states for a journey of a lifetime. We flew back to Sacramento with a sense of accomplishment and a passionate desire to hit the road again. We would soon get our wish.

Angel Stadium, Los Angeles Angels of Anaheim

Wednesday, August 22, 2007

"Baseball is like watching paint dry."
CAROL LUERY

Did I mention I am fanatical about arriving early to baseball games? To me, the first pitch is sacred and something to be cherished. I love the drama of watching the home team endeavor to establish early dominance, while the visitors ratchet up reverse mojo in an attempt to steal their momentum. The starting pitcher for the home team has, for the past four days, been contemplating whether his initial offering to the plate will be a 95-mile per hour fastball under the batter's chin, or a breaking ball low and away that makes the hitter look powerless at the plate. Either way, that first pitch is like the opening salvo in a battle scene I definitely don't want to miss.

I remember years ago, watching Lenny Dykstra of the Phillies drill the very first pitch over the right field wall in Candlestick Park, to crush the Giants' spirits on a blustery San Francisco day.

The first pitch is more than a message, it's the culmination of hours of preparation at the ballpark: the painstaking task of laying down the foul lines with white chalk, the digging of the dirt surrounding the pitcher's mound and the hallowed hosing down of the infield grass. You have to soak in the atmosphere along with the smell of the popcorn to get fully prepared for the first pitch. Miss it and you will lose the magic of the moment.

And for this game in Anaheim between the Angels and the Yankees, my family and I were stuck in a huge traffic jam that kept us miles from the "Big A", as the Angels ballpark used to be known. Our car was packed with Luerys – Carol riding shotgun, while Sarah and Matt were sitting in the back seat. Matt was about to begin his freshman year at USC – while Sarah was now a senior – so we had loaded up the family car with their college gear and drove the 400 miles from Sacramento to Los Angeles to help both kids move in.

The University of Southern California is located in the heart of Los Angeles, just three miles south of downtown. Matt's dorm room was situated on the sixth floor of Birnkrant Hall, where he enjoyed a beautiful view of the entire USC campus. As luck would have it, he was living in the same dorm that Sarah had resided in her freshman year at USC. Sarah was now living on "The Row," the 28th Street enclave that's home to the Greek life made famous by more than a dozen sororities and fraternities. Thursday nights are always rockin' on The Row, but on this Wednesday evening, the Luerys were determined to catch a ballgame in Anaheim – if only the traffic would let us.

But instead of flowing down the freeway, we were stuck like sardines in a sea of chrome that made Interstate 5 look like a parking lot in Anaheim. We crawled to the stadium at a snail's pace, while my frustrations were mounting.

"Damn it, we're gonna be late for the game!" I screamed.

"Dad, chill out," said Sarah.

"Yeah, it's only a baseball game," opined my wife. "And baseball is like watching paint dry."

"That's not helping," I said.

"Dad, you can always get out of the car and walk to the game," Matt suggested.

"That's exactly what I'm going to do!" I shouted. "Who's coming with me?"

Silence.

"Well, don't all sit on your fingers. Let me see a show of hands!" I shouted.

Nothing.

"OK, then. Carol, take the wheel. I'm outta here."

And with that I opened the car door and took off in a sprint along Gene Autry Way, ticket in hand.

I bolted for the ballpark and arrived in just 12 minutes – fully out of breath, but just in time for the national anthem. I ran up the ramp to claim possession of our seats in the second deck.

Angel Stadium of Anaheim has gone through many revisions and name changes since the Angels first abandoned Los Angeles in 1966 for their permanent home in Orange County. Today, the Angels play in a baseball-only park with a capacity of 45,113 seats overlooking a field of bluegrass.

The outfield seats are bleachers underneath two giant video display boards. The one in left field sports a giant red "A" with a halo at the top, symbolizing the Angels. The signature component of the park is the "California Spectacular" located behind the left center field wall, where fans are greeted by gushing geysers and cascading water running down a simulated mountain replete with real trees and man-made rocks.

The ballpark features three club restaurants and a host of other amenities, giving it a modern look but with a retro feel. However, in my estimation, the park also has a design flaw, in the form of two bullpens located immediately behind the left field wall. This creates a visual and physical barrier for the patrons in left field. Fans sitting behind the bullpens are in fact situated a good 75 feet away from the field of play. While it may be fun to rag on the visiting pitchers warming up in the bullpen beneath you, the location makes it much more difficult to catch a home run ball.

Meanwhile, I looked around and realized I was striking out with my family. Carol, Sarah and Matt were now officially missing in action.

I tried to focus on the field, where the Angels and New York Yankees were locked in a scoreless duel with John Lackey, the ace of the Anaheim rotation, battling against Andy Pettitte, the very same pitcher Matt and I had seen taking the mound for the Yanks two weeks earlier in Cleveland.

After the first inning of play, Carol, Sarah and Matt were still AWOL.

I decided to send out an SOS text message to Sarah.

"Where r u?" I demanded.

"Still stuck in traffic."

"Run to the park, ditch the car," I texted.

"Ha!" was Sarah's response.

Finally, with the Yankees batting in the top of the third inning, my family entered the stadium, but they were in no hurry to join me in the seats.

"Where are you?" I asked Carol by phone.

"We're hungry now and in line for food," she said.

Uggh.

John Lackey mowed down the Yanks in the top half of the third, while Pettitte was flawless in the bottom of the frame, with both pitchers tossing goose eggs.

And that's when my family finally decided to make their debut – to see a ballgame that was now officially one-third over.

"What's the score?" Carol asked, oblivious to the fact that zeros were the only digits on the scoreboard.

"It's nothing to nothing," I proclaimed.

"See that," she said pointedly. "We didn't miss a thing."

My wife looks at baseball much differently than I do.

Whereas I believe Carol had missed two nearly perfect pitching performances, she insisted there were only six innings of torture left.

"No one scored and I'm so bored," she needled me.

The Yankees quickly changed that in the top of the fourth, when Alex Rodriguez crossed the plate on a rare throwing error by John Lackey. But the Angels tied the score in the bottom of the sixth when Orlando Cabrera homered over the left field wall, igniting a crescendo of fireworks into the nighttime sky.

But that was really the last hurrah for the Halos. The Yankees hammered the Angels 8-2, highlighted by Jorge Pasada's two doubles and two RBI, along with a solo shot from Bobby Abreu. Andy Pettitte was brilliant as always with six strikeouts, while reliever Joba Chamberlain struck out the side in the bottom of the eighth. The victory was historic for Joe Torre, giving him 1,150 wins as a Yankee manager and undisputed possession of second place on the franchise records list, behind only the legendary Joe McCarthy, with 1,460.

For me, the game was a great way to send Matt off to college. But my son seemed more interested in getting rid of his parents.

"Have a great freshman year at school," I said to him that night in his dorm room. "Let me give you a big hug for good luck."

"You can go now, Dad."

I was sad to be temporarily losing my baseball buddy, but happy for his newfound sense of independence. After 18 years it was time to cut the umbilical cord. Perhaps, I thought, my daughter could use some help moving into her sorority.

"Sarah, is there anything I can get for you?" I asked innocently. I was secretly hoping she might need something that might prolong my stay – maybe even another withdrawal from the Bank of Dad.

"No, Dad, it's time for you and Mom to head back home to Sacramento."

I looked downward and my daughter caught the disappointment in my eyes. "It's not that Matt and I don't want you here," she explained. "It's just that we need our own space so we can grow up."

"I understand," I said. "But Mom and I miss you both so much — and we haven't even left Los Angeles yet. We are about to become empty-nesters; all we'll have is each other."

"Dad!" Sarah exclaimed. "That's exactly how it's supposed to be."

"And don't be too sad," she continued. "You've got the World Series coming up — and then you can look forward to a new baseball season starting again in the spring."

Fenway Park, Boston Red Sox

Sunday, August 3, 2008

"If you come to a fork in the road, take it."
YOGI BERRA

After a long cross-country plane trip, Matt and I finally arrived in Boston, along with my 11-year-old nephew, Shane. It was good to be in Beantown, home of the Red Sawx (as the Fenway Faithful would say) and Fenway Franks. My brother, Russ, drove up from Connecticut to pick us up at Logan Airport. He was excited to see his son, who had been staying in California with Carol and me for most of July. We wanted to give Russ, a single dad, a little break from parenthood. And now the Luery boys – and their boys – were all together.

Cousins Matt and Shane are eight years apart, which is exactly the same age difference between Russ and me. But those eight years can seem like an eternity, especially when it comes to maturity levels.

Arriving at the hotel, we changed into our sleeping clothes and quickly got into a heated argument over something all guys care about passionately: underwear. As it turned out, I was the only one wearing standard briefs or "Tighty Whities," as my antagonists called them. The Boxer Boys – Russ, Matt and Shane – were united in making fun of me.

Matt started the fireworks. "Boxers are so much cooler than those ugly white things you've got on. Why do you wear them?" he demanded.

"Because they are comfortable and give me good support," I said.

That's when Russ let loose his zinger. "Bras give good support too. Are you planning to wear one of those?"

Shane thought that was pretty funny and grossed us all out with a squeaky fart. A pungent odor filled the room.

I knew instantly I had to call him out for that. "That's gross, Shane. Act your age!" I shouted in his direction.

Shane responded quickly, "I am acting my age. I'm only 11. And besides I didn't fart. That was you."

"Nuh uh," I said, reverting back to my 11-year-old inner child.

"Yuh huh," said the real 11-year-old.

"He who denied it, supplied it," was my very mature response.

That prompted Russ to chime in, "He who smelled it, dealt it."

Suddenly I was a kid again, trading insults with my brother over the bodily functions that seem so amusing to pre-pubescent boys. The next thing I knew Russ had me in a headlock and the Luery brothers were wrestling on the floor just like we did when we were kids. Matt and Shane were amused to see their fathers acting like idiots.

Matt decided to channel his inner Mike, saying, "Break it up, Dad and Russ."

Shane piped up, "Dad, stop beating up on Uncle Mike."

Talk about a retro revival – my brother and I were going at each other again, only this time *our sons had to discipline us.* It was a total role reversal that felt liberating to act so silly and just be a kid again.

A baseball trip will do that to you.

154

I woke before sunrise with a sense of urgency. I wanted to get to the ballpark early to show the boys the Green Monster, Boston's famed 37-foot-high outfield wall that turned routine pop flies into home runs.

I quickly herded the three Boxer Boys into action.

"Let's go, boys," I told them as Matt, Russ and Shane followed me down Brookline Avenue on a frantic walk to Fenway.

"Are you sure you know where you're going?" Russ razzed me.

"Just follow the leader."

I was dead certain we were destined to see the baseball monolith in just a few short blocks. But as the shadows grew longer on Brookline Avenue, my confidence began to fade.

"Everyone's going the other way, Dad," Matt said mockingly.

"That's because we're taking a shortcut," was my smart-ass response, even though I knew something didn't feel right.

As I've mentioned before, I have always had a terrible sense of direction. I can get lost anywhere. A walk in the woods for me is a guarantee for getting disoriented deep in the forest. Given a choice, I'll instinctively take the wrong path.

Or as Yogi Berra once said, "If there's a fork in the road, take it."

Then I saw it: The sign that confirmed my worst fears.

"Welcome to Brookline," it said.

Wrong Way Mike had done it again.

"You idiot!" my brother bellowed.

"Uncle Mike, this isn't the ballpark!" Shane shouted.

My terrible sense of direction had done it again. And of all the traits to pass on to your kids, this is the one my daughter, Sarah, inherited from me. Sarah can get lost on her own street and must pray to the GPS gods every time she gets in the car. Have satellite, will travel.

But on Brookline Avenue, there was no graceful way out, so I simply turned around and began backtracking my way to the ballpark, with the Boxer Boys hooting at my heels the whole way there.

Then I flashed back five months earlier to my box office debacle in getting four seats for the game. In my first attempt going online, I found myself shut out, weeks before the season had even started. I called the ticket office only to learn the Sox had sold out the entire season.

I finally reached a ticket representative, who told me there were a few premium seats available at $150 each.

Yikes!

I've never paid that much for baseball tickets in my life, but my entire baseball trip was in jeopardy. Reluctantly, I agreed to fork over the funds, $600 in all on my overloaded credit card. This better be worth it, I thought.

That horrible memory brought me back to present day Brookline Avenue, where the smell of hotdogs filled the air as we approached the park.

"Best saw-sa-giz he-ah on the cornah!" screamed the Bostonese-speaking vendor. "Get yawr Fenway Franks!"

Suddenly we were swallowed up in a sea of red and blue, the Red Sox colors. The Fenway flags proudly proclaimed the championship years 2004 and 2007. Inside the stadium, I admired the manual scoreboard, a throwback to another era, when stadium operators actually chronicled the changing numbers of the ballgame using a ladder.

Fenway, a truly vintage ballpark, is today one of my top three favorites places to see a Major League game.

"You know, the Red Sox have won two championships this century," I informed my brother.

Russ is a diehard hockey fan and responded, "Yeah, but how many Stanley Cups have they brought home?"

"I don't care about hockey!" I shouted. "It's impossible to follow the puck on TV."

"Let's get back to baseball," I said, noting dozens of kids wearing their number 18 Dice K T-shirts, honoring the Red Sox starter Daisuke Matsuzaka. Meanwhile, the Fenway Fanatics were talking smack about their opponents, the lowly Oakland Athletics, my favorite California team. I was conspicuous in my green and gold shirt and A's cap. The Red Sox faithful took some potshots, comparing my club to a minor league team.

"Yeah, nice hat," said one fan. Then he threw the brushback pitch. "Why would anyone come to Fenway and root for the Oakland Triple A's?"

It's hard to respond when your team is mired in last place, so I just laughed and let it go.

Feeling hungry, I ordered something unique to Fenway Park: a New England Lobster Roll! It was buttery and delicious, but most of the Red Sox partisans were chomping away on Fenway Franks. Out on the field, the Beantown boys dominated the Oakland A's in front of a partisan crowd of 37,317, the Red Sox' 444th consecutive sellout, the second longest in baseball history, according to the Fenway scoreboard.

Our mid-afternoon sunshine was soon blocked by black clouds bearing rain, which quickly became a torrential shower in the sixth inning, sending everyone for cover. The Fenway ground crew stormed into action, covering the infield with a tarp in what seemed like record time.

"This is our first rainstorm ever in four years of baseball globetrotting," I mentioned to Matt.

Not a bad track record, but I was praying to the baseball gods that our complete game streak would continue.

And my prayers were answered; after 30 minutes the sun came out and dried everything.

Most of the 37,317 Fenway faithful returned to the fray.

"Play ball!" screamed the home plate umpire.

I looked around and noticed Matt, Russ and Shane were gone. I was suddenly all alone in my sky box seats. And since I had paid such a ransom for these seats, I wasn't going anywhere.

"Where are you?" I yelled at Russ over the phone.

"Oh, we're nice and dry inside a restaurant here just getting something to eat," he said.

"Well, why don't you grab your food and join me in the park?" I demanded.

"Nah, we're not into baseball that much."

"You hockey hoseheads have kidnapped my son. Bring back my baseball buddy!"

"No, we're holding him hostage until the game is over," Russ laughed, and then hung up on me.

Click.

For the remainder of the game I was forced to fly solo. The Boxer Boys had a good laugh on me, but they missed a great rainbow over Fenway Park. And they missed David Ortiz sliding deftly into second for his first stolen base of the season.

That riled up the crowd for the man they called "Big Papi." They saluted him with the Papi Power drinks. Of course in Boston, it's pronounced "Papi Pow-ah."

The Boxer Boys also missed hearing the Fenway Faithful sing their rendition of the Neil Diamond classic "Sweet Caroline" in the eighth inning – with 30,000 people screaming, "Good times never been so good," followed by a loud chorus of "So good, so good, so good." The song has been a Fenway tradition since 2002, when the Red Sox began to realize the value of a good luck charm – and the impact of getting the crowd fired up in the late innings.

The Boxer Boys were definitely not there to see newly acquired Red Sox outfielder Jason Bay fire an armed missile from right field, to throw out Oakland's Mark Ellis at second base, where he was trying to stretch a single into a double.

"Bet you Manny couldn't have done that!" screamed one rabid Red Sox fan. Manny Ramirez, the loony left fielder for the Sox, had worn out his welcome in Boston and found himself traded to the Dodgers. Even though Manny was a monster at the plate, he was also a defensive liability. Manny was not exactly fleet of foot and he never seemed to be in a hurry when roaming the outfield. Red Sox fans would say Manny could often be found tripping over his own two feet and they seemed glad to see him go.

Of course, Manny did take the Dodgers to the next level and guided the team into the National League Playoffs in 2008. Boston hasn't won a World Series since Manny left, but still, most Red Sox fans think they got the better end of the deal. Yet on this day, the Manny-less Red Sox defeated the hapless Oakland A's, 5-2.

After the game, I finally connected with the Boxer Boys and we hopped on the subway at Kenmore Square for our next adventure: Duck Tours, a fun-filled ride on a massive amphibious vehicle that was half jeep and half boat, a living legend from World War II.

Our driver was Howie, a hilarious Bostonian who greeted us with, "Quack, quack! How Ah Yah?" Howie took us past the Italian restaurants and shops of North Boston and the John Hancock Tower downtown. At 791 feet, it is the tallest building in New England.

Howie was a jokester. "How many beans come in a can of Boston Baked Beans?" he asked the crowd.

"Exactly two-hundred thirty-nine," he answered. "Any more and you'd have two-hundred-fahty," he chuckled.

All of us ducks on board roared with laughter. It seems everybody in Boston loves a good fart joke. Especially the Boxer Boys.

New England

Monday, August 4, 2008–
Thursday, August 7, 2008

*"If you don't like the weather in New England,
just wait a few minutes."*
MARK TWAIN

Boston was the Hub for our departure. Russ headed south for Connecticut, while the Boxer Boys and I headed north for Maine. It was good to be on the road again. Matt was riding shotgun in our little rental car and Shane was munching on chips in the back seat. We passed through the industrial towns north of Boston and crossed the border into Seabrook, New Hampshire.

I pulled over at the state visitor center.

"Why are we stopping, Uncle Mike?" Shane asked. "We just started our trip."

"We've got to step out of the car," I said, "so Matt can add New Hampshire to his list of states."

"Dad, are we not in New Hampshire?" Matt demanded.

"Well, technically yes," I blurted before being rudely interrupted.

"Are we not breathing New Hampshire air?" my son snorted.

"Well, yeah. But you have to actually step foot in a state to say you've been there. You can't just fly overhead in a plane and count it as a place you've been," I declared. I thought it was important to clarify the first tenet of the Luery travel rules: "You've got to plant your feet if you don't want to cheat," I declared.

"I'm not buying it," Matt chortled.

He made it clear he had no intention of playing by my rules. "We're in New Hampshire," he asserted. "I don't have to get out of the car to count it."

"Yes you do and besides, I'll buy you a snack."

Shane bolted out of the car. Matt was right behind him.

Click.

Bribery works every time.

Back on the road again, we sailed though the little sliver of New Hampshire real estate along I-95 and arrived on the Maine border in just 30 minutes.

"I can't believe we're in another state already," Matt said.

"It's an Eastern thing," I told him. "The states are much smaller."

"Yeah, not like California," he stated with pride, "where it takes 14 hours to drive the state from top to bottom."

"Now that's a real state," I said to Shane, knowing I could needle him with this zinger. "Not like Connecticut, where you blink and you miss it."

"Shut up!" he shouted. "It's home for me and I'm happy there."

It's hard to argue with that. And since I grew up in Connecticut, I'll always consider it to be my home state too.

"Fair enough," I said. "We'll call it a draw."

No trip to Maine would be complete without a visit to L.L. Bean, the giant apparel and sporting goods store located along the coast in Freeport. Although most people know it as a catalogue company, Bean also has a strong physical presence that includes multiple stores specializing in hunting, camping and fishing gear.

I asked Matt to snap a picture of me in front of the store.

"Here's the author getting booted out of another establishment,"

I said with a laugh to my photographer.

Click.

The boys had a blast looking at the mounted moose heads on the wall and live fish in the indoor pond. It was fun to count the dozens of out-of-state license plates in the parking lot. We spotted South Carolina, Minnesota and Texas – 26 states in all from Maine to California and nearly every place in between.

On the road again, we ran into a heavy rainstorm, followed by sunshine and then another downpour.

"Remember what Mark Twain said," I chimed out to Shane. 'If you don't like the weather in New England, just wait a few minutes.'

"But it's been raining for an hour, Uncle Mike," he pleaded.

"Yeah, but it's changed twice already," I explained. "The weather here is very fickle."

"I'm hungry, Uncle Mike," Shane replied. "When are we gonna get there?"

"Soon," I said. "Very soon. Hey, there's a Dairy Queen," I noted. "Let's stop there."

We pulled over, eager to get some ice cream. Upon entering the DQ we noticed one of the patrons armed with a gun in his holster. There was no effort to conceal the weapon; he flaunted it in open view.

Matt wondered out loud how anyone could carry a weapon in the open – something that would create controversy in California. In Maine, however, the rules are different. No permit is required to possess a rifle, shotgun or even a handgun.

"Well," I said, "maybe he's an off-duty cop. Maine must permit people to carry a weapon as long as it's in plain view. This state firmly supports the Second Amendment, which gives Americans the right to bear arms," I stated in my best professorial tone.

"But that was written centuries ago," Matt noted.

"Yes, it's ancient history – way before Al Gore invented the

Internet," I chuckled. "But the framers of the Constitution saw the value of a well-armed citizen militia to defend itself against a tyrannical government."

"Dad, you sound like Fox News," warned Matt. "Quit the flag waving and drive."

So we finished our ice cream and headed off to our first destination, Reid State Park, located along an isolated stretch of Maine's rocky coastline in Georgetown. We traveled down the dirt road to the beach where the water temperature was a bone-chilling 62 degrees.

It was numbingly cold, but we kicked off our shoes and nudged our toes into the water.

"Aaahhh!" Matt screamed. "It's freezing!"

"Oh come on, you wuss," I needled him. "I'll bet you I can last longer in it than you."

"You're on."

"Come on, Shane," I urged. "Join us in the water."

The rhythm of the waves was broken by a blood-curdling shriek. "Oooooh my God, that's so cold!" Shane bleated.

"OK," I said. "We'll make it a contest. Whoever can last the longest wins five dollars."

Suddenly there were six legs in the ice-cold water.

"Twenty-eight, 29, 30 seconds!" I shouted.

And before I could get to 31, Shane bolted out of the water with blue lips and a cramp in his legs.

"Oh, you're such a girlie man," I said in my best Arnold Schwarzenegger voice.

Shane was speechless and could do nothing but run onto the warm sand. Meanwhile, Matt and I were locked in mortal combat, neither one of us willing to back down.

After 60 seconds, our knees were knocking together from the cold. By the 90-second mark, it seemed we were frozen solid from the frosty ocean lather.

"Let's get out of here, Dad," Matt begged.

"You first."

"Age before beauty."

I tried to break for the beach but found my legs locked in deep paralysis. Using every ounce of strength, I flexed one foot, then the other as I pinched my calves to get the blood flowing. Finally, I found a pulse and started moving like a zombie through the water. Matt was right on my heels as we pushed each other to safety before collapsing on the sand.

"I won!" he shouted.

"No, it was a tie."

"Hand over the five."

I don't know which hurt more, my aching pride or losing the Lincoln. Either way, Matt had a good laugh at my expense. We celebrated our survival by downing a seafood dinner of Maine's finest crustaceans and steamers drowned in butter at the Lobster Dock in Boothbay Harbor. It was a very good day.

⚾ ⚾ ⚾

By the morning I was anxious to hit the highway again. They say the rain in Maine falls mainly in Wayne – the site of that day's destination. Wayne is the home of Camp Androscoggin, where I spent eight summers playing sports and developing some of the best friendships ever. On this rare sunny day, the camp was radiantly beautiful.

Under the leadership of my old campmate and current owner Peter Hirsch, Camp Androscoggin offers a field house for the boys to play street hockey. For those interested in learning cinema, there was a state-of-the-art media center. We stopped in to see the campers making i-Movies using Apple's Final Cut Pro editing program. Outside, the waterfront was pristine and surrounded by pine trees that filled the air with a sweet, pungent odor, while the call of the loons cascaded across Lake Androscoggin. The tennis courts were made of red clay and the baseball diamonds smelled of freshly cut grass.

Shane was engrossed in a game of tetherball with one of the campers while Matt and I walked the waterfront. The counselors were engaged in a fierce game of volleyball.

"It would be fun to be camp counselor here," Matt said.

"It was great for me," I told him. "I was a counselor here for two summers and loved every minute of it. I coached the baseball team and worked with the boys on their hitting and fielding. And at night when the kids were sleeping, you could just go out to the ball field and gaze up at the clear sky, where the shooting stars would put on a show for free."

"But how was your social life? Are there any girls camps around here?" he asked with a gleam in his eye.

"Oh, yes," I said. "I dated girls from Camp Vega and we'd go to the beach on our days off. We had lots of fun."

"Dad, somehow I can't imagine you being young or having lots of fun. I mean after all, your favorite word now is 'No!'"

"Hey, I was your age once."

"I doubt it. You were probably born old."

"Young whippersnapper," I muttered.

As a distraction, I showed Shane some old camp pictures of his father – my brother, Russ, who also attended Camp Androscoggin. Shane was amazed at how much younger his father looked at age 11.

"I can't believe my dad used to look like me," he declared.

"Don't worry," I assured him. "You'll grow out of it."

After a hearty camp lunch in the mess hall, I loaded Matt and Shane into a canoe for an adventure on Lake Androscoggin. With Matt at the bow, I paddled from the rear of the canoe, while Shane played wingman in the middle.

"Where are we going?" Shane demanded.

"You see that island in the middle of the lake?" I asked. "That's where we are headed. It's called Senior Island and it's the former home of Camp Androscoggin Senior, where the older boys lived in rustic cabins in the woods."

The original Camp Androscoggin was founded in 1907 and survived until 1972. That's when the Junior camp, run by the Hirsch family, consolidated the camps by expanding the mainland campus.

As we paddled to the island, I quickly noticed my formerly bucolic camp in the trees had gone through a radical transformation. Upon landing, we discovered all the old wooden cabins had collapsed from the weight of the winter snows, leaving only the framework. The baseball field was overgrown with weeds that reached chest height and the once-walkable trails were now lined with thick vegetation.

But at the far end of the woods, the island's new owner had built a two-story vacation home as a rural retreat. Yes, we were far removed from the cacophony of sounds from city life and for a moment, I could wander down memory lane to hear the joyful noise of the boys of summer from yesteryear, shouting "Play ball!" on a diamond whose glory had faded into overgrown weeds.

My mind was going through a metamorphosis – evolving from childhood memories of a shy, freckle-faced boy who had somehow become a father and a middle-aged man. How could all those years pass so quickly? But as I breathed in the fresh smell of pine trees, for a moment at least, I was young again. Camp Androscoggin will always be my home away from home, a place where my memories are safe from harm.

⚾ ⚾ ⚾

For the boys, memory lane was getting old, so we took off for Maine's Capitol in Augusta. The boys refused to get out of the car, so I snapped a picture.

Next, it was on to Lewiston, an industrial city on the banks of the Androscoggin River. Lewiston is Maine's second largest city and perhaps best known as the site of the famed fight in 1965 between Sonny Liston and Muhammad Ali, then known as Cassius Clay. It was a world championship boxing match that fewer than 2,500 people actually saw, but millions of sports fans have heard the tale of the brash young Cassius Clay/Muhammad Ali yelling "Get up and fight, sucker!" after he floored Liston to the mat. The iconic photograph of that fight captures Ali preening in the ring and celebrating his knockdown victory.

As we left Lewiston, rain filled the sky as we traveled across Maine. We crossed the border and ventured through the White Mountains of New Hampshire, then discovered the Green Mountains of Vermont, where the state name is derived from the French phrase "verts monts." We stopped in Montpelier and took pictures of the State Capitol, but Matt and Shane showed no interest in going inside to see the sights, even though the gold on the dome is the real deal.

Instead, we had lunch with my old friend Roy Bishop, who had been Matt's third grade science teacher in California. Roy had moved back home to Vermont, where he loved the fresh air and rural lifestyle. Vermont is bucolic, beautiful and unique because the state has banned billboards on the highways. As a result, there is nothing to distract your view from the lush, green forest-like setting. The dearth of outdoor advertising makes Vermont radically different from the cluttered commercial landscape of California.

I queried Matt, "Would the Founding Fathers view the ban on billboards here as an expression of state's rights – or a suppression of free speech?"

"It's important to protect the environment."

"What about protecting ideas that can be expressed on a billboard?"

"That's just commercialism."

"Doesn't commercial free speech have a right to be protected?"

"Not in Vermont," said Matt, effectively ending our constitutional crisis.

We grabbed a quick lunch and then headed south on Interstate 91 into the Commonwealth of Massachusetts for a visit to Smith College in Northampton.

Both of Matt's grandmothers – Anita Meyers, my mother, and Liz Kruidenier, Carol's mom – had graduated from the all-women's school in the early 1950s. The Smith College alumnae include some prominent women ranging from feminists Gloria Steinem and Betty Friedan to poet Sylvia Plath and chef Julia Child. Former First Ladies Barbara Bush and Nancy Reagan are also graduates of Smith College. Northampton is a small town, just a few miles down Highway 9 from Amherst, where Matt's other grandfather – Peter Kruidenier – attended Amherst College. We hiked up the historic steps of the Amherst campus at a record clip, as Matt and Shane were getting bored with the family history lesson.

"I'm hungry, Uncle Mike!" Shane bellowed.

"Yeah, Dad, let's go," Matt echoed.

"OK, boys, get in the car," I said.

We wolfed down some fast food and continued our journey down I-91 to Springfield, Massachusetts, home of the National Basketball Association Hall of Fame. The Hall has video tributes, plaques and jerseys from more than 250 players. Springfield is basketball's birthplace – the city where James Naismith, a physical education instructor, invented the sport in 1891.

Matt was excited to hear the famous voiceover of Boston Celtics announcer Johnny Most screaming "Havlicek stole the ball, Havlicek stole the ball!" in describing the final moments of Game Seven of the 1965 Eastern Finals. In that game Boston's John Havlicek stole an in-bound pass to claim victory in the closing seconds of the contest against the Philadelphia 76'ers. The commentary is now considered to be one of the most famous radio calls in basketball history.

While the NBA Hall of Fame fascinated Matt, Shane was painfully bored.

"These guys can't even skate backward," said Shane, the hockey fanatic.

"But hockey players can't jump or soar through the air," was Matt's retort.

I encouraged the boys to settle their argument on the Hall's basketball court, where they had a chance to shoot some free throws. Matt easily won the contest, then we got in the car once again, this time driving through torrential thunderstorms in Connecticut, my home state. I explained to the boys that although I was born in New York, my family had moved to Connecticut when I was nearly two and I had lived there until graduating from high school.

"I consider myself a Nutmegger at heart," I told them.

"So that's where you got the name 'Nutmeg' for your dog!" Shane shouted.

Before long we were in Ridgefield, where Shane lives in a condo with Russ. The Luery Boys were back together again, if only for just one more night.

A Personal Journey
Stamford, Connecticut
Friday, August 8, 2008

"You can't go home again."
THOMAS WOLFE

It was 08/08/08 – a lucky day on the Chinese calendar, but not very lucky for me on separation day. After spending an entire summer with my nephew Shane, it was now time to leave him with my brother, Russ, in Ridgefield. It was hard saying goodbye, but Shane was happy to be back with his dad.

Matt and I drove south to my old hometown of Stamford, Connecticut. Stamford is a medium-sized city of 118,000 people, many of them suburban commuters who travel to New York every day for business. Stamford is a beautiful place, blessed with a rustic reservoir, terrific nature center (the Stamford Museum) and thick woods on the Connecticut coastline.

I wanted Matt to see my childhood home on Newfield Drive, but upon arriving there, we discovered the house had been boarded up. Someone had shuttered the windows with wooden planks. Hoodlums had desecrated my home with graffiti. It was depressing to see the roof literally collapsing over what used to be my parents' bedroom. I stared silently at my boyhood home: a once-beautiful house that had now become a junker, a foreclosure rattrap that vandals had marked as part of their turf.

"Matt," I started to say, but found myself unable to complete the words.

"It's alright, Dad," he said softly. "I understand."

Months later, someone would purchase the condemned property and demolish the house, leaving only an empty lot. From this point forward I would be a housing orphan – a middle-aged man without a childhood home, just a shell of a memory from happier times.

I was feeling very vulnerable, but things were about to get even worse. Our next stop in Stamford would make me even more depressed, as Matt and I drove to the cemetery to visit my family's gravesite. My mom and dad are both buried there, along with my youngest sister, Roberta, who died in a car accident at the tender age of 20.

Roberta had been driving out to college for her senior year at Washington University in St. Louis when she lost control of the wheel along the Merritt Parkway in Connecticut. I can still remember the haunting phone call that came early on a Sunday morning in August. There was a distant voice on the phone, from a stranger informing me my baby sister had just perished in a terrible accident.

I demanded to speak to my mother, but she was too distraught to come to the phone. I dropped to my knees and hung up in disbelief as I burst into tears. The pain was overwhelming, ripping a hole in my heart that even today, more than 20 years later, has still never fully healed.

Roberta was a fiery redhead with a smile that could light up a room. Energetic and vivacious, she was the girl who climbed on stage to plant a kiss on Billy Joel while he was performing in a Sacramento concert back in the 1980s. The crowd gasped in amazement at my little sister's brazen display of affection, but Billy just shrugged it off and kept playing the piano. Roberta darted from the stage into the darkness and then, minutes later, arrived safely back in her seat.

"Did you see me up there on stage?" she asked.

"Yeah," I said, "and so did 20,000 other people who wish it could have been them. It was very cool," I told her before getting into my big brother role. "But don't do it again."

Roberta's gravesite was littered with overgrown weeds and mounds of dust that obscured her nameplate. I hunched down on my knees and began pulling the weeds while scraping through the dirt with a nearby rock. Suddenly, I was overcome with a wave of grief, a sinking feeling that nearly everything from my past had died: my little sister, my parents, my house and my childhood memories.

"Matt, have you ever heard the phrase, 'You can't go home again?'"

He nodded.

"Well, this is what it's like. Sometimes the past is better left as a fond memory. It's not a place you'd really want to revisit. It can dredge up some old issues."

Matt silently acknowledged my pain. Then he put his hand on my shoulder and said, "Dad, it's time to move forward. Let's go."

I looked at him and realized he was right. Our personal histories may shape us, but they don't necessarily define who we are, for life is a journey with plenty of twists, turns and unexpected exits. It was time to get back on the road and let baseball be our guide.

So Matt and I traveled along the scenic Merritt Parkway and in less than 60 minutes, arrived in New York City to drop off our rental car after logging 800 miles through 6 states. Now it was time to explore the Big Apple.

Shea Stadium, New York Mets

Friday, August 8, 2008

"Ohio State will kick your butt this year."
ANONYMOUS BUCKEYE FAN

Bostonians always joke that the initials "NY" stand for "Next Year" and not "New York," but for Shea Stadium there would be no next year. After the 2008 season, the Mets would abandon their home of 44 years for a brand new ballpark known as Citi Field.

I can remember attending ballgames when Shea Stadium first opened (built at a price of $25 million) in 1964. I still have a vision from that inaugural year – a picture of hot dog wrappers swirling around the infield in a voracious whirlpool of wind while the young Mets set records for futility by finishing in last place (for the third year in a row) with 109 losses. The Mets played their first two seasons (1962-1963) in the Polo Grounds, before the park was demolished. Shea Stadium was named after lawyer William Shea, who brought National League baseball back to New York after the painful departure of the Giants and Dodgers.

Indeed the Mets' logo colors of orange and blue are said to represent a stripe from each of the departed teams. Shea Stadium was never really a cozy baseball park, but rather a multi-purpose monolith where fans were bombarded by the monotonous roar of airplanes overhead from nearby LaGuardia Airport (hence the name "Jets" for the football team).

Fast-forward to 2008 and the Mets were hosting a night game, so Matt and I decided to spend our day exploring New York as tourists. We left the comforts of our hotel room in midtown and rode the subway to lower Manhattan, then walked across the Brooklyn Bridge.

"I wonder how old this bridge is?"

"It was built in 1883," Matt said. "It's one of the oldest suspension bridges in the country. I've done a lot of reading about it."

"I can see that."

The Brooklyn Bridge spans more than a mile across the East River, connecting Manhattan and Brooklyn. It truly is an engineering marvel and a great vantage point for seeing the Manhattan skyline. Upon arriving on the Brooklyn side, we decided to hop on the subway and take the "F" train to Coney Island.

"I've always wanted to visit that famous beach," Matt said.

"Yeah, it's got dozens of rides and should be fun."

Coney Island is actually more like a peninsula today and no longer the hub of activity it was in the early 20th century. The wooden boardwalk planks run parallel to the beach, but we found the sand to be dirty and littered with cigarette butts. The amusement park rides also seemed to have lost their luster, so we quickly headed back to the hotel in Manhattan.

After a quick change of clothes, we hopped the "Q" line to Shea Stadium, located at Flushing Meadows in Queens. On the field, we saw "Mr. Met," a giant baseball head mascot that reminded me of a silly song from the Mets' early days.

In my experience, Shea Stadium will always be associated with windy conditions and lousy food. The hot dogs we bought were both pre-cooked and wrapped in foil and tasted like cardboard. The sight lines for the park made it tough to see all the action, depending on where your seats were located. And unlike modern parks, there was no panoramic view of the downtown skyline. The new Citi Field can't correct that problem, but it does recreate the brick façade of Ebbets Field as you enter the park.

The game itself was a good one, with 45,000 fans cheering the Mets to a 3-0 shutout over the Florida Marlins. Mets third baseman David Wright hit a two-run jack in the first, while in the fourth inning, Carlos Delgado had a solo shot over the wall in left center.

The best part of the game was sitting next to four guys from Ohio who just happened to be traveling on their own baseball road trip. Matt and I expressed our admiration for Great American Park in Cincinnati and Jacob's Field (now Progressive Field) in Cleveland. We were getting along just great until someone brought up college football.

"Matt," said one of the guys from Ohio, "where do you go to school?"

Matt proudly proclaimed he was a faithful Trojan from USC.

"Well, Ohio State will kick your butt this year," the Buckeye boasted.

"Doubt it," Matt replied. "We've got Mark Sanchez at quarterback and a great crop of linebackers who will crush your offense."

As it turns out, Matt was right. Five weeks later, USC would destroy Ohio State 35-3 in the opening game of the 2008 season.

Citizens Bank Ballpark
Philadelphia Phillies

Saturday, August 9, 2008

"I've always wanted to play."
ED SPRAGUE, JR.

We left New York's Penn Station via Amtrak and enjoyed the train ride to Pennsylvania in air-conditioned comfort. Along the way, we passed through Newark, Princeton and Trenton, New Jersey's capital, before arriving in Philadelphia, where we lined up to see the Liberty Bell and the Betsy Ross House – the place where, according to legend, a local seamstress designed the American flag.

The Luery boys also explored Independence Hall, where the Founding Fathers signed the Declaration of Independence in 1776.

After feasting on a local treat – a Philadelphia cheese steak – Matt and I walked over to the National Constitution Center, where we got into a heated debate over free speech. The argument was sparked by a legal exhibit involving a case known as Texas vs. Johnson, in which anti-war activists desecrated the American flag and chanted, "Red, White and Blue, we spit on you."

Matt argued that free speech, no matter how spiteful, should be protected at all times. As a journalist, I support the First Amendment wholeheartedly, but for the sake of argument, I decided to challenge Matt. I was curious to see if he could defend his position under pressure.

"Well, what about when the government forces fast food restaurants to disclose their calorie counts? Isn't that limiting free speech rights for businesses, by dictating what the restaurants must say to their customers?"

"No. It's different. Because we have an obesity epidemic in this country and calorie counts help consumers make wise decisions."

"First of all, no one even reads those calorie menus. Are you saying the government's role is to protect people from themselves? Do you really want a nanny state that dictates all your decisions? Whatever happened to individual responsibility and free choice?"

"Stupid people make bad decisions," he said.

"And who are you to decide who's stupid and who's smart?" I snorted. "Now you sound like a pointy-headed intellectual who thinks he should make decisions for everyone else,"

"I'm smart enough to know it's time to head to the ballgame," Matt said, ending the argument. While fathers and sons might fight over the meaning of freedom, at least they can always agree on baseball.

What is it about baseball that brings fathers and sons together?

Two years later, I would ask that very question to Ed Sprague Jr., the baseball coach at the University of the Pacific in Stockton, California. Ed had followed his father into the Major Leagues, with Sprague Senior pitching for the St. Louis Cardinals, while Sprague Junior had been a third baseman for the Toronto Blue Jays.

I took out my trusty reporter's tape recorder and began my interview with a question about fathers and sons.

"How much of an influence was your Dad in your life and what role did he play in your decision to play baseball?" I wanted to know.

Ed told me, "Well, I think he exposed me to it for sure. I grew up around it when he was playing. You know he owned the Stockton Ports here, which brought us to Stockton. I was always constantly around the game so, fortunately, I loved it."

"I've always wanted to play," Ed stated. "So I don't think he ever pushed me in that direction. I was gifted with a little bit of ability and I was fortunate in that I was exposed to it all the time. And then you know, as I became older he became a little bit more of a mentor. I'd bounce things off of him here and there. He would always tell me something about hitting and then he'd be like, 'Well, I was a pitcher; I don't know anything about hitting.' He was always there for me when I was struggling and when I was doing good."

As for baseball's ability to bind fathers and sons together, Ed offered this perspective:

"Well, I think it's one of those things that baseball's a sport — there's a lot going on underneath that you can't really see." He paused for a moment, then added, "Before the pitcher takes a sign, there's a whole lot of things going on. And it's probably true about a father and son's relationship, I mean there's a lot going on beyond what you see, you know, playing catch, so there's a lot to that. Whether you're at the game or you're watching it on TV, you can spend time talking. It's not just father and son; it can be boyfriend and girlfriend or you know, husband and wife or two siblings."

The UOP coach continued, "There's time to relax in between pitches, in between innings. You can have casual conversations. You can talk about strategy or whatever's going on. So I think that part of it, I think it just induces conversation, between father and son. And you know being a father myself now, you know anytime you can sit down and have a conversation with your kids, I think is a great thing."

I think Ed Sprague is right. Baseball is all about timing and the pastoral pace of the game makes it the perfect sport to discuss life between pitches – a chance to have those difficult dialogues with your kid while the batter digs in for the next delivery.

Your conversation with your kid could reach a crescendo or exclamation point, just like a baseball game. You could take a deliberate approach just like a pitcher with perfect control, or you can lob soft questions to your kid, just like a batting practice pitcher. The point is, you want to establish contact and build confidence.

Back in Philadelphia, Matt and I were riding the subway to the south side of town, where the Phillies, 76'ers, Eagles and Flyers are all located in venues that are very close to each other. Citizens Bank Ballpark, the home of the Phillies, is one of the urban jewels of modern baseball, featuring real Kentucky bluegrass with angled seating overlooking a field that is 23 feet below street level, giving everyone a great view no matter where they sit. Most seats from the outfield offer a great view of downtown Philadelphia. There's also a huge video scoreboard that presents highlights and replays with HD clarity.

My favorite feature is the out-of-town game summary that offers up-to-the-minute information, including how many runners are on which base at any ballpark in the Majors. The park also features an electronic Liberty Bell that rocks and chimes after every Phillies home run. The bell is located in right center field, some 50 feet high and 35 feet wide.

Our game tonight would feature the Phillies against their cross-state rival – the Pittsburgh Pirates – and nearly all of the 43,500 seats had a fanny in them. The park was bathed in a sea of red for the hometown Phillies. Philly fans are passionate about their club and very knowledgeable about baseball. One fan told me the Phillies started in 1883. But by August of 2008, they could boast of only one World Championship – and that was in 1980 when the Phillies beat the Kansas City Royals.

Matt and I had no way of knowing, but on this night, we were watching a World Series–bound team. In fact, in the 2008 fall classic, the Phillies would capture their second world title by beating the Tampa Bay Rays in seven games.

By contrast, the Phillies' former rival, the Philadelphia Athletics actually hold the city record with five World Championships. The Athletics lasted just half a century in Philadelphia, departing the City of Brotherly Love in 1954 when the team moved west to Kansas City. In 1968 the team would move west again to California, where they became the Oakland Athletics.

On this night, though, Phillies shortstop Jimmy Rollins was on fire, going 4-4 with two triples and leading the team to a 4-2 victory over the Pirates.

The Phillie Phanatic, the furry green blob and official mascot of the club, led the crowd in a series of cheers throughout the game. The fun family atmosphere at Citizens Bank Ballpark was fantastic!

The Liberty Bell, Philadelphia

Citizens Bank Ballpark, home of the Philadelphia Phillies

Baltimore's Inner Harbor

Old Glory flies proudly
at Fort McHenry

Babe Ruth, Baltimore's native son

Babe Ruth Museum, Baltimore

Boog Powell, American League MVP 1970, Oriole Park at Camden Yards, home of the Baltimore Orioles

Orioles Hall of Fame

Presidential race at Nationals Park, home of the Washington Nationals

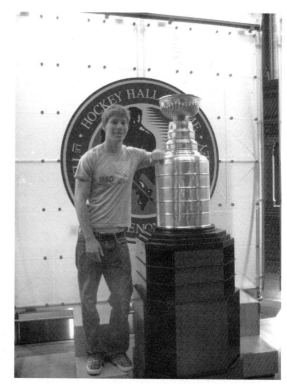

The Stanley Cup, hockey's holy grail,
Toronto, Canada

Ed Sprague Jr., World Series hero 1992

Dave Stewart, World Series champion
1989 and 1993

Opening the dome
in Toronto

Rogers Centre,
home of the
Toronto Blue Jays

Toronto waterfront and skyline

Niagara Falls, Ontario, Canada

Baseball Hall of Fame,
Cooperstown, New York

Matt meets the Sultan of Swat

Fantasy ball with Roy Campanella
at the Baseball Hall of Fame

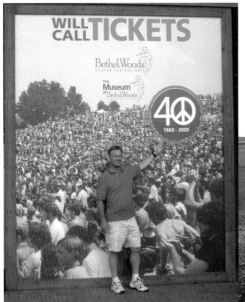

Remembering Woodstock

Site of Woodstock Festival,
August 1969

Studying the
Psychedelic Era

Wavy Gravy's bus

Interviewing Bernie Williams,
five-time All-Star, New York Yankees

Bernie Williams is Moving Forward

Yankee Stadium, home of the New York Yankees

My sister Andrea with Jacob, Alexis and Ethan Fenton and Matt in Connecticut

Lobster lovers
Andrea and Fred Fenton

Bryan Sarner with Matt,
Citi Field, home of
the New York Mets

Mike with Rick Sarner, Citi Field

30 ballparks, or is it 31?

Matt, Mike, Sarah and Carol at Angel Stadium, home of the Los Angeles Angels of Anaheim

Matt at Angel Stadium, home of the Los Angeles Angels of Anaheim

Matt and Sarah in L.A.

Rod Carew, Twins legend

Target Field, home of
the Minnesota Twins

Oriole Park at Camden Yards, Baltimore Orioles

Sunday August 10, 2008

"Oh say does that star spangled banner yet wave?"
FRANCIS SCOTT KEY

Matt and I took the morning Amtrak train from Philadelphia to Baltimore. Along the way, the train stopped in Wilmington, Delaware, where I urged Matt to sprint out to the platform.

"Why?"

"Because you've never been to Delaware before. So run out and touch the ground with your feet so you can count Delaware as your 43rd state."

"Are we not in Delaware now?" Matt argued.

"Yes, technically," I admitted, "but really you have to step foot in the state for it to count."

"Am I not breathing Delaware air right now?"

I knew I had heard this argument before. Nevertheless, I was insistent on Matt getting onto the platform.

"You're still on the train, Matt, and who knows when you're going to be in Delaware again. So do me a favor and just run out there quickly before the train leaves the station."

"Dad, standing on a platform for 10 seconds in Delaware doesn't really mean anything."

"Just go!" I shouted. "You'll be glad you did."

Reluctantly, Matt stood up and walked into the sweltering heat, then instantly came back into the climate-controlled train.

"So what do you think of Delaware?"

"It was hot. And all I saw was the train station!" he said emphatically. "This is so stupid. You can't really say I've experienced the state."

"Well, at least now you can say you've been here. And one of my goals for you is to visit all 50 states, so now we can add one more to the list."

Matt pulled out his iPod and plugged in his earbuds. He was in his own musical world now, oblivious to anything I might say. I suspect that's exactly the way he wanted it.

Upon arriving in Baltimore, we checked into our hotel and found ourselves surrounded by cartoon comic characters. Those rabid fans of Japanese animation buzzed around Baltimore in full costume, masquerading around the city and making it look like Halloween on a hot summer's day.

We walked down to the Inner Harbor area and were impressed by the urban renovation that triggered thousands of tourists to visit the restaurants, clubs and hotels.

"Wow!" Matt said. "Baltimore just shatters my expectations. This is what Oakland should be like. Baltimore seems vibrant and alive, with an impressive skyline."

We walked just a few blocks to Camden Yards, home of Oriole Park. The stadium is an old-school ballpark, converted from a vintage warehouse and made just for baseball with a capacity for 48,876 fans, counting the standing room only seats. Completed in 1992, Oriole Park is considered the first "retro" stadium, built with a brick façade and an asymmetrical field containing all-natural grass turf. The current center field was once home to "Ruth's Café," where Babe Ruth's father had operated his family restaurant a century ago.

Today, it is Boog Powell cooking up a storm at Oriole Park.

The former Oriole All-Star first baseman now runs Boog's BBQ, where fans stand in line to meet and greet the Baltimore legend while chowing down on his delicious barbecue beef and pork. Naturally, I couldn't resist the chance to have my picture taken with the beefy, 6-foot-4, red-haired slugger who won two World Series titles for the Orioles and captured the American League Most Valuable Player award in 1970. I asked Boog to sign my game ticket, which he graciously agreed to do.

Matt and I also checked out the Orioles Hall of Fame, showcasing the careers of Brooks and Frank Robinson, along with Dave McNally, Eddie Murray and Cal Ripken Jr., whose number 8 jersey is still the most popular shirt in Baltimore, even though he retired years ago. Ripken played 2,162 consecutive games without a day off, a Major League record that, in all likelihood, will never be broken.

I noticed Matt was playing with the calculator on his cell phone.

"What are you doing?"

"Do you realize 2,162 consecutive games is the equivalent of playing 14 and a half seasons without missing a day of work?"

Yes," I agreed. "It's a truly remarkable achievement, especially for a shortstop, who played one of the most demanding positions in the game. Ripken played most of his career at short, then he moved to third base in his later years."

The crowd was a sea of orange and black in a park that had attracted nearly 50 million fans since its opening in 1992, according to the center field scoreboard. Singing the national anthem in Baltimore is a unique experience because the fans scream the word "O" in the opening line. In Baltimore, "O" stands for Orioles and the fans punch the "O" for emphasis, then pause dramatically for several seconds before continuing with "say can you see."

Sitting in the upper deck behind home plate, you can see the Baltimore skyline reflecting the sunlight of a beautiful summer day. But it turned out to be a dark day for the Orioles, as they were outslugged 15-7 by the Texas Rangers and Josh Hamilton, who went 3-6, including a three-run homer. But Oriole Park is a winner – a stadium that is truly a great tribute to baseball, the way it's meant to be.

That night we took in the Baltimore nightlife at the Inner Harbor and climbed high up above Federal Hill, which provides a panoramic view of a city that is truly underrated for its charm and beauty.

Matt had been begging for a chance to sleep in. That night he told me, "Dad, you know this is a vacation; we don't have to be out the door every day at 8 in the morning."

"I know, but I feel like there's so much to do and I'd hate to miss it by sleeping in."

"Yeah, and I hate to miss sleep."

So in the spirit of compromise, I promised Matt he could sleep until 10 a.m.

◉ ◉ ◉

By 11 the next morning, we were out the door to take a water taxi ride along Baltimore's Inner Harbor, guiding us to Fells Point, an historic waterfront district lined with cobblestone streets. The next stop was Fort McHenry, where Francis Scott Key wrote "The Star Spangled Banner" in 1814, while the British were invading the city.

But the federal forces held the fort and saved Baltimore from British occupation. Our national anthem poses the question, "O" say does that Star Spangled Banner yet wave? And in Baltimore the answer is definitively yes, because a huge American flag is always flying day and night over Fort McHenry.

After the water taxi trip, we walked to the Babe Ruth Museum, dedicated to arguably Baltimore's most famous native son, although many would claim that Edgar Allen Poe should get that honor. The museum is a fan's delight, replete with pictures, trophies and old uniforms from the New York Yankee legend, whose appeal transcended baseball. During his dominance, Ruth was the highest paid player, making $80,000 a year in 1930, when America was mired deep in the Depression.

The baseball star's salary was $5,000 more than President Herbert Hoover was making at the time. Legend has it that when sportswriters asked the Sultan of Swat how he could justify making more than the president, he answered, "Why not? I had a better year." His comments brought some much-needed laughter to a beleaguered and battered American public.

Indeed Ruth was right, for in 1930 he hit 49 home runs along with 153 runs batted in, while generating 136 walks and maintaining a .373 batting average at the plate. By contrast, Herbert Hoover was proving to be ineffective in combating the economic chaos around him. Hoover was at the helm when the Great Depression would ultimately force nearly one out of every four Americans out of a job.

The Babe Ruth Museum says the Baltimore legend probably didn't say or do everything attributed to him, yet he remains one of the game's most popular players.

⚾ ⚾ ⚾

By late afternoon, it was time to leave Baltimore and head to the Amtrak station, where Washington, D.C., would be our final stop. We checked into the Jury Hotel and grabbed dinner at a nearby Chipotle restaurant.

Matt was wild about the place and ate there regularly in California. To me it was good food at a good price, but nothing special. But my son insisted the vibe was something only his generation could appreciate.

"It just feels like it's designed for us, by people like us," he said.

"Do you mean the two of us?"

"No, Dad, by 'us' I mean young people – definitely not you."

"No need to get all worked up over a meal. You and your generation can claim it for your own."

"But the food is organic and the whole concept is about sustainable living," he stated.

"It's decent food at a decent price; you don't have to get all starry-eyed about it."

"Just leave my Chipotle alone," said the Stinkbug. "Maybe you old folks like your food better when it's strained."

"Hey, I still have my teeth!" I said defiantly. "Now let's get back to the hotel. I need a nap."

Nationals Park, Washington Nationals

Tuesday, August 12, 2008

*"Washington is a city of Southern efficiency
and Northern charm."*
JOHN F. KENNEDY

One of the best ways to see Washington is to board D.C. Ducks, the amphibious relics from World War II, offering an excursion of the city by land and water.

Imagine 30 perfect strangers all shouting "Quack, quack!" in unison outside the U.S. Capitol.

"Are they referring to the members of Congress?" Matt wondered aloud.

The crowd chuckled, but I wondered if he was on to something.

"Yeah, it's not a good time to be an incumbent," I said. "After all, look at their rock-bottom approval ratings."

A Gallup Poll two years later in 2010 would show that a mere 11 percent of Americans had a high level of confidence in Congress.

Duck Tours took us into the Potomac River toward Virginia, where we saw commercial jets taking off from Reagan International Airport, not far from the Pentagon.

Once back in Washington, we walked to the Newseum, a living history of the news business – my dedicated profession for more than a quarter of a century.

"What was news gathering like when you started, Dad?" Matt wanted to know.

"Well, my first live shot was in 1863, when Lincoln delivered his Gettsyburg Address." With tongue planted firmly in cheek, I continued, "We didn't have satellites or microwave trucks back then, so we used telegraph wires to announce the news. It took 22 hours to send the entire transmission, but I got the story. And I had an exclusive interview with President Lincoln," I said, laughing.

"Wow, you *are* old!"

"Yes, I missed George Washington crossing the Delaware by just a few years."

"Really?"

"No!" I insisted.

The Newseum's archival clips of major events from the 20th century captured my attention. Matt was preoccupied with the newspaper display, offering dailies from all the states.

Perhaps most impressive was the twisted steel antenna mast that had once stood majestically over the World Trade Center in New York before the cowardly terrorist attack on 9/11.

From the Newseum, it was an easy walk to the White House grounds, where you could see the president's home from half a mile away. Years ago, tourists could get much closer to the White House, but 9/11 had changed all that by restricting access to some of America's most historic places.

Matt and I took the Metro to Nationals Park, home of baseball's newest team. Formerly the Montreal Expos, the Nationals maintained the tradition of being perennial losers, albeit in a brand spanking new $611 million publicly financed ballpark, featuring a 4,500-square-foot high-definition scoreboard.

"You know what they say about Washington, don't you?" I asked Matt.

"No, what?"

"First in war, first in peace, last in the National League East!"

To be sure, the Nationals were keeping the tradition alive as bottom dwellers in the standings. America's most inept team would finish the season 32½ games behind the first place Philadelphia Phillies, who would ultimately become World Champs in 2008.

Nationals Park seats 41,888 and offers great views of the Capitol and Washington Monument, but it is the park's "green" amenities that excited Matt the most.

"Dad, this park is LEED certified," he announced.

"What does that mean?"

"You don't know what LEED is?"

"I think it's a city in England."

"No that's Leeds," he snorted. "Everyone knows what LEED stands for."

"Well, I don't know, Mr. Smarty Pants."

"LEED means Leadership in Energy and Environmental Design. So the building is energy efficient and the design is very cool," he continued. "Because the field is actually way below street level."

Matt explained to me how fans could enter the park without using elevators, stairs or ramps, making it easy to get to the seats.

I liked the fact several players from the Nationals were actually signing autographs for kids and mingling with the crowd before the game.

At Nationals Park, the hot dogs tasted great off the grill, smothered in Gulden's mustard as a ballpark treat. I love Gulden's because it adds a little spicy kick to the hot dog.

But it's the on-field entertainment that makes Nationals Park so much fun. Whereas Milwaukee has its wiener races, in Washington it's the presidents who run around the track – in this case, small people dressed up in oversized heads of the most popular presidents.

In this presidential race, Teddy Roosevelt won in a landslide over Abe Lincoln, who finished second and not third because he decked George Washington in the chops, sending the Father of Our Country flying to the turf, proving that politics is a full-contact sport – especially in Nationals Park.

As for the ballgame itself, the Nats were naturally inept, falling 4-3 to the New York Mets behind the pitching of Johan Santana – much to the delight of the thousands of New Yorkers in the stands. But the ballpark itself was a terrific treat for our last night in Washington.

After the game, we took a subway ride back to our hotel, where just outside our Metro stop at Dupont Circle, a jazz band serenaded scores of travelers in a sidewalk concert that proved to be the perfect capper to the evening.

But our fabulous journey would be nearly grounded the next day, on our flight back home to California. I had deliberately picked a late afternoon departure from D.C. to give Matt a chance to sleep in for a change. It would prove to be a terrible mistake, because our flight was horribly delayed. The carrier never really told us why the flight was running three hours behind schedule, but Matt and I quickly realized we would arrive in Dallas way too late to make our connection to Sacramento.

Facing a serious dilemma, I was forced to use all my stored-up frequent flyer miles to secure two seats on another carrier for a sure flight home.

It was the one and only glitch in a road trip that would take us to nine states, plus the District of Columbia. And as the wheels finally touched down on the tarmac in Sacramento, I was already starting to plan our 2009 road trip!

Rogers Centre, Toronto Blue Jays

Sunday, August 9, 2009

"I miss my teammates – the guys I had fun with."
DUANE WARD

"Let's make a sign that says number 30," Matt declared.

"Thirty what?"

"Thirty ballparks. You remember that picture of NBA legend Wilt Chamberlain holding up a sign saying 100?"

"Yes, I've seen it."

"Well, Wilt did that to commemorate his 100-point game in 1962. We can make a sign marking our 30th ballpark – once we visit Toronto and the two new stadiums in New York, we'll have every Major League team," he gushed.

We took out a piece of chalk and carefully crafted the number 30 in white letters onto black construction paper.

We were ready now for our 2009 road trip, which would kick off in Toronto.

Our journey from Sacramento to Denver turned out to be much different than I expected, as Matt refused to talk to me. Instead, he hunkered down in his seat with stereo headphones, conveniently drowning out all the sound around him, including me. I think he did that on purpose.

The trip from Denver to Toronto was equally lonely, with both of us listening to our iPods, like two little kids involved in parallel play refusing to acknowledge the other's existence.

But it was the ride to the hotel where things got a little more interesting. I talked to our cabbie, who told me he was going to law school at night to pursue a new career. It was a conversation that would prove to be fortuitous – especially for the guy behind the wheel.

For upon arriving at the Renaissance Hotel in downtown Toronto, Matt tried making a call with his cell phone, only to discover his window to the world had disappeared.

"Dad, my cell phone's gone!"

"What do you mean, 'gone'?"

"Gone, missing, not here."

"Did you check your pockets?"

"Yes, Dad, I think the phone slipped out of my shorts into the back seat of the taxi. It's probably still in the cab. Oh well."

"What do you mean, 'oh well'? Are you just giving up?"

"Dad, it's just a cell phone."

"Oh yeah?" I exclaimed. "That phone has all your connections on it, plus, someone could use it to make free phone calls. We have to try to get it back."

"Don't worry, all my connections are saved on my laptop. I put them there as a backup system, just in case I ever lose my phone."

"Well, aren't you the careful planner," I said sarcastically. "Now someone else has all your friends and family connections."

"Don't worry, we'll just disconnect the service, it's no big deal," he shrugged.

"Well, I'm calling the cab company," I fumed. "And you better hope they have the phone."

I asked the cab company to help us find our lawyer/driver, and somehow we reached him back at the airport. The cabbie told me he found the phone in the back seat and would be happy to make a run downtown to meet us.

"Wow, that's really nice of you to help us out. What a good Samaritan!" I exclaimed.

"Oh, I'm not doing this to be a nice guy," the lawyer part of him explained. "I'm doing it to make 35 bucks."

"Thirty-five dollars just to return a phone?" I asked incredulously.

"Thirty-five in cold Canadian cash," he declared. "That's today's price because I feel sorry for you. Tomorrow it will cost you more."

"OK, please bring it now," I pleaded with the Toronto tough guy who was going to make one heckuva lawyer.

Twenty minutes later, Matt had regained his cell phone, but his wallet had lost some weight. I made him pay the $35 finder's fee as a good lesson about responsibility.

"So now you'll get a holster for your phone, right?" I asked with an edge.

"No, Dad. Holsters are for old men like you. I like my phones wild and free."

"Well, it may be wild, but it certainly wasn't free, now was it?"

My biting comment was met with stony silence.

Check.

I had won the argument and Matt had nothing to say in response.

Checkmate.

The bar at the Renaissance Hotel overlooks the ballfield at Rogers Centre, where the Blue Jays play. The stadium was empty, but the bar was hopping.

"Come on, Dad," Matt said to break the ice. "I'll buy you a beer."

"What do you mean, 'buy me a beer?' You're only 20."

"Exactly. The drinking age in Canada is 19, so let me treat you to a beer."

How could I turn down an offer like that from my son? A

waitress came by to take our order.

"I'll have a Stella," he said, referring to the Belgian brew formally known as Stella Artois. "And my dad will have a Molson, a good Canadian beer."

"How do you know so much about beer?" I asked. "Especially for someone who's underage south of the border?"

"I've done a lot of research."

"You mean in bars?"

"No, in the school library. I'm a good reader."

We clicked glasses and toasted our good fortune to being in Canada and celebrating my son's first legal drink.

"I didn't even have to use my fake ID," he proclaimed.

"You have a fake ID?"

"Ignorance is bliss, eh?"

"Oh, so now you're going Canadian on me?"

"No, I'm just making a toast to Toronto," he said. "Let's drink another."

I smiled at his audacity in flaunting his inner party animal, but found myself agreeing in principal.

"Why not?" I said. "Waitress, another round, please."

After our beer fest, Matt and I took a walk around the hotel. In the lobby we discovered the Blue Jays had made the Renaissance their headquarters for a reunion celebrating the back-to-back World Series championships of 1992 and 1993. We started talking to a tall, athletic man who quickly proved he could identify all of the ballplayers in attendance for the weekend event.

"Yeah, Joe Carter's here," he said. "You know Carter, he's the guy who won the '93 Series with a walk-off homer against the Phillies."

"That's only happened twice in baseball history," I said. "The other guy was Bill Mazeroski, who won the 1960 World Series for the Pirates with a walk-off home run against the Yankees."

"Who else is here?" I asked the stranger, who stood 6-foot-4.

"I heard that guy Duane Ward is here," he whispered.

"I'm not familiar with him," I confided. "I never really followed the Blue Jays."

"Well, he was a top set-up man," the stranger said, "and one of the most reliable middle relievers in '92, when the Blue Jays beat the Atlanta Braves to become the first team from outside the U.S. to win the World Series."

"In 1993," he added, "Duane Ward became the closer for Toronto, with an American League best 45 saves."

"Wow! How do you know so much about Duane Ward?" I asked.

"That's easy," he said. "I'm Duane."

"And this here is Mark Eichorn," he said, pointing to his wingman, a 6-foot-3, right-handed hurler who had been the middle reliever for the Jays, setting up All-Star closer Tom Henke.

"So, Duane," I said, "What are you doing now?"

"I'm retired and living in Colorado."

"What do you miss most about the game?"

"I miss the guys," he said. "I miss my teammates – the guys I had fun with."

Duane Ward retired from baseball at the age of 30 because of tendonitis in his arm, finishing his career with a 3.28 ERA and 121 saves.

⚾ ⚾ ⚾

Former Blue Jay Ed Sprague Jr. was also there celebrating that night with his teammates, although I didn't know it at the time. But months later, I would ask Ed about his memories of the team when I caught up with him in Stockton, California, where he was preparing his University of the Pacific Tigers for the 2010 college baseball season.

I asked Ed what it was like to hang out in Toronto again with Dave Stewart, Duane Ward, Mark Eichorn, Jimmy Key and all the guys who won those back-to-back championships in '92 and '93.

"It was a lot of fun," he told me. "I was really surprised at how much fun I had. You know, I don't miss the game very much. And everybody says, 'Well, I don't miss the game – I miss the guys,' but I've never been like that either. I'd rather be playing, the locker room was the locker room and you know I had great friends, but I don't necessarily miss that part of it."

Ed paused, then added, "But it was interesting how it had been 17 years and we had a golf tournament that day and we kind of got on the bus as a group after the golf tournament and guys started talking and it just felt like we had just finished a three-game series with New York and we swept and we're leaving town."

He stopped for a moment to look up, and then continued his thoughts.

"I mean, the atmosphere, the energy, the guys were kind of fired up. When you hang around different people, you know you kind of speak the language of the people that you're with – then you come home and have a conversation with your wife. It's so funny, you get back into that language with those guys and you haven't seen them in 17 years."

"Did you guys know you had a special club?" I asked. "I mean, to win championships back-to-back is pretty rare."

"Yeah," he said. "You know, in '91 we went to the playoffs and lost to the Twins. It was always just a couple of pieces missing. We just hadn't been able to get over the hump. In '92 maybe with the leadership of Dave Winfield coming in – it just kind of came together. We had obviously a great pitching staff, you know, an All-Star lineup and things went well."

"You had Jimmy Key and Jack Morris on the pitching staff," I said. "Did you realize in spring training that you had something special?"

"I think every year people want to believe that this is the

year," he said. "So anytime you're playing in the A.L. East, you know, it becomes a difficult chore. At the time, the Yankees were down a little bit and Toronto was the team to beat. So you went in with that confidence, like hey, I think we're going to win the division, we're gonna go to the playoffs, but we're looking beyond that. It's not about getting to the playoffs, it's about getting to the World Series, that's never been done [for the Blue Jays] so I think that was kind of the goal from the outset in spring training."

"Who were the guys you missed the most?" I asked.

"Well, you know, I always loved seeing John Olerud, Pat Hentgen, Woody Williams – those guys were probably the guys I was closest to. I still keep in touch with them quite a bit. I haven't seen them in maybe a couple of years," he said. "I hadn't seen John since I played with him in Seattle in 2001. He was a great guy. I liked seeing everybody. I hadn't seen Jimmy Key in forever. Paul Molitor, I hadn't seen him in a long time. I talked to a few guys here and there over the years but some guys I hadn't seen in a long time," Sprague reflected.

"You mentioned about connecting with the game," I said, "and I realize you're still connected with it here at UOP. But what is it that ballplayers miss the most about their playing years?"

"Most people say they miss the camaraderie," Sprague told me. "They probably do. I mean, I was fortunate in that I wasn't 100 percent invested in my relationships with baseball. I came back home (to Stockton). I had friends here at home. It was separate from being a Major League player. And I think that helped my transition into retirement quite a bit. Because I came home and all my friends were here."

Sprague was on a long walk through memory lane, so I let him continue. "I have friends here through my kids' school," he said, "through golfing buddies or whatever, so I still had that connection. I certainly miss being in the locker room with the guys. I like being around people and competing at the highest level. Being able to talk to guys and hear their different approaches. To be honest with you, I love to stand in the batter's box, facing a guy that is the best at what he does and see how I can do," the former Blue Jay stated.

Sprague looked right at me and said, "You can't recreate competitive juices that you get when you're facing a guy like Randy Johnson. I miss that part of it. I certainly don't miss the travel. I don't miss going from city to city. I don't miss the grind of getting home at two and three in the morning and then coming to a day game the next day. So those things I don't miss. You're always going to miss the players and the relationships there, but mostly for me it was just competing."

"Now you're the head baseball coach here at the University of the Pacific," I said. "You have a chance to be a mentor to guide some young men who could end up in the Major Leagues. What do you enjoy most about your current job?"

"Well, I think that's probably it, just the development, trying to find ways to help guys succeed. It can be challenging at times, not only the physical aspects of it but also the mental aspects of just trying to get through – you know, watching them learn something and then apply it in a competitive situation and have it work and then when the light goes on – you know, you're just really excited for them," Sprague said.

He stopped for a moment and then picked up where he left off. "We had a pitcher on Friday night – he had been working on a change-up and he just learned it the other day – and it was just one of those things where it all of a sudden felt good coming out of his hand," he said with a smile. "You could see his face just light up," he continued. "He struck out five guys with that pitch. He was like, 'Yeah, that really feels good.' So those little things like that when you see guys getting over the hump or take one step to the next level in their own ability, that's exciting. I still think baseball is America's pastime."

"Yes," I agreed. "Baseball is America's pastime – even if it's played in Canada."

⚾ ⚾ ⚾

O Canada!

It was suddenly 8 o'clock on Sunday morning – game day in the Eastern Time zone, and I was trying to wake up Matt for a full day of activities in Toronto. Of course his body knew it was actually 5 a.m. in California, and he was not getting out of bed.

"Come on, Matt," I pleaded. "We've got to skate over to the Hockey Hall of Fame."

"I'm trying to get up," he moaned, "and stop looking at me."

The Stinkbug was back in rare form, refusing to get out of bed in a new country.

I decided to let the poor kid sleep for a change and headed downstairs to the lobby of the hotel, hoping to get some coffee and maybe bump into another ballplayer.

And as the elevator doors opened to the hotel lobby, my heart started pounding; sitting there all by himself was Toronto pitching great Dave Stewart, checking out his BlackBerry.

Stewart was an integral part of the 1993 Toronto Blue Jays championship team, going 12-8 that year and leading them into the World Series, where they won it all.

"Hey, Dave," I said as I introduced myself to the All-Star. "I'm on a baseball road trip with my son and traveling across North America to visit every Major League Baseball stadium."

Stewart quietly nodded, but his eyes never really left his BlackBerry.

"I'm writing a book about my travels; would you have just a few minutes to talk?" I asked.

Stewart pondered my request but seemed transfixed with his electronic device. Sensing I was losing the battle, I pulled out my secret weapon.

"I'm from California," I declared, "and I used to watch you pitch all the time in Oakland."

"Oh yeah, where in California?" Stewart said, his eyes more animated now.

"Sacramento," I said proudly.

"Really, my mom lives in Elk Grove."

The two cities are just 20 minutes apart. Stew suddenly seemed receptive to talking, so I took out my tape recorder and began asking questions before he could change his mind.

"What was it like playing on that Toronto team that beat the Phillies in the World Series?" I asked.

"It was a great year to play baseball up here in this city," Stewart began as he reflected on the 1993 baseball classic. "A lot of great things took place for our ballclub at that time," he continued. "We had Olerud, Molitor and Alomar, to finish 1-2-3 in the League batting title, which I don't think has ever been done before and I don't think it will ever be done again."

Indeed, first baseman John Olerud won the American League batting crown that year after finishing with Ty Cobb–type numbers, hitting .363. Designated Hitter Paul Molitor came in second with a .332 average, while the scrappy second baseman Roberto Alomar was the third best hitter that year at .326. For baseball, it was the first time in 100 years that three teammates had finished the season as the top three hitters, but the '93 Blue Jays were a very special club, as Dave Stewart would reveal.

"You know, playing for (manager) Cito Gaston was something that I had looked forward to, as a player from across the field and then to finally get an opportunity to play with Cito was a great experience," he said. "Everything that I had heard about him being a player's manager, easygoing guy with an intense nature, was true.

There were some guys on the ballclub that I had competed against and looked forward to playing with as well," he added.

"And you can start with Joe Carter."

The lanky right fielder for the Jays had 396 lifetime home runs, but none more famous than his walk-off bomb to win the 1993 World Series. It was a ninth-inning blast, with the Jays trailing 6-5 against Phillies closer Mitch Williams, just two outs away from a decisive Game Seven. The 3-run homer sparked a huge celebration and 8-6 victory for Toronto, with Carter jumping for joy as he rounded the bases.

I asked Dave Stewart to recall the famous homer.

"I mean, that's exciting if it ends a World Series," Stew said. "It's exciting if it finishes the final game in your regular season. I mean walk-off home runs – you dream about that type of ending. It's a fairy tale ending," he continued. "And then you just highlight that, multiple times, billions of times in a World Championship game and the winning game. I mean, there are just no words to explain the emotion of when that's the way you finish it."

I asked Stew about his pitching role for the Jays, after a storied career with the Oakland A's, which included a World Championship in 1989.

"I came here from the Oakland A's and jumped on the back of a ballclub that had the opportunity to win another championship," he stated. "The Toronto club had lost David Cone." Stew explained he had been brought on board to fill the hole in the rotation.

"I had a great League Championship series," he added. "Beat the Chicago White Sox twice and being named Most Valuable Player in the League Championship series. I threw a pretty good ballgame the first start (in the World Series). And actually, the game that Joe hit the home run was a game I started as well. And I pitched deep into the game and got a No Decision out of it, but gave us a chance to win it."

Time was running short, so I asked Dave what he was doing now and what he missed most about baseball.

"Now I'm representing players," Stewart said. "I'm an agent in the business with my own company. I'm still close to the game and so I get an opportunity to be around the athletes and be around the game."

And like most players, Dave Stewart really missed his teammates. "I think if you talk to anybody about the thing they miss most about playing the sport, it's the camaraderie," he said.

Camaraderie is a key ingredient in the glue that holds baseball teams together.

Stew continued, "Being around the fellows, talking baseball, being in the clubhouse, the smell of cut grass."

Yes, that was the beauty of baseball.

I thanked him for his time and asked for one final favor. "Would you mind if I took a quick picture of you?"

Stew smiled and stood up, stretching out his full 6-foot-2, athletic frame.

Click.

"Thanks again, Dave," I said, and with that I rushed to the elevator to tell my son about my good fortune.

"Matt!" I blurted while bursting into the room. "I just interviewed Dave Stewart."

Matt was still sleeping, curled up into his Stinkbug pose.

"Wake up, Matt, I just met a player with two World Series rings."

"That's nice," he groaned and quickly rolled over.

"Oh, let him sleep," I said to myself. After all, nothing can top this.

Three hours later we enjoyed breakfast overlooking the ballpark, then hightailed it down Front Street to the Hockey Hall of Fame. Once inside, we saw a remarkable replica of the Montreal Canadians' locker room. The highlight, though, was posing for a picture in front of the Stanley Cup, hockey's holy grail.

Next we took turns shooting pucks at a virtual goalie. Matt arched his back for a powerful righty slap shot that thrust the puck at 45 mph past the imaginary goalie.

"That was fun!" he said. "I'm going to call Uncle Russ and tell him I scored five times and that it was the easiest thing I've ever done," he said with a laugh.

Russ would argue that Matt was successful only because he was on concrete instead of ice, but the whole thing was a giant ruse just to rile my brother.

We had entered the Hockey Hall of Fame in bright sunshine, but upon leaving the building we were caught in the middle of a torrential downpour and arrived back at the hotel soaking wet.

We quickly dried off and entered the Rogers Centre, which is actually part of the hotel. I'm not a big fan of domed stadiums, but on this day, I was glad to have a roof over our heads.

The Rogers Centre used to be known as the SkyDome, where it's been the home of the Blue Jays since 1989. Its most striking feature is the retractable roof, the first of its kind in the world – and it takes just 20 minutes to open fully or close. It is 282 feet high, tall enough to enclose a 31-story building in center field with the roof closed. The video screens are massive (110 feet long and 33 feet wide) and can display up to 4.3 *trillion* colors, according to the Blue Jays.

And on this day, Matt and I received free Tom Henke figurines, honoring one of the game's premier closers from the late '80s and early '90s. The 6-foot-5 giant was there in person to throw out the ceremonial first pitch at our game, where he was honored as Toronto's "Terminator." In his illustrious 14-year career, Henke averaged 9.8 strikeouts for every nine innings he pitched.

Our game turned out to be a slugfest, with Marco Scutero, Kevin Millar and Vernon Wells all going deep for the Jays in a 7-3 rout of the hapless Baltimore Orioles. Toronto's ace, Roy "Doc" Halliday, got the win, but the highlight occurred in the fifth inning, when the roof started to rumble.

The dome gods had decided to open the roof, revealing blue skies and the majestic CN Tower!

It was fascinating to watch the stadium transform into a dynamic display of shadows and light as the sunshine sliced its way through the park, enveloping the entire structure with living colors in just 20 minutes' time. Suddenly our gloomy inside "night" game had become an outdoor day game – just the way baseball is supposed to be played.

"I really like this park a lot," I told Matt. "But my top five are still San Francisco first with Pittsburgh a close second, followed by Boston, Baltimore and Detroit. What are your fave five?"

"I don't do rankings. I just like to experience things." Then he threw me the zinger. "Why do you have to always quantify everything? You just ruin things when you do that."

"Well," I backpedaled, "it's my nature as a news reporter to process, sort and evaluate. I can't help it – that's just who I am."

There was no response from Matt, making me think I had either won the argument or effectively neutralized his opposition. Either way, we were off to the waterfront for a harbor cruise of Toronto. The city is actually surrounded by 14 small islands that form a natural barrier where the small cruise ships can glide around the port, showcasing Toronto's impressive skyline.

After returning to land, we ate Thai food at a small outdoor café, then headed up the CN Tower for a panoramic view from Toronto's "Pride in the Sky." At 1,815 feet, it is considered to be North America's tallest building. The Observatory is roughly 1,100 feet above the earth and while our visit began with sunny skies, the weather quickly began to change.

Dark clouds were swarming in and by the time we reached the Observatory, we were battered by gale-force winds so strong the building managers ordered everyone off the observation deck. Just as soon as we got inside, we were treated to a massive lightning display and torrential rainstorm that flooded two of the elevator shafts. The powerful winds literally blew one of the Observatory doors off its hinges, creating a wind tunnel effect that sent tourists scurrying for cover. Matt told me the CN Tower, built by the Canadian National Railway, was his favorite observation deck anywhere. The question was, would it survive this violent attack from Mother Nature?

Our lightning storm experience triggered, for some reason, a philosophical discussion about reality.

"How do you know what's real?" Matt wanted to know. "How do you know I'm really here?"

"Well, I saw you enter the world. And we're together in this scary storm. That's as real as it gets."

"But how do you know I'm not a figment of your imagination and you're really here on your own? In fact, maybe you're all alone and everything else is just a dream."

"You've been having too many late-night hookah parties," I said.

"Dad, I'm challenging you to leave your comfort zone and asking you: How do you tell the difference between what's real and what's imagined?"

When in doubt, I always relied on my inner Yogi, who said, "I wish I had an answer because I'm tired of answering that question."

Baseball Hall of Fame, Cooperstown, New York

Monday, August 10 – Tuesday, August 11, 2009

*"Today I consider myself the luckiest man
on the face of the earth."*
LOU GEHRIG

We picked up our rental car at the Toronto train station. It was a scarlet red Kia that tracked our odometer readings in kilometers, not miles. We drove through the labyrinth of Canadian cities from Mississauga to Hamilton, then down to St. Catharine and eventually Niagara Falls, Ontario. The Canadian side of the Falls is considered by most travelers to offer the best vantage points – including Horseshoe Falls, a spectacular gushing waterway that is approximately 12,000 years old. The Falls are about 180 feet high and push 6 million cubic feet of water over the edge every minute – enough for a million bathtubs.

We took the "Tunnel Tour" into the depths of the Falls, where we could see mountains of cascading water.

"I'm getting wet," Matt proclaimed, despite donning the obligatory Niagara Falls poncho.

"Well, don't stand under the funnel of water!"

It was Matt's first trip to Niagara Falls and he was intent on getting a firsthand look at the awesome power and beauty of this natural wonder.

"Dad, I'm getting soaked; this is great!"

"Just don't tell your mother."

Once we were back on dry land, we drove across the border to U.S. Customs, where we displayed our passports to get through to the American side.

"Purpose of your trip to the United States?" demanded the Customs agent.

"We're on a baseball road trip," I proudly proclaimed. "My son and I are on our way to the Baseball Hall of Fame in Cooperstown, New York."

"Take Interstate 90 east, all the way to Exit 30 at Herkimer," the agent stated. "Then take Route 28 south to Cooperstown," he added before waving us through to the Empire State.

We followed the agent's directions, taking the New York State Thruway across Buffalo, Rochester, Syracuse and Utica, before weaving our way to the tiny hamlet of Cooperstown, home of the Baseball Hall of Fame.

We checked into the Lake Front Motel, located conveniently on the shores of Otsego Lake and then walked along the historic main street.

"Look, Dad," Matt said. "This whole town is comprised of baseball memorabilia shops with trading cards, jerseys and posters of players from all eras."

"Yes. It's the New York State version of heaven."

We walked past Doubleday Field, where Cooperstown resident Abner Doubleday is said to have invented baseball back in 1839. Of course, as we would learn later that day, legends are not always based on facts.

But for a baseball fan, Cooperstown is the perfect place to be – with wooden statues of Ted Williams and Babe Ruth and with the chance to catch a glimpse inside Lou Gehrig's locker, for a moment, I too felt like "the luckiest man on the face of the earth." There were also artifacts from Hank Aaron, Sandy Koufax, Bob Gibson, Willie Mays, Roberto Clemente and every legend of Major League Baseball from the game's beginnings to the modern era.

The Museum has displays from all the teams, with plaques and statistics for every Hall of Famer. Baseball's showcase venue is located in a charming lakeside hamlet, a picturesque slice of Americana with baseball card shops up and down Main Street, a tribute to small towns everywhere.

Right outside the Hall is a bronze statue of Brooklyn Dodgers pitcher Johnny Podres, throwing a strike to All-Star catcher Roy Campanella. I asked Matt to step up to the plate for a picture.

"You're facing the ace of the Brooklyn Dodgers, who helped them win their only World Series, in 1955," I told him. "Take a swing," I said while delivering an imaginary pitch.

Matt covered his eyes in humiliation.

"There's a drive deep to left," I said in my best play-by-play voice. "It's way back, it's going, going, gone. A three-run walk-off homer for Matt Luery!" I intoned into the virtual microphone.

I hoped my son would play along and embrace the baseball fantasy I was creating. "Run the bases, Matt!" I said.

Instead, he ran off the field in total embarrassment.

"Come on! It's just a baseball dream. You know, build it and they will come."

"I don't know you."

"Matt, it's just a script in my head."

But he marched away, pretending we were strangers.

"Damn," I muttered. There's nothing like humiliating your own kid at the Hall of Fame.

I finally caught up with my son as he entered Doubleday Field, which honors the man who they say invented America's pastime. Abner Doubleday may have grown up in Cooperstown, but most historians believe he had little to do with creating the game of baseball – yet the story has become urban legend.

At the Baseball Hall of Fame I learned that a rascal named Abner Graves had invented the story. Graves responded to an Akron, Ohio, newspaper advertisement claiming he had seen Doubleday's drawings of a rudimentary diamond in the dirt while the two were classmates at school in Cooperstown in 1839. In reality, Doubleday didn't live in Cooperstown in 1839. Instead, he was enrolled as a cadet at West Point. Doubleday never claimed to have "invented" the game and he reportedly never mentioned baseball in any of his diaries, but somehow his name is closely linked to the game's genesis.

The urban myth grew as the game gained popularity, with National League president Ford Frick proposing that Cooperstown should be home to the "Hall of Fame," and indeed the museum was dedicated in 1939, marking the supposed 100th anniversary of baseball.

"Maybe," I suggested to Matt, "we should put an asterisk by the name 'Hall of Fame' – as a slap against the baseball commissioner who orchestrated a similar slight against Maury Wills and Roger Maris."

"Now that would be justice," he agreed.

As a point of fact, baseball probably evolved from other popular bat-and-ball games in the early 19th century, including an English game called Rounders. But there's no mistaking that Cooperstown has become the epicenter for baseball stories big and small, with some 350,000 fans visiting the Hall of Fame each year.

Woodstock Nation

Tuesday, August 11, 2009

"What's an LP?"
MATT LUERY

Matt and I were exhilarated after experiencing baseball's living history museum but now hunger was taking control. We quickly wolfed down a meatball wedge on Cooperstown's Main Street and were soon on the road again. We drove south through the Catskill Mountains until we came to the tiny town of Bethel, New York, home to the Woodstock music festival in 1969.

Bethel is actually more than an hour from Woodstock – the town in Ulster County where the festival was supposed to be held – until the musical promoters had their permit denied just weeks before the event. They were forced to scramble to find a new place, this time just over the border of Sullivan County, in Bethel, New York. The hippie entrepreneurs finally struck a deal with Max Yasgur, a dairy farmer in Bethel; his Back Forty would quickly become the epicenter of the free love and music celebration that transformed an entire generation.

Of course, there was no time left to include the name "Bethel" on any of the promotional materials, so the printed tickets and posters all proclaimed the name Woodstock Music Festival – a name that would stick.

Woodstock was home to more than 400,000 hippies for three days of peace, love and music in August 1969. Joni Mitchell wrote the definitive "Woodstock" song in a New York City hotel room. She never attended the music fest – but heard firsthand accounts from her then boyfriend, British musician Graham Nash. The anthem would later become a major hit for Crosby, Stills, Nash & Young.

Woodstock musicians included Jimi Hendrix, The Jefferson Airplane, The Who and The Grateful Dead, along with Santana, Credence Clearwater Revival, Janis Joplin, Joan Baez, John Sebastian, Richie Havens, Sly & the Family Stone, Crosby, Stills, Nash & Young and many more.

The festival is memorialized now in a museum called the Bethel Woods Center for the Arts. Matt and I entered just in time for the 40th anniversary celebration of the concert that changed the world.

Inside the Bethel Woods Center, there were psychedelic posters, album covers and video clips of the people who made the music come alive, along with a 20-minute film about the festival. Matt and I watched the split-screen movie while reclining on beanbag chairs, designed to evoke the spirit of the '60s.

"This is a really cool way to experience Woodstock," Matt said.

"Well, you know the expression?"

"What's that?"

"If you remember Woodstock, you probably weren't there," I said with a laugh. "So for an entire generation, this museum helps to connect the dots. It's a modern-day flashback."

"You mean like an acid flashback?"

"How do you know about that?"

"I've done a lot of reading."

"Reading about it is fine," I told him. "Just don't do any original research."

We walked outside the museum to the iconic festival site, where hundreds of thousands of kids had marched through the mud to commune with their favorite bands. In my head, I was playing the Woodstock double-record set that had practically burned a hole in my turntable decades ago.

"*Woodstock* used to be one of my favorite LPs," I said.

"What's an LP?"

I rolled my eyes in disbelief. "It's a Long Playing record, with two sides," I explained. "You had to physically get up and turn it over after side one was done, in order to hear side two. You played it on a turntable with a needle and a groove."

"How primitive."

"Yes, definitely pre-digital. It was long before Compact Discs were invented."

We strolled back into the museum to examine the rainbow-colored school buses Wavy Gravy and his followers utilized to get to Woodstock from their commune in New Mexico. I was especially glad that Matt could experience the '60s without taking an acid trip to get there.

I was also certain that my daughter, Sarah, if she had been alive in 1969, would have been working at Woodstock, making sure the musicians were ready to take the stage. Sarah loves music and for two years she worked in Los Angeles for the Mitch Schneider Organization, a firm that provides publicity for retro bands from the '70s including The Dead, The Allman Brothers, Aerosmith and David Bowie.

Talk about a cool job – she was authorized to go backstage to meet Bob Weir and Greg Allman before they performed in front of thousands of people. So naturally, I purchased the *Woodstock* CD for Sarah in the museum store. And now my little flower child plays it incessantly, saying she really digs Joe Cocker. While I have bonded with my son over baseball, Sarah and I will always have music between us.

I was lost in '60s nostalgia but Matt was getting bored with yesteryear, so we headed south for the Big Apple. Upon arriving in Manhattan, we enjoyed two slices of authentic New York pizza. We were now ready for the world of baseball.

Yankee Stadium, New York Yankees

Wednesday, August 12, 2009

*"I don't think there's a lot of things
that can beat playing center field
for the New York Yankees for 16 years."*
BERNIE WILLIAMS

The sun! It was a beautiful sight over midtown Manhattan and I couldn't wait to walk outside and soak it in. But Matt had a totally different agenda: one that involved pillows, blankets and plenty of darkness. The Stinkbug was sleeping in and wouldn't get up.

Imagine that.

Nine o'clock became 10, then finally 11 and I could wait no longer.

"Matt, it's time to get up," I said in my best indoor voice.

No response.

"Matt, we've got to get going," I said a little louder. "We're headed to Yankee Stadium today."

"Oh, let me sleep in," the Stinkbug pleaded. "I am getting up but it's very gradual."

"Yeah, so was the Ice Age. And you're moving at the same glacial pace."

"Oh, you're all talk," he groaned.

"Why?"

"Because you said I could sleep in today and relax. But you never follow through with your promises."

Ouch!

"We'll be out of here by 11:45," the Stinkbug promised.

Of course, things didn't work out that way.

Matt was soon busy on the computer, answering e-mails and finding his friends on Facebook.

"I'm getting anxious," I said. "It's 11:45 and time to go to the ballpark."

"Would you stop pacing, Dad? I'm just downloading a file."

"That wasn't our agreement. You promised we'd be out the door at 11:45 for the game, which starts, by the way, at 1:05."

Since my positive, motivational approach clearly wasn't working, it was time to bring out my secret weapon.

Guilt.

"I can't take it anymore," I said. "Here you made a promise and you can't keep it. I'm going down to the lobby."

"Good, go," said the Stinkbug.

Sometimes you've got to give a kid some space and generally he'll come around. It took 15 minutes, but Matt did make it to the lobby at the stroke of noon, ready to go.

We hopped on the "D" line subway outside our hotel at 35th Street and 6th Avenue. The subway cars were packed with Yankee fans. Everyone, it seemed was wearing the team's pinstriped jerseys, hats and shirts. I proudly wore my Yankee blue Mickey Mantle number 7 T-shirt with my hero's name on the back.

I expected to see hundreds of fans wearing the legendary Mantle shirt, but to my chagrin I spotted only a few. I noticed just a smattering of fans sporting Lou Gehrig's number 4 blue T-shirt and but a handful wearing Babe Ruth's number 3 or Joe DiMaggio's legendary number 5. But clearly the most popular Yankee T-shirt was Derek Jeter's number 2, not surprising given his status as the longtime Yankee captain.

I also noticed dozens of Jorge Posada's number 20 shirts, along with newly acquired first baseman Mark Teixeira's number 25. Then it dawned on me: I was experiencing a generational gap, a shift in popularity based on age. Yankee fans today love the modern-day Yankees, the players they see day in and day out. It was only "old guys" like me who would want to wear a Mickey Mantle shirt, because he was my Yankee hero when I was growing up. But clearly, the fan base from my era was getting smaller. Suddenly, I was reminded of my own mortality. When the subway deposited us at 162nd street, I looked first at the old Yankee Stadium, where I had seen dozens of games as a kid. It was now decommissioned and destined for demolition, although my memories could never be destroyed.

I flashed back two months, to a chance meeting with a guy who played his entire career at the original Yankee Stadium. The baseball gods were kind enough to grant me an interview with Yankee legend Bernie Williams, in my adopted hometown of Sacramento.

"Meet former Yankee great Bernie Williams tonight at 6," the radio announcer said.

I practically jumped out of the driver's seat.

"Yes, Bernie will be signing his new CD this evening," the announcer continued.

"I'll be there!" I shouted, even though I was the only one in the car. "I'm going to meet Bernie Williams today," I said to myself.

I made a beeline for the bookstore, where I met the manager, who fortunately, recognized me as a Sacramento TV news reporter.

"I'm here to interview Bernie Williams," I stated.

"Of course you are," he said. "You're here to do a story on him for the news."

"Well, let's just say this is more of a personal story," I told him.

"I'll leave that out when I talk to Bernie's publicist," the manager said with a wink. "Just tell a good story when you write it up," he urged.

Bernie Williams bounced across the floor with a major league swagger. I had to run just to catch up with him and quickly introduced myself. "Hi, Bernie," I said. "I'm writing a book about baseball and would love to talk to you about your careers – both on the diamond and in the studio."

He paused for a moment, and then gave me a big grin. "Sure," he said. "Right after my sound check."

Bernie Williams was on the road again, only this time he was armed with a jazz guitar instead of his trusted Gold Glove that made him one of baseball's top defensive players four years in a row. Yes, the five-time All-Star center fielder for the New York Yankees was on another winning streak, scoring points first with talk show host Craig Ferguson during a television taping in Los Angeles, then lighting up the crowd in Sacramento, where his new musical release was generating buzz.

From 1991 to 2006, Bernie Williams patrolled the hallowed grounds of Yankee Stadium, tracking down fly balls in center field with God-given speed and amazing grace. In 1998, he hit .339 to win the batting crown and became the first player to be proclaimed the best hitter, the best fielder (a Gold Glove Award) and a World Series champion all in the same year. In fact, Bernie would earn four World Series rings with the Yankees before hanging up his spikes. He finished with 449 doubles, the third most in Yankee history, behind only Lou Gehrig and Derek Jeter. But the 6-foot-2, muscular Williams is now "Moving Forward" into a successful musical career.

Williams' first album made the Billboard Top 100. His second release on Reform Records features jazz legend Dave Koz, singer Jon Secada and a live performance of "Glory Days" with the Boss, Bruce Springsteen. But the inspiration for *Moving Forward* comes from somewhere else. The album "marks being in a sort of transitional period between being a professional athlete and just kind of segueing in this other career," Williams told me.

And the person who best personified that transition for Williams was another talented athlete turned jazz musician. Wayman Tisdale played power forward for the Sacramento Kings from 1989 to 1994, before launching his own jazz/funk career. Wayman teamed up with Bernie on this album, playing bass on the title track in one of Tisdale's last performances before tragically, he died of cancer on May 15, 2009 – at the age of 44.

"He was a great influence," Williams reflected. "He was the person I modeled myself after. He was a person who was very successful in sports, yet he made a very successful transition into the music arena. Then he was in jazz, even though he could probably play everything. And you know, I'd look at that example and I'd say, 'Well, if he can do it, why can't I?'"

If Tisdale was the starting inspiration for the aspiring musician, then Bruce Springsteen was his closer. The two stars met at Yankee Stadium following a ballgame. Williams' teammate, Paul O'Neil, brought Springsteen into the clubhouse where Bernie just happened to have his guitar on hand. "It was actually a brand new Telecaster," he recalled. "I had a pen and I said I would like for him to sign a ball, but you know, he might as well sign my guitar."

Springsteen handled the request like a pro. "Oh, this is great," he said. "This is kind of unusual to sign a guitar in a clubhouse, a baseball clubhouse." Then he wrote, "To Bernie, if you ever get tired of baseball – Bruce Springsteen."

Williams and Springsteen would team up again a decade later, sharing the same stage, this time as dueling musicians at the original Yankee Stadium. "We were playing at the Joe Torre Safe at Home Foundation Dinner," Williams explained. "It was a charity dinner honoring former Yankee manager Joe

Torre, and Bruce Springsteen was the guest entertainer." What happened next took Williams by surprise.

"He brought me over to the stage, I mean we sat and played 'Glory Days,'" Williams gushed. "And we asked for his permission to put it as a bonus track on the album, and he was nice enough to say yes, so he's very proud of that." The track is on Williams' new release.

Tisdale and Springsteen definitely helped advance Williams' career, but it was Paul McCartney who actually loaded the bases for him. "I had an opportunity to meet with 'Sir' Paul one time," Williams fondly remembered. "He was at Yankee Stadium watching a game. He is an avid baseball fan, and I had an opportunity to say hi to him. Actually, it was after we signed a deal for his company to do the publishing of the record – that lasted for about four or five years."

Williams is now with Reform Records, a company that he says was "interested in me as a person first and then my music second. The baseball aspect of it was a far third. When they heard the demos and they heard the music, they said, 'Well, we believe we can work with this, with you as a music artist.'"

The praise from Reform Records rang true for Bernie. It was the affirmation he needed. He remembers the company saying, "We don't want to take anything away from the baseball side, but we think you have some potential here." The record company wisely signed Bernie Williams to a musical contract.

Bernie Williams has been performing all his life. He grew up in Puerto Rico, where he played Little League ball and dreamed one day of making it to the Bigs. When Yankee Stadium closed down in 2008 to make way for the new ballpark, it was Bernie Williams who gave the very last performance there, not as a ballplayer, but a musician.

"For me, it was such a surreal situation," he said. "It was a nice, clear afternoon in the fall and the stadium was totally empty. It was a little chilly and I was in street clothes recording and taping some video of 'Take Me Out to the Ballgame,' which is sort of melancholic." That song is also on the new album.

Bernie was also there for opening day of the new Yankee Stadium in April 2009. He describes it as an amazing experience.

"I was supposed to be there with pinstripes and a glove in my hand. Instead, I was with a big wedge speaker in front of me playing 'Take Me Out to the Ballgame,' just kicking off the beginning of the new home of the Yankees over there in the Bronx."

Unlike Williams' previous performance when Yankee Stadium was empty, this time it was packed with more than 50,000 fans. "And they were New York fans," he said. "You know, they get all crazy in celebration of the momentous occasion, but when that sun came out and I started playing, everything got quiet. It was such a great treat for me to see, among all that craziness, a moment of peace and quiet, and calm, in that stadium."

If you gave Bernie the choice between performing in Yankee Stadium as a musical artist or a baseball player – there would be no contest. "I would have to say playing baseball," he told me emphatically. "I mean, not a lot of things can beat being able to be the guy that saves the game, you know? It doesn't matter what game it is, whether it's regular season or playoffs – or the World Series. I mean, it's just a great treat to be able to be the hero of that particular game on that particular day," he stated.

There's no doubt Bernie Williams' heart and passion are still linked with baseball. "I don't think there's a lot of things that can beat playing center field for the New York Yankees for 16 years, man no!" he gushed with enthusiasm.

For Williams, the magic of baseball is "just the thrill and

the rush of the competition. To go out there in some sort of a psychological battle. Me against the pitcher. From one at-bat to the other, you can strike out three times or you can hit two homers in a game and be the hero of the game. You never know what's going to happen!" he exclaimed.

"To me, it's living at about 100 miles an hour every day, for 6 months, or 162 games. Very high intensity. They expect you to produce and you expect the best out of yourself. It was a very thrilling thing for me."

And no doubt a thrill for the millions of fans he entertained while on the diamond.

For Bernie Williams, the thrill of baseball will never be gone, but now he is Moving Forward to the sound of a musical pitch.

I awoke from my Bernie Williams reverie to look up at the new Yankee Stadium and instantly fell in love with it. The new park is a modern architectural triumph that artfully links the past to the present. Inside the stadium are huge banners of historic Yankee legends from Babe Ruth to Bernie Williams. The pennants seemed to span the decades of fans both young and old.

The new stadium features a spectacular high definition scoreboard, yet the field dimensions are exactly the same as the original park, blending the old with the new in a creative way.

Yankee Stadium's signature arched façade is respectfully recreated in the new ballpark, paving the transition from the House That Ruth Built to the Stadium the Steinbrenners insisted upon (to generate revenue from luxury suites).

Ticket prices range from $5 for a seat in the nosebleed section (if you can even get one) to more than $2,600 for a single seat behind home plate. Imagine taking a family of four to a ballgame for more money ($10,400) than what most people make in several months.

Matt and I sat high up in the third deck, but we were just happy to have two seats. For lunch, I treated myself to a mouthwatering Philly cheese steak, a surprising find in the heart of Yankee territory. Matt wolfed down a humdrum hotdog that he described as underwhelming.

He didn't complain, though, as we were caught up in the pre-game ritual of watching the fans in the right field bleachers shout out the name of every Yankee starter on the field.

"Der-ek Je-ter, Der-ek Je-ter!" they chanted, until the All-Star shortstop turned around to tip his hat and acknowledge the crowd. The fans went around the horn and across the field until they had honored every Yankee on the diamond.

The game itself was very exciting, with the Yanks winning 4-3 in extra innings over the very same Blue Jays we had seen just three days earlier in Toronto. The game clincher came in the eleventh inning, when Robinson Cano doubled off the right field wall to drive in the winning run. Cano had also hit a home run earlier in the game, along with Johnny Damon, but two Yankee stars were injured.

Derek Jeter was hit by a pitch in the second inning and actually had to leave the game – something that rarely happens. Meanwhile A-Rod (Alex Rodriguez) was tagged by an errant fastball in the left elbow in the eleventh, causing him to lose feeling in his left hand, but he stayed in the game to take first base. Jorge Posada followed with a single and that's when Cano delivered his game-winning hit.

As soon as the winning run crossed the plate, the Yankees swarmed the field to the sounds of Frank Sinatra's "New York, New York" blaring loudly on the stadium speakers.

Matt and I were elated to have visited our 29th ballpark in a game that was nearly rained out. Storm clouds had moved in during the fourth inning and let loose a light rain that lasted until the sixth inning, but the game was never delayed.

As the clouds lifted, I looked toward my son.

"Do you realize we've never been rained out over 5 years and 29 ballparks?"

"Shhhhh. Don't say anything more, Dad. You'll jinx it."

I bit my lip, realizing we still had one more ballpark to go.

"I've got someplace special to take you, Dad," Matt announced after the Yankee victory.

"Where's that?"

"Just follow me."

We hopped the subway and headed back into the Manhattan madness, where we began walking toward Central Park. Matt stopped abruptly on 59th Street, in front of a bright blue awning, sporting the distinctive design of the Yankee Stadium porch and a script signature that said "Mickey Mantle."

"This is one of the best sports bars anywhere, Dad. It's Mickey Mantle's restaurant, and I picked it just for you."

"Matt, this is the perfect choice. And what a great way to celebrate our journey."

Inside the restaurant were dozens of photos of Mickey Mantle, my boyhood hero, along with 32 high definition screens featuring games from baseball parks all across the country. This sports bar is like a museum, with 300 pieces of baseball memorabilia on display, including original uniforms worn by Mantle and Joe DiMaggio. Ted Williams' jersey is featured there, along with Jackie Robinson's and a life-size cutout of the Babe.

I was so drunk on the atmosphere I don't even remember ordering lunch, but I'm sure it was delicious. I was too busy reviewing the posters and autographed baseballs from dozens of players – or as Yogi Berra would say, "You can observe a lot, just by watching."

"Matt, thank you so much for taking me here," I said. "How did you know about this place?"

"I saw it this summer when I was working here in New York," he answered.

Matt had lived for three weeks on his own in Manhattan, where he was part of a crew working on drywall at several high-rise buildings. The construction firm was owned by one of my brother's best friends, who was nice enough to give my son, a budding architect, the opportunity to gain some on-the-job training. The experience was, in Matt's words, life altering — opening up a whole new world for him.

"I'm so glad we took this trip together!"

"Me too, Dad. I've definitely caught the baseball bug."

Citi Field,
New York Mets

Friday, August 14, 2009

*"I knew I was going to take
the wrong train, so I left early."*
YOGI BERRA

Matt was looking forward to sleeping in after a night of exploring the sights and sounds of New York's Times Square, the self-proclaimed "crossroads of the world" where millions of electric lights illuminate your every move. Portions of Times Square are blocked off, reserved just for pedestrians, providing the perfect path for travelers to explore the sparkling incandescence of New York and its infinite array of clubs, restaurants and souvenir shops.

We had an off day on the baseball calendar, which proved to be good timing to fit in a family visit. I was eager to see my sister Andrea and her family in Connecticut. I had planned for us to board the Amtrak train at Penn Station for an 11 a.m. departure. Naturally, I wanted to get there by 10:30 to grab some coffee and a bagel, but Matt wasn't buying into my plan.

"We'll leave at 10:30," he informed me.

"But it takes 20 minutes to walk there from our hotel, so we should leave by 10:15 at the latest."

"What's the rush? You waste so much time arriving early — only to end up waiting around."

"Well, it's important to get a good seat on the train."

"Dad, any seat is a good seat. It's a train, not a movie."

"Matt, we have a deal. We have goals to reach and shared expectations for this trip."

"There are no shared expectations with you, old man. You always come out on top. Then you try to manipulate the system by guilt-tripping me about things like honor."

He paused for a second, then fired off his next round.

"We've never missed a bus, train or plane on any of these baseball trips," he reminded me.

"Exactly," I said. "So you see, my system works."

Bang.

Matt slammed the door to the bathroom. He had no retort. But I heard a faint laugh as he disappeared behind the door.

"He knows I'm right," I thought to myself. "There's no effective comeback to what I just said, so he just decided to go along with the program."

Sometimes parenting has its rewards.

We finally reached the Amtrak station and enjoyed the train ride along the Connecticut shoreline. It took us just two hours to reach Old Lyme, where my sister and her family greeted us at the station. My nephew Jacob was now 12, while Ethan was 10 and newly adopted Alexis was 3.

"How ya doing, Uncle Mike?" Jacob wanted to know.

"Wow, Uncle Mike, Matt's taller than you!" Ethan declared.

"Yes, you're very observant, Ethan," was my pained reply.

We headed back to Andrea's house and took a wonderful walk along the shoreline, observing the nautical nuances of Long Island Sound. The waterway was filled with birds and boaters and the countryside was green from all the recent rain. Along the way, we noticed dozens of stone walls that marked the property lines surrounding the houses.

"Go up, Uncle Mike?" Alexis said.

"Sure, Alexis, hold my hand and you can walk on the stones."

After completing our shoreline walk, my sister was adamant about showing us her barnyard animals.

"These are my pride and joy," Andrea informed me.

"They're chickens!" I protested. "Are we having them for dinner?"

"No, they are family pets. We don't eat family pets," she insisted. "Would you like to hold one, Matt?"

"Do I have to?"

"Yes, you have to," she said. "Here."

And with no formal introduction, Andrea thrust the robust rooster into Matt's rib cage.

"Can I wash my hands now?" he begged afterward.

Just at that moment, my brother, Russell, drove onto the pebbled driveway with my nephew Shane. The Luery boys quickly took out the whiffle ball equipment. Russ threw an assortment of curves and sliders that baffled the batters. But Matt got a hold of one junk pitch and lined it deep into the marsh surrounding Andrea's house.

"I'll get it," I said, stretching for the errant ball that was just out of my reach. I leaned forward and suddenly found myself tumbling into the marsh. I landed in a swampy soup laced with briars, my family howling with laughter.

"It's not funny," I said. "Help me out of here."

After the laughter subsided, Matt stuck his hand into the bushes and pulled me to safety.

"I hope everyone is amused," I said, checking my clothes for snakes and frogs. "Are there any animals on me?" I asked my sister.

"No," Andrea said, "but sometimes there's a little poison ivy in there."

Sure enough, two weeks later I would end up sporting a rash

on my legs, which I'm sure originated from my tumble into Andrea's marsh.

After regaining my balance on solid land, I rejoined the group to walk across the street – this time to invade another family playing whiffle ball. My brother-in-law, Fred, invited us to cross over his neighbor's stone wall and into the game, already in progress. We began swinging for the fences. The Luery/Fenton clan teamed up for a resounding 16-5 victory, sending our hosts back to the barn with their heads held low. My family is ultra competitive, even in whiffle ball – and we always play to win.

Meanwhile, my sister had prepared a festive New England feast, featuring 10 lobsters, a bushel of steamers, corn on the cob and fresh zucchini from her garden. I clipped the lobster shells with a nutcracker and dipped the tender seafood into the melted butter, which made for a delectable treat. For dessert, we picked fresh blackberries off the vine. It was a fabulous family visit.

⚾ ⚾ ⚾

The next morning, Russ drove us to Stamford, where Matt and I boarded the train to New York.

Or so I thought.

As we pulled out of the station, the conductor took our tickets and announced, "Oh, you're on the wrong train. This one is going eastbound to New Canaan, Connecticut."

Wrong Way Mike had done it again. Somehow, I had misdirected us to Track 3 instead of Track 5, and now my son and I were heading in the wrong direction.

"Sorry, Matt. I really blew it."

"Don't worry, Dad, this is what makes traveling with you so interesting – it's always an adventure."

All I could do was channel my inner Yogi and quote my favorite philosopher, who had been in this very predicament.

"I knew I was going to take the wrong train, so I left early," Yogi had said.

Matt let out a laugh that made me chuckle at the absurdity of it all. "Dad, sometimes you just got to let it go and go with the flow."

"And now you know why Sarah has such a terrible sense of direction," I explained. "She inherited it from me."

Of all the traits you'd want your kids to develop, getting lost early and often has got to be dead last on the list. I felt like apologizing to my daughter, even though she was not on board our wayward train. What would I tell her? "I'm sorry, Sarah, but getting disoriented just comes naturally to me. It's an ailment called Luery-itis. Yes, it's very contagious – and now you've got it too."

She'd probably laugh it off, but I really wish I had a better sense of direction.

Fortunately, it took only 15 minutes for the pair of wrong-way passengers to arrive at the New Canaan station. After a short break, the train reversed course and began heading west. Finally, we were back on track.

We arrived an hour later at New York's Grand Central Station – an architectural triumph that's home to a sea of humanity. Matt and I walked to our hotel; I could sense he was hungry.

"Dad, how 'bout if we eat at Chipotle? I know there's one on the ground floor of the Empire State Building."

"Sure," I said. "Let's go."

After lunch, Matt and I walked to the United Nations Building and explored some of the exhibits inside. My thoughts, however, were on the Mets game.

"Matt," I said, "I'd like to leave for the game by 5:30."

"Why?" he challenged me. "The game doesn't start until 7. You spend so much energy being early, when you could just relax and be on time. We'll leave at 5:45."

"But what if there's a traffic delay? We might be late!"

"Dad, we're taking a subway that goes right to the park. Just chill out."

"OK."

I let Matt take charge, so naturally we didn't leave our hotel until 5:50. As we walked the four blocks to Grand Central Station, I worried about missing the first pitch. With a sense of urgency, we boarded the "7" line express train that took us directly to Citi Field and fortunately, we arrived a full 30 minutes before game time. All was good in the world.

Citi Field features a beautiful brick façade entrance that's reminiscent of the old Ebbets Field, where the Dodgers once played. The façade takes you to Jackie Robinson Rotunda, a marvelous mix of pictures and videos honoring the former Dodger great.

The Mets have incorporated the Dodger Blue into their uniforms, along with the orange hues from the Giants, to make their jerseys a perfect blend of the two clubs that captivated New York for so many years, before both teams abandoned Gotham for the West Coast.

The Mets' new stadium is a massive improvement over Shea, where the swirling winds would often lift hot dog wrappers and small children into the air in a dusty vortex of negative energy. By contrast, the seats at Citi Field are a couple of inches wider than Shea, accommodating the more massive girth of today's fans. Citi Field is also a more intimate park, seating just 41,800 fans compared to the 57,333 capacity at Shea.

Citi Field includes a structural steel "bridge" that's designed to symbolize New York's five boroughs. The new stadium also features a high definition scoreboard to track the action and on this night, the Mets wore retro jerseys with huge NY letters sewn on front, just as the early New York Giants had done decades earlier.

Best of all, the Mets were playing the San Francisco Giants, my favorite National League team. Barry Zito was on the mound for the Giants and he quickly surrendered a home run to the Mets leadoff batter Angel Pagan, who drove the ball into the left field seats just 10 rows in front us, giving the New Yorkers an early 1-0 lead. It was the only run the Mets would need; rookie pitcher Bobby Parnell shut out the Giants 3-0.

My old high school buddy Rick Sarner joined us for the game, along with his son Bryan, who was born just three days before Matt.

We enjoyed seeing the giant bobble head known as Mr. Met run around the stadium, while the speakers blared out his theme song. Mr. Met is a leftover from the days of Shea Stadium, but a welcome distraction at Citi Field, where the team has successfully blended the old with the new.

Matt and I scrambled down to the edge of the left field stands, where Rick took our picture. Matt held up our sign that proclaimed "30," symbolizing all 30 Major League ballparks we had visited over the years. The spirit of Wilt Chamberlain lived on, at least for a moment.

"Dad, do you realize Citi Field is actually our 31st ballpark?"

"How can that be? There are 30 Major League teams and we've now been to every ballpark."

"Yes, but this is our second time seeing the Mets at home. So if you count Shea Stadium and Citi Field, it makes 31 ballparks."

"You're right," I conceded with a sheepish grin. "I guess we can roll up that cardboard poster now. It's already out of date."

"But look at it this way," Matt said with a hint of grace. "We've now visited every single Major League park – and never once did we have a rainout."

"Yes, that's true."

We had come close to a rainout in Boston, where a torrential downpour had halted the game for 30 minutes before the sun returned to shine on Fenway.

"And then we were nearly drizzled out at Yankee Stadium just two days ago," Matt observed.

"Right," I said. "But we're true baseball fans, so we stuck it out – except at Fenway Park, where you bailed on me over a minor rain delay."

"Is this really the end of the line?"

"No. It turns out we need to make one more stop before our journey is complete."

"Where's that?"

"Minnesota, here we come."

L.A. Road Trip

Saturday, April 10–Sunday, April 11, 2010

Angel Stadium, Los Angeles Angels of Anaheim

"The music scene today, Dad, is the indie bands."
SARAH LUERY

I had Minnesota on my mind. I was just starting to plan our 2010 road trip, when an e-mail invitation arrived in my inbox.

"Dad, I know this is pretty short notice," Matt wrote, "but if you were to come down to L.A. next weekend, we could see the Angels play the A's on Saturday night – then see USC play Cal on Sunday."

My heart was racing.

"Not sure if this is possible," Matt continued, "but it's just a thought…"

I picked up the phone and speed-dialed my son.

"Yes, I'm coming to L.A.!" I shouted. "I can't wait to see you and Sarah."

How could I pass up an invitation to see my kids – and watch two baseball games in two days?

"Woo hoo! I've just hit the Dad Daily Double at Hollywood Park!" I shouted out loud.

"Did you say something, hon?" my wife asked from the living room.

"Yes, I'm going to Disneyland!" I screamed. "Well, not really Disneyland, but Anaheim – to see the Angels play – and that's way better than Fantasyland."

My son had actually initiated our 2010 baseball odyssey. As Matt greeted me at the Burbank airport, I gave him a big hug.

"Thanks for inviting me down to see you," I said enthusiastically.

"Well, Dad, you're my baseball buddy and I had a free weekend – so I thought it might be fun to follow the wisdom of Ernie Banks, who said—"

"Let's play two," I interjected as we both laughed.

Our first stop was Los Feliz, a friendly L.A. neighborhood that's home to Fred 62, a small breakfast café with outdoor seating. Matt and I secured a table and waited eagerly for Sarah.

"There she is," I said as my daughter raced into my arms and gave me a big bearhug.

"Daddy, I'm so glad you're here," she said.

Suddenly the world was in perfect harmony. We sampled a delicious bowl of berries while Matt and I also ordered eggs benedict to accompany our spirited discussion about music and mysticism.

"What kind of music are you guys listening to these days?" I asked my children.

"The music scene today, Dad, is the indie bands," Sarah informed me.

"You mean musical bands from Indiana – like John Mellencamp and the Jackson Five?" I inquired.

"No, Dad," Sarah snorted. "I mean independent bands. Groups you've probably never heard of that are making great music."

"Like who?" I asked.

"No, Dad, not The Who," Matt countered. "Bands like Arcade Fire, and the Arctic Monkeys."

"Never heard of them," I said.

"Exactly," Matt and Sarah said in unison. "You are running the risk of becoming tragically unhip."

"I brought you both a present," I said. "For your musical pleasure, I am giving you the complete Jimi Hendrix collection, replete with digitally remastered versions of all his original albums."

"That's awesome!" Sarah said.

"You may be a dinosaur, but you rock," Matt confirmed.

"Thank you, I think," I said softly, then asserted, "Yes, you'll find *Are You Experienced?*, *Axis: Bold As Love,* and *Electric Ladyland* – the three albums released before Jimi's death in 1970."

Both kids were beaming.

"And they have a special DVD that takes you behind the scenes, with never-before-seen interviews with Jimi's band mates Noel Redding and Mitch Mitchell. And you get to hear from Jimi's producer, Chas Chandler and sound engineer, Eddie Kramer," I said enthusiastically.

"I'll listen to the tunes on the way home," Sarah said. "I've got to go now."

"Okay, babe, let's have brunch tomorrow then?" I asked hopefully.

"Of course, Dad, see you then," she said before driving off.

Matt and I hopped in his Honda Civic and headed to the USC campus for a much-anticipated visit to the architecture studio where he spent most of his waking hours.

It was there he showed me his architectural 3-D model depicting a community center in Los Angeles. Matt explained the design intricacies of his crafted model, which seemed to come to life before my eyes.

"I'm so impressed with what you've created," I proudly told him.

"Thanks, Dad. I think it's time to go to the game."

Was my son actually prompting me to head for the ballpark? What a role reversal. What a thrill!

On the drive down to Anaheim, I plugged in my iPod to provide Matt with a musical overview of the Jimi Hendrix collection.

"Let's start with Jimi's first album, *Are You Experienced?* said the middle-aged musical guide in the passenger seat.

I cranked up the volume for "Love or Confusion," letting Jimi's guitar overdubs fill the car with the psychedelic sounds of the '60s. Then I shuffled the iPod to the album's title track. Jimi's reverse guitar licks reverberated through the car woofers.

Matt was blown away by the magic of the music, which I sequenced chronologically to document the growing sophistication of each album. He was enchanted by the beautiful ballad of "May This Be Love" and inspired by the brilliance of "Voodoo Child (Slight Return)," which really rocked his world. I turned him on to the nuances of "Night Bird Flying" from *First Rays of the New Rising Sun* followed by the heartfelt passion of "Hear My Train A Comin'" from the latest release, *Valleys of Neptune.*

"Jimi Hendrix was truly the greatest rock guitarist who ever lived," I said to Matt. "And if there's any doubt about that, then listen to this," I stated emphatically as I cranked up "Lullabye for the Summer," a raucous rocker from the *Neptune* CD.

The electrical energy of wailing guitars filled the car instantly with a contagious beat that had us hopping in our seats.

"Dad, this is great!" Matt shouted over the dueling decibels.

All I could do was nod and smile as the music rocked us into the early evening.

We glided on what seemed like a magical musical carpet ride all the way to Anaheim, where a crowd of 40,239 was eagerly anticipating the clash between two California rivals – the hometown Angels versus the Oakland Athletics. Fortunately, I was able to score two great seats, in front of the right field foul pole, giving us a perfect vantage point for watching the Angels' Bobby Abreu and Oakland's Ryan Sweeney in action.

The moment we sat down, Matt said, "I'm hungry, let's get something to eat."

So we raced to the nearby concession stand for two hot dogs and a pair of ice-cold beers.

"I can't believe we're actually enjoying brewskis together at a ballpark!" I exclaimed.

"Well, we did that in Toronto last year, remember?"

"Yes, the drinking age is 19 in Canada, but this is our first American ballpark beer together," I said. "After all, you're 21 now."

Matt smiled as we settled into our seats, just in time for the national anthem.

The two teams were armed with aces: Ben Sheets for the A's and Jared Weaver for the Halos. Neither pitcher surrendered a hit until the third inning. That's when the Angels broke the scoreless tie as Hideki Matsui slapped a double in front of us down the right field line, scoring Bobby Abreu.

With the Angels leading 1-0, Matt shared his baseball wisdom. "I like the pace of the game," he said. "You know, how managers can strategize between pitches – debating whether to bunt or hit and run."

He was on a roll. "And depending on the situation – managers can try a squeeze play to bring home that runner from third base. It's a thinking man's game," he opined.

"That's the beauty of baseball," I agreed. "You know, Matt, we've got to get to Minnesota this summer to see the Twins' new ballpark. I hear Target Field is a beautiful place to watch a game."

"I can't wait to go."

"Besides, if we don't go, then you can't say you've seen baseball in Minnesota," I said to needle him.

"Well, we've been to the Hubert Humphrey Metrodome," was his retort.

"But you don't count stadiums unless they're current," I reminded him.

"I take it back. I'm older and wiser now."

"Now you know how I feel," said the Old Man. "There's wisdom in each passing year."

"Then you must be the wisest guy in the ballpark; you're the oldest one here."

I looked around and realized he was right. Everyone around me, it seemed, was younger.

"I'm not ancient," I said, "just more experienced in life."

My retort was weak, but the best I could muster on short notice. We watched the two teams battle back and forth for the lead, with the score knotted at three in the ninth.

That's when Hideki Matsui knocked his third hit of the game, a screaming liner down the right field line, scoring Bobby Abreu once again for the winning run in a 4-3 victory for the Angels. Instantly the stadium erupted in a pyrotechnic celebration, with fireworks filling the sky. It was only a single, but a walk-off hit nevertheless – and a great way to end a ballgame.

And the best thing was that tomorrow would bring another game.

⚾ ⚾ ⚾

Matt picked me up in the morning at the Los Angeles Midtown Radisson, conveniently located across from the USC campus. It was my home away from home – earning me a free overnight stay this time around, thanks to the 97,000 Gold Points my wife and I had accumulated from our frequent visits over the years. Matt glided us down Figueroa Boulevard where thousands of Lakers fans were filling the Staples Center for a game against the Portland Trailblazers. We just kept moving forward until we got to 9th Street, for our rendezvous with Sarah at Panini's Café.

"Dad, I've got some very exciting news," she said.

"What is it?"

"I've been accepted into grad school. I'm enrolling at Cal State Northridge to get my master's degree in sociology."

"Congratulations, babe!" I beamed while giving my daughter a big hug. "That means you'll be getting the degree you've always wanted – and I'll get to see plenty of Dodger games. You planned this really well."

"Dad!" she said with an exasperated look. "I didn't pick the school because it's close to Dodger Stadium. I chose Northridge because of its outstanding program in gender studies."

"You know, you can study genders at the ballpark," I said innocently. "It's called people watching, and I do it all the time."

"Ugggh," she said in frustration. "Some things never change, but I still love you, Dad."

After brunch, Matt and I headed back to campus where the USC Trojans were hosting the Cal Bears at Dedeaux Field.

"Matt, did you know that Mickey Mantle once hit two home runs here at USC?"

"How did that happen?"

"Well in 1951, when Mantle was a 19-year old rookie, the Yankees played an exhibition game against the USC Trojans. And in the first inning, he hit a mammoth 550-foot home run that took off like a rocket and landed on the football practice field. Then in the sixth inning, he launched another monster shot that traveled more than 500 feet."

"Wow, right here at my school?"

"Yes, and that's where the legend of Mickey Mantle's tape-measure home runs first began."

USC's baseball legacy is proudly showcased on its wall of fame which includes a virtual All-Star lineup of Major Leaguers. Tom Seaver is a decorated Trojan on the wall, along with Fred Lynn,

Mark McGwire, Barry Zito and the Boone brothers – Aaron and Brett. Pitchers Randy Johnson and Bill Lee are also on the list, along with slugger Dave Kingman – nearly 100 names in all, dating back to the 1920s. The entrance to the stadium features the Trojans' baseball championship flags, 12 total – the most of any team in the nation. The reign started in 1948 and ended in 1998.

The 2010 Trojans were unfortunately last in the Pac 10 Conference, generating a small turnout of perhaps only 200 fans for the game. Taking full advantage of the situation, Matt and I plopped right behind home plate, where we could hear the umpire call every ball and strike.

"I'm going to teach you how to score a game," I told Matt. With my $1 scorecard in hand, I explained how each position on the field corresponded with a number from one to nine, starting from the pitcher to the catcher, then the first baseman and around the diamond in a counter-clockwise fashion, until you finished with the right fielder. The only exception to the rule is that the shortstop (6 on the scorecard) comes after the third baseman (5). Baseball is filled with exceptions, just as in life.

"So a simple ground out to the third baseman would be marked 5-3," I explained.

"What about a strikeout?" he asked as the USC hitter whiffed at the plate.

"Give him a K for a swinging strikeout and a backward K for a called strike three," I said. "And a single is one line, while a double is two and a triple three lines."

"And a home run is four lines?"

"Exactly. You got it."

And with just a little help from dear old Dad, Matt scored the game, in which the Trojans went down to defeat 5-4 before a crowd that was mostly decked in blue and gold from the visiting Cal Bears fans.

"Better Bear than with a Trojan," they taunted.

Matt and I chuckled over that one.

"Well, Matt, we may have lost the game, but at least I passed on the torch to you. Now you can take your kids to a game one day and teach them how to keep score."

"Dad, you are such a hopeless romantic. Why do you see everything as poetry, but in a corny kind of way?"

"That's just who I am," I said proudly. "Yes, I'm an old-fashioned baseball fan who lives for the crack of the bat and the roar of the crowd."

"But that's exactly why I love going to games with you!" Matt exclaimed. "And I can't wait to meet you in Minnesota."

Target Field,
Minnesota Twins

Saturday, July 17–Sunday, July 18, 2010

"We will always have baseball between us."
MATT LUERY

I set the alarm for 4 a.m. but found myself wide-awake and wound up with anticipation. I was terrified I might oversleep and miss my 6:30 flight on Saturday morning. I had big plans to meet Matt in Minneapolis to see the Twins play two games (naturally, that's what Twins do) over the weekend at Target Field.

And for the first time ever, the Luery boys would begin their road trip in two separate cities. I was flying from my home in Sacramento; Matt would be leaving from Los Angeles, where he had a summer job as a marketing intern for a lumber company.

"Make sure you go to bed early," I warned my son over the phone. "It's important that you get a good night's sleep for your early morning flight."

"Dad, I'm 21 now. I can handle a late night out before boarding a plane. You can't."

"What are you talking about?" I asked indignantly. "When I was your age, I was the life of the party."

"I doubt you were ever my age. And you're no party animal."

In fact, you are the eternal party pooper," said the Stinkbug. "You're in bed by 10:30 every night. That's when my evening is just getting started," he added for emphasis.

"Just meet me in Minnesota on time. Our flights should arrive 10 minutes apart. Mine comes in first, so I'll look for you at your gate."

Our rendezvous unfolded just the way I had scripted it. I landed at 1:25 Minnesota time and then bolted from my terminal to Matt's gate, just as he arrived.

"Hey, Matt," I said, "perfect timing." I gave my son a big hug. "You seem a little tired today," I said.

"Well, I went to a movie with my friends last night in Hollywood. We saw *Inception*, the new film with Leonardo DiCaprio. The 10:30 show was sold out. So we saw the midnight performance. I didn't get home until 3 in the morning."

"No wonder you're listless," I bristled. "You were getting home just about the same time I was getting up."

"Well, the movie was great," he countered. "It was well worth it."

"We'll see if you can make it to the game."

The Twin Cities are thoroughly modern and multi-modal when it comes to transportation. You don't need a car to get around and in fact, many people rent bikes for the day. Matt and I took a Light Rail train (the Hiawatha line) from the airport directly to the warehouse district of downtown Minneapolis, where our hotel was located. I had scored a free overnight stay at the Radisson, thanks to my Gold Points and a zillion visits to the sister hotel opposite USC in Los Angeles.

The Radisson is located only two blocks from the Light Rail station – but instinctively I took off in the wrong direction.

"Dad, where are we going?"

"We're looking for 7th Street," I said with confidence.

"It's the other way."

Wrong Way Mike had done it once again. Given a choice

between two destinations, I will inevitably select the wrong course of action. Even if I try to fake myself out by going against my gut, I always seem to end up in the wrong direction. There was no way out of my embarrassment, except to use food as a weapon.

"Are you hungry?"

"Starved. All I had today was a croissant."

"Then let's go find a place to eat."

We wandered along the Nicollet Mall, a pedestrian walkway that takes you through 11 blocks of downtown Minneapolis. It is the second oldest downtown pedestrian mall in the United States – highlighted by the famous Mary Tyler Moore statue at 7th and Nicollet, the very spot where fictional TV character Mary Richards tossed her hat into the air, celebrating her independence as a female television news producer in the popular 1970's *Mary Tyler Moore Show*, which took place in Minneapolis.

Being a news guy myself, I was drawn to the nearby "Newsroom," which features vintage newspaper headlines and a 32-foot sailboat that serves as a bar. Matt and I both ordered the Kobe burgers smothered in mushrooms and grilled onions. We sat outside on the patio, breathing in the sultry, humid Minnesota air.

"It's 85 degrees, but it feels like 100," I observed.

"I don't mind it," said Matt.

Just a few bites into my thick mushroom burger, the sky turned dark and rain began pouring down. We rode out the storm underneath an awning that kept us – and our food – dry.

"I hope we don't have a rainout tonight," I said with concern.

"Be positive, Dad. We haven't had a rainout yet."

The skies opened up for a 20-minute downpour, but then the baseball gods intervened to turn off the spigot. We walked back to the hotel to check in and get ready for the game. Matt plopped down on the bed and I quickly sensed he was fading fast.

"I'm just gonna take a quick power nap," he said.

"Hey, I thought you were Mr. Late Night," I said mockingly. "Aren't you the guy who can stay out until the cows come home?"

Silence.

"Matt, are you up?"

Zzzzzzzz.

He was off in dreamland. I debated my dilemma, wondering if I should wake the kid to make tracks to the ballpark, or let him recharge his batteries.

I decided that batting practice could wait. So I let him sleep – for the moment. By 4:30, I was getting edgy; game time was 6:10 and I wanted to arrive early to explore the park.

By 5 p.m., I could wait no longer.

"Time to get up, Matt," I said to the zombie on the bed. "Let's go now."

I shook Matt repeatedly to awaken him. Finally, after 23 futile attempts, he began to show signs of life.

We walked the five blocks to the park and noticed multiple Twins Around Town – life-sized statues depicting catcher Joe Mauer – with each figure featuring decoupage headlines and pictures representing different years in Twins' history.

We found ourselves in the middle of a sea of pinstriped Twins jerseys. Many of the fans wore Twins T-shirts with Justin Morneau's number 33 embossed on the back. The Twins first baseman was very popular – but the crowd favorite was clearly the kid from St. Paul, the All-Star catcher for the American League who wore number 7.

"We like that Joe Mauer, don't ya know," a Twins fan told me in his Minnesota dialect. He said his name was Tommy.

"He's a great player," I agreed. "He can hit, field and throw with the best. Mauer could be one of the all-time great catchers if he stays healthy."

"OK then," said Tommy the Twins fan, sporting his dark

blue Twins jersey. He wore a hat with the initials TC (for Twin Cities).

"Then what?" I wondered.

"Just OK then," Tommy responded. "There's a sports bar here named Hrbek's," the Twins fan pointed out. "It's operated by Twins' legend Kent Hrbek, who helped us win a World Series in 1987 and again in '91. If you want to see it now, I can go with."

"Go with me?" I asked innocently. "Is that what you mean?"

"That's what I said," Tommy stated emphatically. "I can go with."

"Well, I'm sure I can find it, but thanks anyway," I countered.

"Well, alrighty then," declared Tommy the Twin. "I'm gonna go get me a walleye sandwich and some pop now."

"Pop?" I asked. "Is that the aging shopkeeper who minds the store?"

"Ohhhh nooooooo," Tommy said with pronounced o's. "Pop is what we drink when we get thirsty, don't ya know, like Coke or Pepsi. It's a good way to wash down the walleye."

Walleye is a delicate and flaky freshwater fish that's a fan favorite in Minnesota.

"OK then," I said. "It's been nice to meet you, don't ya know."

"Gooooo Twins!" Tommy said as he darted off into the night.

Target Field is filled with a wide variety of cuisine ranging from Asian wok cooking to bratwurst on the grill. Matt and I savored the flavor of "Twins Brews," featuring lagers from Minnesota and Wisconsin, including my personal favorite, Leinenkugel. "Leinie" is an American premium Pilsner beer with a rich, creamy taste representing the "Legend of the Northwoods." The Chippewa Falls, Wisconsin, beer maker is in fact the seventh oldest brewery in the United States.

"This beer has a great taste," Matt observed.

I clicked my glass with his in a display of agreement.

"Let's celebrate the fact," I said, "that we can sip these delicious brewed beverages together here at the ballpark. And since this is the Twins stadium," I added, "let's have two."

As for the ballgame, the 39,504 fans in attendance were treated to a pitching duel between two aces – Carl Pavano for the Twins and Mark Buerhle for the Chicago White Sox. Pavano gave up a solo shot to slugger Paul Kanerko in the fourth inning, while Buerhle was bested by a three-run second inning. Both pitched complete games, though, in a lightning-quick hour and 52 minutes. Lightning is the key word here; just minutes after Pavano nailed down the final out in the ninth inning for a 3-2 victory over the Sox, the sky became electric.

No sooner had the fans screamed, "Twins win, Twins win!" then a steady rain cascaded across the stadium, sending us scurrying to the exits. A huge lightning bolt lit up the sky, followed by a thundercrack that rocked the Twin Cities.

"Carl Pavano for President in 2012!" screamed one fan.

"Ka-boom!" was the response from above as the heavens opened up with a river of water.

"If Pavano can save the Twins," shouted the fan, "then he can save the country!"

"KA-BOOM!" roared the thunder as another lightning bolt streaked across the sky. The winds picked up in intensity, howling with gusts up to 40 mph.

In all the confusion, I took off at a record clip, with Matt nipping at my heels. Two blocks into our dash for dryness, I realized I had lost my bearings – we were actually sprinting *away* from the hotel.

Wrong Way Mike had done it again!

Maybe it's funny to get lost on a sunny day, but in the middle of a torrential mini-tornado, Matt was not amused. But rather than berate me for being a bonehead, my son offered a simple solution.

"Let's find a place to eat."

I nodded as we turned into the House of Thailand for a warm meal and shelter from the storm. But instead of dissipating, the wind and rain only got stronger, blowing out power in portions of the city. We sipped our soup and hoped the storm would fade, but after an hour, it was actually getting more intense. We finished our meal and then bolted to the hotel, only to get drenched in the process.

We arrived wet and tired, but elated to have survived the tempest. We watched the weather coverage on TV that night and saw video of golfball-sized hail destroying crops and snapping tree limbs around the Twin Cities. We had truly dodged a bullet that would have stopped the ballgame had the monster storm begun just 10 minutes earlier. I went to sleep that night with the contentment of knowing we'd be back at the ballpark in less than 12 hours.

◇ ◇ ◇

On Sunday morning I awoke early, but Matt begged for more time in dreamland.

"Let's skip breakfast," he pleaded. "We'll eat brunch at the ballpark."

"That lack of sleep is catching up with you," I sneered.

No response.

I'd proven my point.

Two hours later, when Matt finally did wake up, we loaded our backpacks and headed back to the ballpark, where we stopped to look at the Rod Carew statue.

"Rod Carew, the legendary infielder, played 12 seasons for the Twins," I explained. "Then he played another 7 years for the California Angels. He was a slap hitter who won 7 American League batting titles and finished with a .328 lifetime batting average."

"Did the Twins retire his number?" Matt inquired.

"Yes, his number 29 is retired," I said. "And so is Harmon Killebrew's number 3, Tony Oliva's number 6 and Kent Hbrek's number 14. And number 34 is also retired — it belonged to outfielder Kirby Puckett, who is considered by most fans to be the greatest Twins player ever. Puckett was a 10-time All Star who scored more hits and runs than any other player in team history."

I could tell Matt's attention was focused elsewhere — on a wall of metallic squares outside the park.

"What is that?"

"That's The Wave," I said. It's a giant wind veil comprised of thousands of metallic panels — all lit up by LED lights. And when the wind blows—"

"The panel moves to simulate the effect of the prairie winds," said Matt, completing my thought.

Inside the park is the fourth largest video board in the Majors. It features a 5,800-square-foot high definition screen. In center field is the "Celebration Sign," showcasing the original team logo with Minnesota Twins "Minnie and Paul" on opposite sides of the Mississippi River. The sign comes alive and the Twins actually shake hands every time a Minnesota player hits a home run.

Matt and I ate lunch on the patio of the Town Ball Tavern, overlooking the oncoming trains. The Tavern features pictures of semi-pro parks from around Minnesota and includes the original floor from the Minneapolis Armory — where the Lakers hosted basketball fans from 1947 to 1960 before moving to Los Angeles.

"Let's celebrate," I said.

"Are you thinking what I'm thinking?"

"Yeah, two Leinies, please," I told the waitress.

After savoring the local lagers, we found our seats in the upper deck, offering a panoramic view of the downtown Minneapolis skyline. The sun emerged from the clouds to light up the park, reminding me of the Beatles tune "Rain." In my head, John and Paul were singing they were fine with either rain or shine.

"I don't like to rank ballparks," said Matt, "but I will tell you, this is one of my favorites."

"Really, what do you like best about it?" I asked.

"Good integration with the existing urban fabric," said the architecture major.

"What does that mean in English?"

"It means I love how Target Field is a hub for mass transit and serves as a magnet for bringing people downtown, unlike other ballparks that are islands unto themselves, even though they are located in a city center. You don't need a car here. You can ride a bike to the game or take Light Rail right from the airport to get here – it's environmentally friendly and I like that."

"Me too."

As for the game, the Twins took an early lead in the second inning when Delmon Young hit a two-run homer off Sox starter Freddy Garcia. The crowd went crazy as Young circled the bases, while Minnie and Paul celebrated in center field with their home run handshake. But Chicago would beat up on Nick Blackburn, the Twins star-crossed starter, and the White Sox took a 6-3 lead into the ninth inning.

Suddenly I realized we had a Major League dilemma.

"Well as Yogi Berra would say," I whispered to Matt, "it gets late early out there."

"What are you talking about?"

"You know I've never left a game before the final out. But our planes leave in two hours and I'm afraid Light Rail will be jammed with Twins fans if we don't leave now."

"OK, whatever you say."

"Don't you want to argue with me?" I said with a hint of disappointment. "Can't you convince me we should stay longer?" I begged.

"Dad, it's your call. We can bolt for the airport now and play it safe – or we can live dangerously and see if the Twins might rally in the bottom of the ninth."

"I'm afraid we'll miss our flights if we don't leave right now."

"Alrighty then," said Matt in his best Minnesota dialect.

We boarded the train with the outcome still hanging in the balance. As the Light Rail train left the ballpark, we heard a roar from the crowd that seemed to only get louder. There was a buzz in the air signaling that something special was happening. A Twins fan on the train let out a yell.

"What's happening now?" Matt asked.

We both dialed up our BlackBerries in search of an Internet connection.

"Oh my God!" I said. "The Twins are staging a comeback. Delmon Young just looped a single to center to score the tying run!" I exclaimed as I clicked my phone for an instant update. "And Alex Rios just threw the ball away, allowing Michael Cuddyer to score the winning run!" I screamed. "I can't believe it. The Twins just staged a four-run rally in the bottom of the ninth, for one of the most dramatic come-from-behind victories of the year. And we missed it. I blew it, Matt. I just botched the most beautiful ending for the road trip!"

"No you didn't, Dad. That's the Hollywood ending. You're such a romantic. Life is not always glowing sunsets and fairy tale finales. This is a much more realistic way to end the journey."

"Why do I always have to play it safe? Why can't I roll the dice once in a while and be more daring?"

"Because that's who you are. And I really value the time we've had together on this road trip," he said softly as he put his hand on my shoulder.

"We saw 2 games in 2 days," he stated. "And 32 ballparks altogether in 16 years," he said with consolation. "I added it up last night: we attended 35 Major League games in 29 states and the District of Columbia – plus a foreign country. We traveled some 43,000 miles on one of the greatest road trips a father and son could ever experience."

I looked into my son's face and saw passion in his eyes.

"Dad, you've given me a love for the game of baseball that I will pass on to my children."

He paused for just a moment and then looked me in the eye.

"And Dad, from my heart I can tell you this – no matter how much we may argue about bedtime, wakeup calls or music on the radio, we will always have baseball between us."

Epilogue

By Matt Luery

When I look back on the 30+ Major League Baseball stadiums I have visited with my dad over the last 10 years, I find myself simultaneously flooded with memories, yet hard-pressed to form even a single sentence describing the experience. Family members or friends sometimes ask questions such as, "Wow, what was that like?!" or inevitably, "Which places were your favorite?" But answering these questions is as difficult as singling out your favorite childhood memory or attempting to describe what people call "the college experience." Reflection can be an overwhelming activity, whether you are put on the spot by a curious grandparent or taking time to write down thoughts for a book, so I will do my best to describe what the baseball travels I have shared with my dad mean to me now as I prepare to graduate from college.

To begin with, I want to come clean and say that in addition to some exciting experiences I will always remember – baseball and otherwise – I have only a vague recollection of many of the details from our trips. While I do vividly recall reading the plaque on the statue of Ty Cobb at Comerica Park in Detroit and visiting the birthplace of Babe Ruth in Baltimore, I probably couldn't tell you a single score of a game we saw. With little difficulty I could describe in depth the exact night in Texas when, at my dad's behest, I listened to Led Zeppelin and then fell in love, but I would likely stumble if tasked with naming all the stadiums we visited and in which order. Meeting former Dodger Maury Wills? Another solid memory. Meeting former Blue Jay Dave Stewart? Not nearly as strong.

As a final complication, some insignificant events from the trips have stuck with me through the years (seeing *Mr. and Mrs. Smith* in South Dakota which, by the way, I also remember thinking was just OK; a group of flight attendants delaying the check-in process for over an hour at a hotel in Miami) while a few significant ones, such as seeing a game at Wrigley Field, are rather hazy.

But from out of this mishmash some enduring realizations about travel, baseball, and my relationship with my dad have taken shape. My family's insistence on the importance of travel, which I have since learned was one of my dad's not-so-hidden motives in visiting baseball stadiums, is summed up best by something Mark Twain said over 150 years ago: "Travel is fatal to prejudice, bigotry, and narrow-mindedness." The idea that seeing the world in person can be as educational as sitting in a classroom is not earth-shattering by any means, but I think people sometimes discount the amount of culture and history in North America. This is especially true in regard to the parts of the United States some coastal residents insist on calling the "flyover states." The single biggest thing I took away from traveling with my dad is that I could learn much more about my own prejudices and biases than I ever expected without having to take an epic study abroad–style trip overseas.

When I was in high school I once made a trek to Montana to visit the childhood buddy of one of my good friends in California. The subject of school dances came up as we were talking. I remember being fascinated to hear that his Montana high school had California-themed dances. He went on to tell me enthusiastically how everyone would show up at the dances dressed as either surfers or movie stars. How ridiculous, I thought...my home state of 37 million diverse people was being stereotyped into two pop culture clichés! Then it dawned on me that at my high school we have an annual Hawaiian-themed dance where everyone comes dressed in flowery shirts and leis (I've since learned that dressing like this is a surefire way to identify yourself as a tourist on the islands). Stereotypes like this seem to exist for most states and even some cities, but it wasn't until leaving California and traveling across the country that I realized how much more interesting the truth is.

Some of my favorite unexpected discoveries were the beautiful hills surrounding Cincinnati; the stock of early 20th century architecture in Kansas City and St. Louis; serene lakeside neighborhoods east of Detroit and across the U.S.-Canadian border; Mt. Washington in Pittsburgh; a chain of islands a ferry ride away from Toronto; desert hiking in Phoenix; and a crowded Lake Michigan beach (complete with sand dunes) in Indiana. One by one my preconceived notions and judgments were shattered as we traveled, and I learned a whole lot of American history in the process.

Looking at red and blue Electoral College maps every four years seems more and more like a gross oversimplification of America when you've been served breakfast by farmers on a field in South Dakota; listened to New Yorkers argue about football on the 7 Train all the way from Queens to Manhattan; watched a ballgame with a family from Texas; and made friends in the nosebleed section of Target Field in Minneapolis. The point is my dad and I encountered good people in every city and every stadium we went to, and it didn't matter which side of the Mason-Dixon line, which side of the Mississippi River, or which side of Chicago we were in. Baseball is baseball everywhere, and people are people everywhere (just try to avoid the subject of presidential elections, if possible).

We all know that ESPN broadcasts to national audiences and *Sports Illustrated* has subscribers in every city, but I didn't really appreciate the remarkable role of sports in binding America together until I experienced it firsthand. There are definitely rivalries, arguments, trash talking, and even genuine hatred in regard to opposing teams, but these emotions are what make the bind so strong, not examples of fracture within it. Would Red Sox fans really want a world where the Yankees finish in last place every season? Well, maybe for a couple of years it would be entertaining, but I suspect anybody in Boston would rather beat the Yankees in the American League Championship Series than settle for another opponent. Our sports teams are something we identify with, and I feel blessed that through baseball my dad and I have had the opportunity to visit and begin to understand these various identities. Without a doubt this has had the effect of making a large and diverse continent feel like a much smaller, more personal space.

Another thought about baseball games is how my dad and I found their notoriously slow pacing to be something we really looked forward to. It's true someone could do a tour of football stadiums or basketball arenas, but the excitement and constant activity in these games make it quite a different experience when it comes to talking to the person next to you or even doing some thinking. It's a glass half empty or half full type thing. If you read sports news even occasionally, you probably know it's become fashionable to take the half-empty point of view, going on about the demise of baseball as "America's pastime" due to its slow, low-scoring games at a time when people can't wait in line for two minutes without pulling out their cell phone to browse the Internet.

At the beginning of our trips I shared this perspective for the most part: I loved *playing* baseball but was unconvinced of the benefit of watching it. My dad insisted that watching a slow game could be more rewarding than watching a fast game, however, and set out to show me how. Years later and by the time we posed for a picture at a Mets game in Citi Field, our 30th ballpark (or was it actually 31?) I was convinced. What had changed? I learned to appreciate the game for its slow pace—and suddenly the glass was half full.

Instead of viewing sports as a crazed extension of an already hectic, unpredictable part of my life (high school and college) I started to view sports as an opportunity for relief. Taking three hours on a Sunday to watch a calculated, methodical game and just let my mind wander while talking to my dad turned out to be an excellent antidote to the fast-paced world beyond the ballpark. Throw in the fact that you get to sit outside, and that you experience being part of something with so much tradition, and all of a sudden a baseball game becomes more like a meditation session. Plus, it even makes it possible to enjoy a game when you have no emotional stake in who wins. I don't mean to say I abstain from watching "fast sports" anymore, only that when studying for multiple finals or trying to secure a summer internship gets stressful, I find the thought of watching a ballgame out in the sun on a lazy weekend day to be much more calming than fretting about my team's third down conversion rate on the gridiron. The meditation factor, I think, is why I have come to love baseball so much.

As far as the father-son aspect of our trips, I'm grateful for all the time I got to spend with my dad, even if we did have our disagreements every now and then. High school can be a pretty awkward time, especially when it comes to your relationship with your parents, but the fact that we were traveling and had only each other for companionship meant we had no choice but to talk and get to know each other a bit more. There were times when the whole thing started to feel contrived, like a manufactured activity, but when you think about it, a lot of things in life actually are that way. There's nothing *authentic*, for example, about the mixers that colleges arrange in the first weeks of school so that freshman can make friends, but that doesn't mean you won't meet some of your future best friends there. Ditto for the process of joining a fraternity or going on a blind date or anything else of that nature: it may start off contrived but it often ends up feeling very real.

I think my dad and I covered just about every topic we could along the way. Conversations starting with sports or music would turn into political debates or career advice and planning for the future. Every now and then he would offer up a story from his past, slowly letting me know that he wasn't perfect either. And learning that my dad pulled pranks in high school or had some crazy nights in college was a cool way of building trust. I shared some of my best stories too, but I think I'll let a bit more time pass before I reveal them all. There seems to be a magic period (sort of like the statute of limitations) when something that used to get me in major trouble—throwing a house party when my parents were out of town—becomes a story everyone can laugh about a few years later. I've found it's best to err on the side of caution with these things.

Learning not only about my dad's strengths, like his political knowledge, but also his weaknesses, like his sense of direction, has made our relationship stronger and more equal; he certainly knows all of my faults from 22 years of raising me. And I'm proud that we can relate to each other well enough now to be able to joke around—just like I do with my friends. I also admire my dad for being able to put up with me constantly challenging his authority throughout the trip. Based on what my aunt and uncle have told me in recent years though, it seems the fruit doesn't fall far from the tree.

So how do I answer the unanswerable question of what it was like to go to every Major League ballpark in North America with my dad? I usually get jolted all at once by the memories of almost everything I've just described. But then I think about how fortunate I am that my dad and I got to do something he never got to do with his dad.

And so in my best understated tone I answer that question by simply saying "It was one hell of a trip."

Los Angeles, California
January 9, 2011

Baseball Lingo

Ace: The #1 starting pitcher on a team.

Bag: Base.

Bases Loaded: Runners on first, second and third.

Bronx Cheer: When fans boo a team, an umpire or a play.

Brushback: A pitch designed to deliberately intimidate the batter by nearly hitting him.

Bunt: A deliberate small hit, in which the batter does not swing, but rather squares the bat to strike the ball downward. In a successful bunt the batter will place the ball in between fielders, allowing him to reach first base safely.

Can of Corn: A fly ball hit directly to a fielder, who can snag it in his glove without moving.

Chin Music: A fastball delivered near the batter's chin as a warning to back off the plate.

Closer: The "ace" reliever, who must shut down a scoring threat and save the game, usually in the eighth or ninth inning.

DL: Disabled List. A player on the DL is injured and not on the active roster.

Double: A two-base hit in which the batter safely reaches second base.

Doubleheader: Two games played back to back, for the price of one. Doubleheaders are now nearly obsolete, except for makeup games following a rainout.

Double Play: When the defense records two outs on one hit ball.

Ducks on the Pond: Fenway Park slang for bases loaded, especially with Red Sox.

Going Deep: Hitting a home run.

Grand Slam: A home run with the bases loaded, scoring four runs in one blow.

Heat: A fastball with zip.

Hit and Run: A play when the runner on first base tries to advance to second base before the pitch, forcing the second baseman to cover the bag, while leaving his territory unprotected. The hitter then tries to place the ball in the gap for a base hit. This play should really be called a Run and Hit.

Home Run: A ball hit out of the park. Also called a homer, dinger, four-bagger, tater, jack or moon shot (if it's a high, arcing drive).

Inside the Park Home Run: A ball hit between fielders, allowing the batter to advance all the way around the bases to score a run.

K: A strikeout. The term is said to be derived from the term Knock Out.

Let's Play Two: Ernie Banks' coined this phrase about playing a doubleheader.

No Hitter: A game in which no batter gets a base hit, but runners may manage to get on base by a fielder's error, a hit batsman or a base on balls.

Perfect Game: A game in which all 27 batters are retired consecutively without reaching base.

Passed Ball: An error by the catcher, in which he loses control of a pitched ball, thereby allowing runners on base to advance.

Pinch Hitter: A substitute batter used to replace a weaker hitter in key situations.

Rainout: When rain or inclement weather forces the postponement of a game.

Relief Pitcher: A pitcher brought in to replace a tired, ineffective or injured starting pitcher.

RBI: Run Batted In

Sacrifice Fly: A deliberate out, hit deeply to an outfielder, allowing a runner to tag up and advance to the next base, at his own risk. A sacrifice fly can occur only with fewer than two outs in an inning.

Single: A one-base hit in which the batter safely reaches first base.

Slump: A prolonged batting drought in which the batter is unable to get a base hit over the course of many games.

Stolen Base: The pilfered prize of a base runner, who uses speed and deception to advance to another base just as the ball is pitched. Runners must avoid a pitcher's pickoff move and beat the catcher's throw to the base to be declared safe. The most common base to steal is second, then third, but rarely home— unless your name is Jackie Robinson.

Southpaw: A lefty pitcher.

Triple: A three-base hit in which the batter safely reaches third base.

Triple Play: A rare defensive maneuver in which the team on the field records three consecutive outs on one play.

Utility Player: A player who is versatile enough to play multiple positions in the field during the course of a season.

Walk: A base on balls in which the batter reaches first base after the pitcher delivers four balls.

Whiff: A strikeout.

Wild Pitch: An errant pitch that is so far out of the strike zone it cannot be contained by the catcher, allowing any base runners to advance.

Baseball Bullets

A compilation of fun and family-friendly things to do
and places to stay in every Major League city.
(All contact information was valid as of press time for this book.)

AMERICAN LEAGUE

BALTIMORE ORIOLES
Oriole Park
333 West Camden Street
Baltimore, MD 21201
(410) 685-9800
www.orioles.com

BOOG'S BBQ
Oriole Park
Center Field Bleachers
Baltimore, MD 21201
www.boogsbbq.com

BABE RUTH MUSEUM
216 Emory Street
Baltimore, MD 21201
(410) 727-1539
www.baberuthmuseum.com

SPORTS LEGENDS MUSEUM
AT CAMDEN YARDS
301 W. Camden Street
Baltimore, MD 21201
(410) 727-1539
www.baberuthmuseum.com

INNER HARBOR
baltimore.org/about-baltimore/
inner-harbor

FT. MCHENRY
2400 East Fort Avenue
Baltimore, MD 21230
(410) 962-4290
www.nps.gov/fomc/index.htm

FEDERAL HILL
(*Historic neighborhood overlooking
the Inner Harbor*)
www.historicfederalhill.org/www

FELLS POINT
(Historic waterfront community)
www.fellspoint.us

BOSTON RED SOX
Fenway Park
4 Yawkey Way
Boston, MA 02215
(617) 267-9440
www.redsox.com

THE FREEDOM TRAIL
(*Walking history tour of America's
Revolutionary War*)
99 Chauncey Street
Suite 401
Boston, MA 02111
(617) 357-8300
www.thefreedomtrail.org/

BOSTON DUCK TOURS
4 Copley Place
Suite 4155
Boston, MA 02116
(617) 267-DUCK
www.bostonducktours.com/

MUSEUM OF SCIENCE
1 Science Park
Boston, MA 02114
(617) 589-0100
www.mos.org/

BOSTON PUBLIC GARDEN
(*Ride the Swan Boats, See
Make Way for Ducklings*)
9 Arlington Street,
Boston, MA 02116
(617) 522-1966
www.swanboats.com/

JFK PRESIDENTIAL LIBRARY
(*Honoring John F. Kennedy*)
Columbia Point
Boston, MA 02125
(866) JFK-1960
www.jfklibrary.org

HARVARD UNIVERSITY
Massachusetts Hall
Cambridge, MA 02138
(617) 495-1000
www.harvard.edu

CHICAGO WHITE SOX
U.S. Cellular Field
333 West 35th Street
Chicago, IL 60616
(312) 674-1000
www.whitesox.com

CHICAGO ARCHITECTURE
FOUNDATION RIVER CRUISE
224 South Michigan Avenue
Chicago, IL 60604
(312) 922-3432
caf.architecture.org/Page.
aspx?pid=574

WILLIS-SEARS TOWER SKYDECK
Willis Tower
Suite 3530
Chicago, IL 60606
(312) 875-9696
www.theskydeck.com/

NAVY PIER
600 East Grand
Chicago, IL 60611
(312) 595-5100
www.navypier.com/

MAGNIFICENT MILE
401 North Michigan Avenue
Chicago, IL 60611
www.themagnificentmile.com

FIELD MUSEUM
(*One of the best natural history
museums in the U.S.*)
1400 South Lake Shore Drive
Chicago, IL 60605
(312) 922-9410
www.fieldmuseum.org

SHEDD AQUARIUM
1200 South Lake Shore Drive
Chicago, IL 60605
(312) 939-2438
www.sheddaquarium.org

THE HANCOCK OBSERVATORY
875 North Michigan Avenue
Chicago, IL 60611
(888) 875-VIEW
www.hancockobservatory.com

SLICE OF CHICAGO PIZZA TOURS
(*Chicago's Deep-Dish pizza
lover walking tour*)
(312) 623-9292
www.sliceofchicagopizzatours.com

PIZZERIA UNO
29 East Ohio Street
Chicago, IL 60611
(312) 623-9292
www.sliceofchicagopizzatours.com

GIORDANO'S FAMOUS STUFFED
PIZZA
35 Chicago locations
www.giordanos.com

GINO'S PIZZA
Numerous Chicago locations
www.ginoseast.com

SMITH AND WOLLENSKY
STEAKHOUSE
318 North State Street
Chicago, IL 60610
(312) 670-9900
www.smithandwollensky
steakhouses.com

BANDERA RESTAURANT
535 North Michigan Avenue
Chicago, IL 60611
(312) 644-3524
www.hillstone.com/#/
restaurants/bandera

CLEVELAND INDIANS
Progressive Field
2401 Ontario Street
Cleveland, OH 44115
(216) 420-4200
www.indians.com

ROCK & ROLL HALL OF FAME
1100 Rock and Roll Boulevard
Cleveland, OH 44114
(216) 781-7625
rockhall.com

GREAT LAKES SCIENCE CENTER
601 Erieside Avenue
Cleveland, OH 44114
(216) 694-2000
www.glsc.org

CLEVELAND ZOO
3900 Wildlife Way
Cleveland, OH 44109
(216) 661-6500
www.clemetzoo.com

THE FLATS
(*Cleveland's entertainment district,
filled with pubs, music and
restaurants*)
www.cleveland.com/flats

PRO FOOTBALL HALL OF FAME
2121 George Halas Drive NW
Canton, OH 44708
(330) 456-8207
www.profootballhof.com

DETROIT TIGERS
Comerica Park
2100 Woodward Avenue
Detroit, MI 48201
(313) 962-4000
www.tigers.com

MOTOWN HISTORICAL MUSEUM
(*Rhythm & Blues/Soul sounds
of the '60s*)
2648 West Grand Boulevard
Detroit, MI 48208
(313) 875-2264
www.motownmuseum.com

THE DETROIT PEOPLE MOVER
AND RIVER WALK
1420 Washington Boulevard
Detroit, MI 48226
(313) 224-2160
www.thepeoplemover.com

HILTON GARDEN INN
(*One block from Comerica Park*)
351 Gratiot Avenue
Detroit, MI 48226
(313) 967-0900
www.hiltongardeninn.hilton.com/en/
gi/hotels/index.jhtml;jsessionid=KPP
B404DLQACCCSGBIXMVCQ?ctyhoc
n=DETDHGI

HENRY FORD MUSEUM
(*Tribute to the American Automobile*)
20900 Oakwood Boulevard
Dearborn, MI 48124
(313) 982-6001
www.hfmgv.org

AMBASSADOR BRIDGE
(*to Canada*)
Detroit, MI 48201
(586) 467-0117
www.ambassadorbridge.com

WINDSOR, ONTARIO
www.windsorontario.worldweb.com

UNIVERSITY OF MICHIGAN
515 East Jefferson
Ann Arbor, MI 48109
(734) 764-1817
www.michigan.edu

KANSAS CITY ROYALS
Kauffman Stadium
One Royal Way
Kansas City, MO 64129
(816) 921-8000
www.royals.com

NEGRO LEAGUES BASEBALL
MUSEUM
1616 East 18th Street
Kansas City, MO 64108
(816) 221-1920
www.nlbm.com

AMERICAN JAZZ MUSEUM
1616 East 18th Street
Kansas City, MO 64108
(816) 474- 8463
www.americanjazzmuseum.com

KANSAS CITY BBQ
www.gatesbbq.com
www.arthurbryantsbbq.com

COUNTRY CLUB PLAZA
(*KC's dining, shopping
and entertainment center*)
4750 Broadway
Kansas City, MO 64112
(816) 753-0100
www.countryclubplaza.com

HARRY TRUMAN PRESIDENTIAL
LIBRARY
500 West U.S. Highway 24
Independence, MO 64050
(800) 833-1225
www.trumanlibrary.org

**LOS ANGELES ANGELS
OF ANAHEIM**
Angels Stadium
2000 Gene Autry Way
Anaheim, CA 92806
(714) 940-2000
www.angelsbaseball.com

DISNEYLAND
1313 South Disneyland Drive
Anaheim, CA 92802
(714) 781-4565
www.disneyland.disney.go.com

DISNEY'S CALIFORNIA ADVENTURE
Anaheim, CA 92801
(714) 781-4101
www.disneyland.disney.go.com

KNOTT'S BERRY FARM
8039 Beach Boulevard
Buena Park, CA 90620
(714) 220-5200
www.knotts.com

MINOR LEAGUES MAJOR DREAMS
(*Discounts on caps and jerseys for
Major League and Minor League
teams*)
1733 South Douglass Road
Suite A
Anaheim, CA 92806
(714) 939-0939
www.minorleagues.com

FLIGHTDECK AIR COMBAT CENTER
(*Pilot an F-16 flight simulator*)
1601 South Sunkist Street, Unit A
Anaheim, CA 92806
(714) 937-1511
www.flightdeck1.com

MINNESOTA TWINS
Target Field
1 Twins Way
Minneapolis, MN 55403
(612) 659-3400
www.twinsbaseball.com

TOWN BALL TAVERN
Target Field
1 Twins Way
Minneapolis, MN 55403

HRBEK'S
(*Kent Hrbek's sports bar*)
Target Field
1 Twins Way
Minneapolis, MN 55403

SMALLEY'S 87 CLUB
(*Sports bar tribute to 1987 World Champion Minnesota Twins and Roy Smalley, one of the stars of the '87 team. Located directly behind right field fence at Target Field*)
100 North 6th Street
Minneapolis, MN 55403
(612) 877-7799
www.smalleys87club.com

THE NEWSROOM
(*Fresh baked breads, pastries and sandwiches*)
990 Nicollet Mall
Minneapolis, MN 55403
(612) 343-0073
www.thenewsroommpls.com

NICOLLET MALL
700 Nicollet Mall
Minneapolis, MN 55402
http://www.mapquest.com/maps?city=Minneapolis&state=MN&address=700+Nicollet+Mall

MARY TYLER MOORE STATUE
7th and Nicollet
Minneapolis, MN 55403
www.tvacres.com/statues_mary.htm

MALL OF AMERICA
60 East Broadway
Bloomington, MN 55425
(952) 883-8800
www.mallofamerica.com

MINNESOTA STATE CAPITOL
75 Dr. Rev. Martin Luther King Jr. Boulevard
St. Paul, MN 55155
(651) 296-2881
www.mnhs.org/places/sites/msc

MINNEAPOLIS QUEEN
(*Paddle wheel cruise on the Mississippi River*)
700 Sibley Street NE
Minneapolis, MN 55413
(612) 378-7966
www.twincitiescruises.com

SCIENCE MUSEUM OF MINNESOTA
120 Kellogg Boulevard W
St. Paul, MN 55102
(651) 221-2550
www.smm.org

UNIVERSITY OF MINNESOTA
100 Church Street SE
Minneapolis, MN 55455
(612) 625-5000
www.umn.edu/tc

TARGET CENTER
(*Minnesota Timberwolves*)
600 North 1st Avenue
Minneapolis, MN 55403
(612) 673-1600
www.targetcenter.com

HUBERT H. HUMPHREY METRODOME
(*Minnesota Vikings*)
900 South 5th Street
Minneapolis, MN 55415
(612) 332-0386
www.msfc.com

HIAWATHA LIGHT RAIL TRANSIT
(*From MSP Airport to Target Field*)
(651) 602-1000
www.metrocouncil.org/
transportation/lrt/lrt.htm

RADISSON PLAZA HOTEL
MINNEAPOLIS
35 South 7th Street
Minneapolis, MN 55402
(612) 339-4900
www.radisson.com/hotels/mpls_dt

NEW YORK YANKEES
Yankee Stadium
One East 161st Street
Bronx, NY 10451
(718) 293-4300
www.yankees.com

YANKEE STADIUM TOUR
Yankee Stadium
One East 161st Street
Bronx, NY 10451
(718) 293-4300
http://newyork.yankees.mlb.com/
nyy/ballpark/stadium_tours.jsp

EMPIRE STATE BUILDING
350 5th Avenue
New York, NY
(212) 736-3100
www.esbnyc.com

STATUE OF LIBERTY
National Park Services
Liberty Island, NY 10004
(212) 363-3200
www.nps.gov.stli

MICKEY MANTLE'S RESTAURANT
& SPORTS BAR
42 Central Park South
New York, NY 10019
(212) 688-7777
www.mickeymantles.com

TIMES SQUARE
Times Square Alliance
1560 Broadway
Suite 800
New York, NY 10036
(212) 768-1560
www.timessquarenyc.org

PENN STATION
Metropolitan Transit Authority
7th Avenue (at 33rd Street)
New York, NY 10001
(212) 630-6401
www.mta.info/

GRAND CENTRAL STATION
87 East 42nd Street
New York, NY 10017
(212) 340-2583
www.grandcentralterminal.com

UNITED NATIONS BUILDING
760 United Nations Plaza
(First Avenue at 46th Street)
New York, NY 10017
(212) 963-TOUR (8687)
www.un.org/tours

OAKLAND ATHLETICS
(O.co) Oakland-Alameda
  County Coliseum
7000 Coliseum Way
Oakland, CA 94621
(510) 638-4900
www.oaklandathletics.com

LAKE MERRITT/LAKESIDEPARK
552 Bellevue Avenue
Oakland, CA 94610
(510) 238-7275
www.oaklandnet.com/parks/parks/
lakemerritt.asp

USS HORNET MUSEUM
707 W. Hornet Avenue
Alameda, CA 94501
(510) 521-8448
www.uss-hornet.org

JACK LONDON SQUARE
1956 Webster Street
Oakland, CA 94612
(510) 645-9292
www.jacklondonsquare.com

CHABOT SPACE & SCIENCE
CENTER
10000 Skyline Boulevard
Oakland, CA 94619
(510) 336-7300
www.chabotspace.org

UNIVERSITY OF CALIFORNIA –
BERKELEY
110 Sproul Hall
Berkeley, CA 94720
(510) 642-6000
www.berkeley.edu

AMOEBA MUSIC
(*Independent music store*)
2455 Telegraph Avenue
Berkeley, CA 94704
(510) 549-1125
www.amoeba.com

RASPUTIN MUSIC
(*Independent music store*)
2401 Telegraph Avenue
Berkeley, CA 94704
(800) 350-8700
(510) 848-9004
www.rasputinmusic.com

SEATTLE MARINERS
Safeco Field
P.O. Box 4100
Seattle, WA 98104
(206) 346-4000
www.mariners.com

SPACE NEEDLE
400 Broad Street
Seattle, WA 98109
(206) 905-2100
www.spaceneedle.com

SEATTLE UNDERGROUND TOUR
608 First Avenue
Seattle, WA 98104
(206) 682-4646
www.undergroundtour.com

(JIMI HENDRIX) EXPERIENCE
MUSIC PROJECT
325 5th Avenue North
Seattle, WA 98109
(206) 770-2700
www.empsfm.org

JIMI HENDRIX MEMORIAL
350 Monroe Avenue Northeast
Renton, WA 98056
(425) 255-1511
www.jimihendrixmemorial.com

SEATTLE DUCK TOUR
516 Broad Street
Seattle, WA 98109
(800) 817-1116
(206) 441-DUCK
www.ridetheducksofseattle.com

TAMPA BAY RAYS
Tropicana Field
One Tropicana Drive
St. Petersburg, FL 33705
(727) 825-3137
www.raysbaseball.com

BOEING FACTORY TOUR
8415 Paine Field Way
Mukilteo, WA 98275
(800) 464-1476
www.futureofflight.org

BUSCH GARDENS THEME PARK
3605 East Bougainvillea Avenue
Tampa, FL 33612
(888) 800-5447
www.buschgardens.com/Bgt

SALTY'S SEAFOOD GRILL
1936 Harbor Avenue Southwest
Seattle, WA 98126
(206) 937- 1600
www.saltys.com

SUNKEN GARDENS
1825 4th Street North
St. Petersburg, FL 33704
(727) 551-3102
www.stpete.org/sunken

ELLIOTT BAY BOOK COMPANY
(*For those rainy Seattle days*)
1521 10th Avenue
Seattle, WA 98122
(800) 962-5311
www.elliottbaybook.com

THE FLORIDA AQUARIUM
701 Channelside Drive
Tampa, FL 33602
(813) 273-4000
www.flaquarium.org

GEORGE M. STEINBRENNER FIELD
(*Winter home of the New York
Yankees with same dimensions as
Yankee Stadium*)
Home of the Tampa Yankees
3802 West Dr. Martin Luther King
Boulevard
Tampa, FL 33614
(813) 875-7753
www.steinbrennerfield.com

EBBETTS FIELD FLANNELS
(*Authentic baseball jerseys, caps
and jackets from yesteryear*)
408 Occidental Avenue South
Seattle, WA 98104
(888) 896-2936 (toll free for orders)
www.ebbetts.com

UNIVERSITY OF WASHINGTON
1410 NE Campus Parkway
Seattle, WA 98195
(206) 543-2100
www.washington.edu

FLORIDA STATE LEAGUE
(*Minor League Baseball*)
http://web.minorleaguebaseball.com/
index.jsp?sid=l123

TEXAS RANGERS

Rangers Ballpark in Arlington
1000 Ballpark Way
Arlington, TX 76011
(817) 273-5222
www.texasrangers.com

FORT WORTH STOCKYARDS
NATIONAL HISTORIC DISTRICT
130 East Exchange Avenue
Fort Worth, TX 76164
(817) 626-7921
www.fortworthstockyards.org

COWBOYS STADIUM
900 E. Randol Mill Road
Arlington, TX 76011
(817) 892-4000
www.stadium.dallascowboys.com

THE SIXTH FLOOR MUSEUM AT
DEALY PLAZA
(*Kennedy assassination site*)
411 Elm Street
Dallas, TX 75202
(214) 747-6660
www.jfk.org

SIX FLAGS OVER TEXAS
(*Amusement park*)
2201 Road to Six Flags
Arlington, TX 76011
(817) 640-8900
www.sixflags.com/overTexas

CROWN PLAZA SUITES
Arlington Ballpark Stadium
700 Avenue H East
Arlington, TX 76011
(817) 394-5000
www.crowneplaza.com

TORONTO BLUE JAYS

Rogers Centre
1 Blue Jay Way, Suite 3200
Toronto, Ontario, Canada
M5V1J1
(416) 341-1000
www.bluejays.com

CN TOWER
301 Front Street West
Toronto, Ontario, Canada
M5V 2T6
(416) 868-6937
www.cntower.ca

HOCKEY HALL OF FAME
Brookfield Place
30 Yonge Street
Toronto, Ontario, Canada
M5E 1X8
(416) 360-7765
www.hhof.com

TORONTO HARBOUR CRUISES
5 Queens Quay West
Toronto, Ontario, Canada
M5J 2H1
(416) 361-9159
www.torontoharbour.com

NATIONAL LEAGUE

ARIZONA DIAMONDBACKS
Chase Field
401 East Jefferson Street
Phoenix, AZ 85004
(602) 462-6500
www.dbacks.com

PIESTEWAH PEAK
(*Formerly Squaw Peak –
a great day hike*)
1411 East Orangewood Avenue
Phoenix, AZ 85020
www.phoenix.gov/PARKS/
hikephx.html

HEARD (INDIAN) MUSEUM
2301 North Central Avenue
Phoenix, AZ 85004
(602) 252-8848
www.heard.org

RAWHIDE WESTERN TOWN &
STEAKHOUSE
5700 West Tham Yog North
Loop Road
Chandler, AZ 85226
(480) 502-5600
www.rawhide.com

TALIESIN WEST
(*Former studio of architect
Frank Lloyd Wright*)
12621 North Frank Lloyd Wright
Boulevard
Scottsdale, AZ 85259
(480) 860-8810
www.franklloydwright.org

ALICE COOPERSTOWN
(*Sports/Rock and Roll restaurant
owned by Alice Cooper*)
101 East Jackson Street
Phoenix, AZ 85004
(602) 253-7337
www.alicecooperstown.com

DESERT BOTANICAL GARDEN
(*More than 130 rare desert plants*)
1201 North Galvin Parkway
Phoenix, AZ 85008
(480) 481-8159
www.dbg.org

ARIZONA STATE UNIVERSITY
University Drive and Mill Avenue
Tempe, AZ 85287
(480) 965-9011
www.asu.edu

ATLANTA BRAVES
Turner Field
755 Hank Aaron Drive
Atlanta, GA 30315
(404) 522-7630
www.braves.com

MARTIN LUTHER KING JR.
NATIONAL HISTORIC SITE
450 Auburn Boulevard NE
Atlanta, GA 30312
(404) 331-5190
www.nps.gov/malu

STONE MOUNTAIN PARK
(*Georgia's top tourist attraction with
rides and natural wonders*)
Highway 78
Atlanta, GA 30086
(770) 498-5690 / (800) 401-2407
www.stonemountainpark.com

UNDERGROUND ATLANTA
(*Guided history tour of downtown Atlanta*)
50 Upper Alabama Street
Suite 007
Atlanta, GA 30303
(404) 523-2311
www.underground-atlanta.com

INSIDE CNN ATLANTA
1 CNN Center
Atlanta, GA 30303
(404) 827-2300
www.cnn.com/tour/atlanta

GEORGIA STATE CAPITOL
206 Washington Street
Atlanta, GA 30344
(404) 463-4536
www.sos.ga.gov/archives/tours/
about.html

WORLD OF COCA-COLA
121 Baker Street NW
Atlanta, GA 30313
(800) 676-COKE
www.worldofcoca-cola.com

GEORGIA INSTITUTE OF
TECHNOLOGY
225 North Avenue
Atlanta, GA 30332
(404) 894-2000
www.gatech.edu

MARGARET MITCHELL HOUSE &
MUSEUM
(*Author of Gone with the Wind*)
990 Peachtree Street NE
Atlanta, GA 30309
(404) 249-7015
www.MargaretMitchellHouse.com

COMFORT INN
(*Turner Field*)
795 Pollard Blvd. SW
Atlanta, GA
(404) 658-1610
www.turnerfielddowntowninn.com

CHICAGO CUBS
Wrigley Field
1060 West Addison
Chicago, IL 60613
(773) 404-2827
www.cubs.com

THE CUBBY BEAR
(*Sports bar opposite Wrigley Field*)
1059 West Addison Street
Chicago, IL 60613
(773) 327-1662
www.cubbybear.com

MURPHY'S BLEACHERS
(*Sports bar opposite Wrigley Field*)
3655 North Sheffield Avenue
Chicago, IL 60613
(773) 929-7061
www.murphysbleachers.com

SLUGGERS WORLD CLASS
SPORTS BAR
(*Wrigleyville area sports bar*)
3540 North Clark Street
Chicago, IL 60657
(773) 248-0055
www.sluggersbar.com

WRIGLEY BUILDING
410 North Michigan Avenue
Chicago, IL 60611
www.thewrigleybuilding.com

LINCOLN PARK ZOO
2001 North Clark Street
Chicago, IL 60614
(312) 742-2000
www.lpzoo.org

FRANK LLOYD WRIGHT HOME &
STUDIO
951 Chicago Avenue
Oak Park, IL 60302
(312) 994-4000
www.gowright.org

ERNEST HEMINGWAY BIRTHPLACE
HOME
339 North Oak Park Avenue
Oak Park, IL 60302
(708) 848-2222
www.ehfop.org

NORTHWESTERN UNIVERSITY
633 Clark Street
Evanston, IL 60208
(847) 491-3741
www.northwestern.edu

CINCINNATI REDS
Great American Ballpark
100 Main Street
Cincinnati, OH 45202
(513) 765-7000
www.reds.com

CINCINNATI REDS HALL OF FAME
& MUSEUM
100 Main Street
Cincinnati, OH 45202
(513) 765-7576
http://cincinnati.reds.mlb.com/cin/
ballpark/museum/index.jsp

KROHN CONSERVATORY
(*Featuring 3,500 plant species*)
1512 Eden Park Drive
Cincinnati, OH 45202
(513) 421-5707
www.cincinnatiparks.com/krohn-
conservatory/index.shtml

ROEBLING SUSPENSION BRIDGE
(*Gateway to Kentucky*)
Ohio River
Cincinnati, OH 45202
www.cincinnati-transit.net/
suspension.html

FOUNTAIN SQUARE
(*Heart of downtown Cincinnati*)
5th and Vine Streets
Cincinnati, OH 46203
(513) 621-4400
www.myfountainsquare.com/

NATIONAL UNDERGROUND
RAILROAD FREEDOM CENTER
(*American Civil War history*)
50 East Freedom Way
Cincinnati, OH 45202
(513) 333-7500
www.freedomcenter.org

WILLIAM HOWARD TAFT NATIONAL
HISTORIC SITE
(*Honoring America's 27th president*)
2038 Auburn Avenue
Cincinnati, OH 45219
(513) 684-3262
www.nps.gov/wiho/index.htm

CAREW TOWER
441 Vine Street
Hilton Cincinnati Netherland Plaza
Cincinnati, OH 45202
(513) 241-7700
www.cincinnati-oh.gov/cdap/
pages/-3743

COLORADO ROCKIES
Coors Field
2001 Blake Street
Denver, CO 80205
(303) 292-0200
www.coloradorockies.com

LODO
Lower Downtown Denver
(*Restaurants, shopping and
entertainment*)
1616 17th Street
Denver, CO 80202
(303) 628-5428
www.lodo.org

WYNKOOP BREWING COMPANY
(*LoDo BrewPub*)
1634 18th Street
Denver, CO 80202
(303) 297-2700
www.wynkoop.com

BUCKHORN EXCHANGE
(*LoDo restaurant offering alligator,
rattlesnake and Rocky Mountain
oysters*)
1000 Osage Street
Denver, CO 80204
(303) 534-9505
www.buckhornexchange.com

LARIMER SQUARE
(*Shopping, restaurants and
entertainment*)
1430 Larimer Street
Denver, CO 80211
(303) 534-2367
www.larimersquare.com

BLACK AMERICAN WEST MUSEUM
AND HERITAGE CENTER
3091 California Street
Denver, CO 80205
(720) 242-7428
www.blackamericanwestmuseum.
com

COLORADO STATE CAPITOL
200 East Colfax Avenue
Denver, CO 80203
(303) 866-2604
www.colorado.gov/cs/Satellite/
CGA- LegislativeCouncil/
CLC/1200536135302

DENVER INSIDE & OUT
(*Scavenger hunt based on 1892
robbery of the Denver Mint*)
1835 West 40th Avenue
Denver, CO 80211
(303) 330-9871
www.denverinsideandout.com

UNIVERSITY OF COLORADO
Regent Drive at Broadway
Boulder, CO 80309
(303) 492-1411
www.colorado.edu

RED ROCKS AMPHITHEATRE
18300 West Alameda Parkway
Morrison, CO 80465
(720) 865-2494
www.redrocksonline.com

COORS BREWERY TOUR
12th Street and Ford Street
Golden, CO 80401
(303) 277-2337
www.coors.com

FLORIDA (MIAMI) MARLINS
Sun Life Stadium
2269 Dan Marino Boulevard
Miami, FL 33056
(305) 626-7400
www.marlins.com

MARLINS BALLPARK
(*2012 projected open*)
1501 Northwest 3rd Street
Miami, FL 33125
(305) 626-7400
www.marlins.com

VIZCAYA MUSEUM AND GARDENS
3251 South Miami Avenue
Miami, FL 33129
(305) 250- 9133
www.vizcayamuseum.org/

SOUTH BEACH
www.visitsouthbeachonline.com/

ART DECO HISTORIC DISTRICT
www.miamibeach411.com/news/
index.php?/news/comments/
southbeach-artdeco/

EVERGLADES NATIONAL PARK
40001 State Road 9336
Homestead, FL 33034
(305) 242- 7700
www.nps.gov/ever/index.htm

LITTLE HAVANA
(*Cultural center of Miami's Cuban
community*)
www.miamiandbeaches.com/visitors/
little_havana.asp

UNIVERSITY OF MIAMI
1252 Memorial Drive
Coral Gables, FL 33146
(305) 284-2211
www.miami.edu

HOUSTON ASTROS
Minute Maid Park
501 Crawford Street
Houston, TX 77002
(713) 259-8000
www.astros.com

JOHNSON SPACE CENTER
1601 NASA Parkway
Houston, TX 77058
(281) 244-2100
www.spacecenter.org/

SAN JACINTO MONUMENT
(*Marks decisive battle of Texas
Revolution*)
One Monument Circle
La Porte, TX 77571
(281) 479-2421
www.sanjacinto-museum.org/

USS TEXAS
10000 Memorial
Suite 700
Houston, TX 77024
www.usstexas.org/

HOUSTON MUSEUM
OF NATURAL SCIENCE
1 Hermann Circle Drive
Houston, TX 77030
(713) 639-4600
www.hmns.org

UNIVERSITY OF TEXAS
2400 Inner Campus Drive
Austin, TX 78712
(512) 471-3434
www.utexas.edu

LBJ LIBRARY & MUSEUM
(*Presidential Library for Lyndon Johnson*)
2313 Red River Street
Austin, TX 78705
(512) 721-0200
www.lbjlibrary.org

LYNDON B. JOHNSON NATIONAL
HISTORICAL PARK (LBJ Ranch)
(*Boyhood home and final resting place of Lyndon Johnson*)
Ladybird Lane
Johnson City, TX 78636
(830) 868-7128
www.nps.gov/lyjo/index.htm

LBJ RANCH
(*Texas White House*)
100 Park Road 49
Stonewall, TX 78671
(830) 868-7128 ext. 231
www.nps.gov/lyjo/planyourvisit/visitlbjranch.htm

RUBY'S BBQ
512 West 29th Street
Austin, TX 78705
(512) 477-1651
www.rubysbbq.com

DOUBLE TREE AUSTIN
303 West 15th Street
Austin, TX 78701
(512) 478-7000
http://doubletree1.hilton.com/en_US/dt/hotel/AUSLNDT-Doubletree-Hotel-Austin-Texas/index.do

LOS ANGELES DODGERS
Dodger Stadium
1000 Elysian Park Avenue
Los Angeles, CA 90012
(323) 224-1500
www.dodgers.com

HOLLYWOOD WALK OF FAME
Hollywood Boulevard and Vine Street
Hollywood, CA 90028
(323) 469-8311
www.hollywoodchamber.net/walk-of-fame-welcome

L.A. LIVE
(*Entertainment Center*)
800 West Olympic Boulevard
Los Angeles, CA 90015
(866) LIVE4LA
www.lalive.com

WALT DISNEY CONCERT HALL
111 South Grand Avenue
Los Angeles, CA 90012
(213) 972-7211
www.laphil.com

LA BREA TAR PITS
(*Dinosaur graveyard*)
5801 Wilshire Boulevard
Los Angeles, CA 90036
(323) 934-7243
www.tarpits.org

THE J. PAUL GETTY MUSEUM
(*Art museum*)
1200 Getty Center Drive
Los Angeles, CA 90049
(310) 440-7300
www.getty.edu

UNIVERSAL STUDIOS
100 Universal Terrace Parkway
Universal City, CA 90068
(800) 864-8377
www.universalstudioshollywood.com

OLVERA STREET
(*Birthplace of the City of Los Angeles
– A village with 27 historic buildings*)
El Pueblo De Los Angeles
Historic Park
845 North Alameda Street
Los Angeles, CA 90012
(213) 628-1274
www.olvera-street.com

LA LUZ DEL DIA
(*Authentic Mexican food*)
W-1 Olvera Street
Los Angeles, CA 90012
(213) 628-7495
www.calleolvera.com/directory/w1/

PHILIPPE'S
(*The original birthplace of the
French Dip sandwich*)
1001 North Alameda Street
Los Angeles, CA 90012
(213) 628-3781
www.philippes.com

GRIFFITH OBSERVATORY
2800 East Observatory Road
Los Angeles, CA 90027
(213) 473-0800
www.griffithobs.org

HOLLYWOOD SIGN
Mount Lee in Griffith Park
Los Angeles, CA 90027
(213) 469-8311
www.hollywoodsign.org

FRED 62
(*Restaurant*)
1850 North Vermont Avenue
Los Angeles, CA 90027
(323) 667-0062
www.fred62.com

RADISSON HOTEL
Midtown Los Angeles (USC)
3540 South Figueroa Street
Los Angeles, CA 90007
(800) 395-7046
(213) 748-4141
www.radisson.com/losangeles_
midtown

THE GROVE
(*Shopping, restaurants, movies*)
189 The Grove Drive
Los Angeles, CA 90036
(323) 900-8080
www.thegrovela.com

PANINI CAFÉ DOWNTOWN
600 West 9th Street
Los Angeles, CA 90015
(213) 489-4200
www.mypaninicafe.com

MILWAUKEE BREWERS
Miller Park
One Brewers Way
Milwaukee, WI 53214
(414) 902-4400
www.brewers.com

MILLER BREWING COMPANY TOUR
4251 West State Street
Milwaukee, WI 53208
(414) 931-BEER
www.factorytour.com/tours/miller-brewing.cfm

MILWAUKEE PUBLIC MUSEUM
800 West Wells Street
Milwaukee, WI 53233
(414) 27802701
(888) 700-9069
www.mpm.edu

MILWAUKEE MUSEUM OF ART
700 North Art Museum Drive
Milwaukee, WI 53202
(414) 224-3200
www.mam.org

CAPTAIN FREDERICK PABST
MANSION
(*Founder of Pabst Beer*)
2000 West Wisconsin Avenue
Milwaukee, WI 52302
(414) 931-0808
www.pabstmansion.com/

LAKEFRONT BREWERY
1872 North Commerce Street
Milwaukee, WI 53212
(414) 372-8800
www.lakefrontbrewery.com

HARLEY DAVIDSON MUSEUM
(*More than 400 motorcycles on display*)
400 West Canal Street
Milwaukee, WI 53203
(414) 287-2700
www.harley-davidson.com

MILWAUKEE HYATT REGENCY
(*Site of attempted assassination of Teddy Roosevelt*)
333 West Kilbourn Avenue
Milwaukee, WI 53203
(414) 276-1234
www.milwaukee.hyatt.com

NEW YORK METS
Citi Field
126th Street and Roosevelt Avenue
Flushing, NY 11368
(718) 507-6387
www.mets.com

BROOKLYN BRIDGE
www.nycroads.com/crossings/brooklyn

CONEY ISLAND
1000 Surf Avenue
Brooklyn, NY 11235
www.coneyisland.com/tourism.shtml

CHINATOWN
www.chinatown-online.com

CENTRAL PARK
Central Park Conservancy
14 E. 60th Street
New York, NY 10022
(212) 310-6600
www.centralparknyc.org

AMERICAN MUSEUM
OF NATURAL HISTORY
Central Park West at 79th Street
New York, NY 10024
(212) 769-5100
www.amnh.org

GREENWICH VILLAGE
(*New York's bohemian
neighborhood*)
www.nycgv.com/about.asp

PHILADELPHIA PHILLIES
Citizens Bank Ballpark
One Citizens Bank Way
Philadelphia, PA 19148
(215) 463-6000
www.phillies.com

INDEPENDENCE NATIONAL
HISTORIC PARK
(*Liberty Bell and U.S. Constitution*)
143 South Third Street
Philadelphia, PA 19106
(800) 537-7676
www.nps.gov.inde

NATIONAL CONSTITUTION CENTER
525 Arch Street
Philadelphia, PA 19106
(215) 409-6600
www.constitutioncenter.org

BETSY ROSS HOUSE
239 Arch Street
Philadelphia, PA 19106
(215) 686-1252
www.betsyrosshouse.org

FRANKLIN INSTITUTE
AND SCIENCE MUSEUM
222 North 20th Street
Philadelphia, PA 19103
(215) 448-1200
www.2.fi.edu

GENO'S STEAKS
(*Cheese steaks*)
1219 South 9th Street
Philadelphia, PA 19147
(215) 389-0659
www.genosteaks.com

THE ROCKY STATUE AND
ROCKY STEPS
2600 Benjamin Franklin Parkway
Philadelphia, PA 19130
www.visitphilly.com/museums-
attractions/philadelphia/the-rocky-
statue-and-the-rocky-steps

PHILADELPHIA MUSEUM OF ART
Benjamin Franklin Parkway
Philadelphia, PA 19101
(215) 763-8100
www.philamuseum.org

PATS KING OF STEAKS
(*Cheese steaks*)
1237 East Passyunk Avenue
Philadelphia, PA 19147
(215) 468-1547
www.patskingofsteaks.com

MITCHELL AND NESS
(*Authentic sports apparel*)
1318 Chestnut Street
Philadelphia, PA 19107
(866) 879-6485
www.mitchellandness.com

PITTSBURGH PIRATES
PNC Park
115 Federal Street
Pittsburgh, PA 15212
(412) 323-5000
www.pirates.com

MT. WASHINGTON INCLINES
(412) 442-2000
www.portauthority.org/PAAC/
CustomerInfo/Inclines/tabid/119/
Default.aspx

PITTSBURGH WATER LIMO
Railroad Street and 23rd Street
Pittsburgh, PA 15222
(412) 221-LIMO
www.pghwaterlimo.com/index.html

RIVERBOAT TOURS
Gateway Clipper Fleet
350 West Station Square Drive
Pittsburgh, PA 15219
(412) 355-7980
www.gatewayclipper.com

CARNEGIE MUSEUMS OF
PITTSBURGH
(*Art, science, natural history
and pop culture*)
4400 Forbes Avenue
Pittsburgh, PA 15213
(412) 622-3131
www.carnegiemuseums.org

THE ANDY WARHOL MUSEUM
(*Honoring Pittsburgh's pop
culture icon*)
117 Sandusky Street
Pittsburgh, PA 15212
(412) 237-8300
www.warhol.org

ROBERTO CLEMENTE BRIDGE
(*Sixth Street Bridge*)
www.pghbridges.com/pittsburgh
W/0584-4477/sixth_st_br.htm

DOUBLETREE HOTEL
PITTSBURGH CITY CENTER
(*Delicious, warm chocolate chip cookies*)
1 Bigelow Square
Pittsburgh, PA 15219
(412) 281-5800
www.doubletree.com

SAN DIEGO PADRES
Petco Park
100 Park Boulevard
San Diego, CA 92101
(619) 795-5000
www.padres.com

SAN DIEGO ZOO
2920 Zoo Drive
San Diego, CA 92101
(619) 231-1515
www.sandiegozoo.org

SAN DIEGO ZOO SAFARI PARK
15500 San Pasqual Valley Road
Escondido, CA 92027
(760) 747-8702
www.sandiegozoo.org/park

SAN DIEGO HARBOR EXCURSIONS
(*Flagship Cruises*)
1050 North Harbor Drive
San Diego, CA 62101
(800) 44-CRUISE
www.flagshipsd.com

SEAWORLD
500 SeaWorld Drive
San Diego, CA 92109
(800) 25-SHAMU
www.seaworld.com

BALBOA PARK
(*15 major museums*)
1549 El Prado
San Diego, CA 92101
(619) 239-0512
www.balboapark.org

GASLAMP QUARTER
(*Shopping, dining and entertainment*)
614 5ᵗʰ Avenue
San Diego, CA 92101
(619) 233-5227
www.gaslamp.org

BIRCH AQUARIUM AT SCRIPPS
INSTITUTION OF OCEANOGRAPHY
2300 Expedition Way
La Jolla, CA 92037
(858) 534-3474
www.aquarium.ucsd.edu

SAN DIEGO HALL OF CHAMPIONS
(*Relive the early days of San Diego
native Ted Williams' career*)
2131 Pan American Plaza
San Diego, CA 92101
(619) 234-2544
www.sdhoc.com

SEAPORT VILLAGE
(*Shopping and dining with a sea
breeze*)
849 West Harbor Drive
Suite D
San Diego, CA 92101
(619) 235-4014
www.seaportvillage.com

SAN FRANCISCO GIANTS
AT&T Park
24 Willie Mays Plaza
San Francisco, CA 94107
(415) 972-2000
www.sfgiants.com

PIER 39
(*Dining, shopping and entertainment*)
Suite 39, 39 Pier
San Francisco, CA 94133
(415) 981-7437
www.pier39.com

ALCATRAZ ISLAND
National Park Service
Golden Gate National Recreation
Area
Fort Mason, B201
San Francisco, CA 94103
www.nps.gov/alca/index.htm

Alcatraz Cruises
(415) 981-ROCK
www.alcatrazcruises.com

SAN FRANCISCO CABLE CARS
www.sfcablecar.com

GHIRARDELLI SQUARE
(*Ghirardelli chocolate*)
900 North Point Street
San Francisco, CA 94109
(415) 775-5500
www.ghirardellisq.com

COIT TOWER
1 Telegraph Hill Boulevard
San Francisco, CA 94133
www.sftravel.com/coit-tower-san-
francisco.html

UNION SQUARE
www.unionsquareshop.com

LOMBARD STREET
(*Crookedest street in the world*)
www.lombardstreetsf.com

CHINATOWN
www.sanfranciscochinatown.com

NORTH BEACH
(*Restaurants and bohemian
San Francisco scene*)
www.northbeachchamber.com

HAIGHT ASHBURY
(*Former hippie haven*)
www.lovehaight.org/

ST. LOUIS CARDINALS
Busch Stadium
700 Clark Street
St. Louis, MO 63102
(314) 345-9600
www.cardinals.com

ST. LOUIS GATEWAY ARCH
Gateway Arch Riverfront
St. Louis, MO 63102
(877) 982-1410
www.gatewayarch.com

(LEWIS & CLARK) MUSEUM OF
WESTERN EXPANSION
Gateway Arch Riverfront
St. Louis, MO 63102
(877) 982-1410
www.gatewayarch.com/Arch/info/act.
museum.aspx

HISTORIC OLD COURTHOUSE
(*The place where Dred Scott, a
slave, sued for freedom and lost*)
Gateway Arch Riverfront
St. Louis, MO 63102
(877) 982-1410
www.gatewayarch.com/Arch/info/act.
courthouse.aspx

MISSISSIPPI RIVER CRUISES
Gateway Arch Riverfront
St. Louis, MO 63102
(877) 982-1410
www.gatewayarch.com/Arch/info/act.
riverboat.aspx

THE MUNY
St. Louis Outdoor Theatre in Forest
Park
1 Theatre Drive
St. Louis, MO 63112
(314) 361-1900
www.muny.org

DRURY INN
2 South 4th Street
St. Louis, MO 63102
(314) 231- 3003
wwws.druryhotels.
com/PropertyOverview.
aspx?Property=0103

WASHINGTON NATIONALS
Nationals Park
1500 South Capitol Street SE
Washington, D.C. 20003
(202) 349-0400
www.nationals.com

WHITE HOUSE TOURS
1600 Pennsylvania Avenue
Washington, D.C. 20500
(202) 456-7041
www.whitehouse.gov/about/tours-
and-events

U.S. CAPITOL VISITOR CENTER
East Capitol Street NE and
1st Street NE
Washington, D.C. 20001
(202) 226-8000
www.visitthecapitol.gov

U.S. SUPREME COURT BUILDING
One First Street NE
Washington, D.C. 20543
(202) 479-3000
www.supremecourt.gov/visiting/
visitorservices.aspx

THE SMITHSONIAN INSTITUTION
1100 Jefferson Drive SW
Washington, D.C. 20013
(202) 633-3030
www.si.edu

WASHINGTON MONUMENT
Constitution Avenue and
15th Street SW
Washington, D.C. 20024
(202) 426-6841
www.nps.gov/wamo

LINCOLN MEMORIAL
Lincoln Memorial Circle SW
Washington, D.C. 20037
(202) 426-6841
www.nps.gov/linc

JEFFERSON MEMORIAL
900 Ohio Drive SW
Washington, D.C. 20024
(202) 426-6841
www.nps.gov/thje

THE NEWSEUM
555 Pennslyvania Avenue NW
Washington, D.C. 20001
(888) NEWSEUM (toll free)
www.newseum.org

KENNEDY CENTER FOR THE
PERFORMING ARTS
2700 F Street NW
Washington, D.C. 20566
(800) 444-1324
www.kennedy-center.org

BEN'S CHILI BOWL
1213 U Street NW
Washington, D.C. 20009
(202) 667-0909
www.benschilbowl.com

DUCKTOURS
Union Station
50 Massachusetts Avenue NE
Washington, D.C. 20018
(800) 213-2474
www.dcducks.com

GEORGE WASHINGTON'S
MT. VERNON ESTATE AND
GARDENS
3200 Mount Vernon Memorial
Highway
Mount Vernon, VA 22309
(703) 780-2000
www.mountvernon.org

ARLINGTON NATIONAL CEMETERY
State Highway 110 and
Memorial Drive
Arlington, VA 22201
(703) 607-8000
www.arlingtoncemetery.org

Baseball Bullets
Extra Innings
The Dakotas

Fun adventures outside Major League Baseball

FARGO-MOORHEAD REDHAWKS
Newman Outdoor Field
1515 15th Avenue North
Fargo, ND 58102
(701) 235-6161
www.fmredhawks.com/

ROGER MARIS MUSEUM
West Acres Shopping Center
3902 13th Avenue South
Fargo, N.D. 58103
(701) 282-2222
www.rogermarismuseum.com/

ROGER MARIS BURIAL SITE
HOLY CROSS CEMETERY
1502 32nd Avenue North
Fargo, ND 58102
(701) 237-6671
www.findagrave.com/cgi-bin/
fg.cgi?page=gr&GRid=1599

MAURY WILLS MUSEUM
Newman Outdoor Field
Fargo-Moorhead RedHawks
1515 15th Avenue
Fargo, ND 58102
(701) 235-6161
www.nlfan.com/fargo/maury/

FARGO AIR MUSEUM
1609 19th Avenue North
Fargo, ND 58102
(701) 293-8043
www.fargoairmuseum.org

HOLIDAY INN EXPRESS –
WEST ACRES
(*Opposite Roger Maris Museum*)
1040 40th Street
Fargo, ND 58103
(701) 282-2000
www.hiexpress.com/hotels/us/en/
farex/hoteldetail

WORLD'S LARGEST BUFFALO
Jamestown, ND
www.realnd.com/
jamestownbuffaloindex.htm

NORTH DAKOTA STATE CAPITOL
600 E. Boulevard Avenue
Bismarck, North Dakota 58505
(701) 328-2200
http://www.nd.gov/content.
htm?parentCatID=75&id=State%20
Capital

SOUTH DAKOTA STATE CAPITOL
500 East Capitol Avenue
Pierre, SD 57501
(605) 773-33688
www.sdpb.org/capitolidea/Tour.asp

BADLANDS NATIONAL PARK
25216 Ben Reifel Road
P.O. Box 6
Interior, SD
(605) 433-5361
www.nps.gov/badl/index.htm

WALL DRUG
510 Main Street
P.O. Box 401
Wall, SD 57790
(605) 279-2175
www.walldrug.com

MT. RUSHMORE
NATIONAL MEMORIAL
13000 Highway 244
Building 31, Suite 1
Keystone, SD 57751
(605) 574-2523
www.nps.gov/moru

CRAZY HORSE MEMORIAL
12151 Avenue of the Chiefs
Crazy Horse, SD 57730
(605) 673-4681
www.crazyhorsememorial.org

BLACK HILLS BALLOONS
P.O. Box 210
Custer, SD 57730
(605) 673-2520
www.blackhillsballoons.com

RUSHMORE CAVE
13622 Highway 40
Keystone, SD
(605) 255-4467
www.rushmorecave.com

WOOLY MAMMOTH SITE
1800 U.S. Highway 18 Bypass
P.O. Box 692
Hot Springs, SD 57747
(605) 745-6017
www.mammothsite.com

BLACK HILLS MUSEUM OF
NATURAL HISTORY
117 Main Street
Hill City, SD 57745
(605) 574-4505
www.blackhillsvacations.com

Baseball Bullets
New England

MAINE

MAINE STATE HOUSE
State Street
Augusta, ME 04333
(207) 287-2301
www.mainestatemuseum.org

L.L. BEAN
95 Main Street
Freeport, ME 04033
(877) 755-2326
www.llbean.com

THE LOBSTER DOCK
49 Atlantic Avenue
Boothbay Harbor, ME 04538
(207) 633-7120
www.thelobsterdock.com

REID STATE PARK
375 Seguinland Road
Georgetown, ME 04548
(207) 371-2303
http://www.maine.gov/cgi-
bin/online/doc/parksearch/
search_name.pl?state_
park=13&historic_site=&public_
reserved_land=&shared_use_
trails=&option=search

CAMP ANDROSCOGGIN
126 Leadbetter Road
Wayne, ME 02484
(207) 685-4441
www.campandro.com

NEW HAMPSHIRE

MT. WASHINGTON COG RAILWAY
(*Highest peak in the Northeast*)
Base Road
Six Miles off Route 302
Bretton Woods, NH 03575
(800) 922-8825
http://www.thecog.com/

NEW HAMPSHIRE STATE HOUSE
107 North Main Street
Concord, NH 03301
(603) 271-2154
www.gencourt.state.nh.us

DARTMOUTH COLLEGE
Hanover, NH 03755
(603) 646-1110
www.dartmouth.edu

VERMONT

VERMONT STATE HOUSE
115 State Street
Montpelier, VT 05633
(802) 828-2228
www.vtstatehouse.org/tours

MASSACHUSETTS

MASSACHUSETTS STATE HOUSE
24 Beacon Street
Boston, MA 02108
(617) 727-7030
www.cityofboston.gov/freedomtrail/
massachusettshouse.asp

BASKETBALL HALL OF FAME
(*Naismith Memorial Basketball Hall
of Fame*)
1000 W. Columbus Avenue
Springfield, MA 01105
(413) 781-6500
www.hoophall.com

SMITH COLLEGE
7 College Lane
Northampton, MA 01063
(413) 584-2700
www.smith.edu

AMHERST COLLEGE
103 Converse Hall
Amherst, MA 01002
(413) 542-2000
www.amherst.edu

RHODE ISLAND

RHODE ISLAND STATE HOUSE
82 Smith Street
Providence, RI 02903
(401) 222-2357
www.rilin.state.ri.us/statehousetour

BROWN UNIVERSITY
Providence, RI 02912
(401) 863-1000
www.brown.edu

CONNECTICUT

STAMFORD MUSEUM
AND NATURE CENTER
39 Scofieldtown Road
Stamford, CT 06903
(203) 322-1646
www.stamfordmuseum.org

CONNECTICUT STATE CAPITOL
210 Capitol Avenue
Hartford, CT 06106
(860) 240-0222
www.cga.ct.gov/capitoltours

YALE UNIVERSITY
246 Church Street
New Haven, CT 06520
(203) 432-9300
www.yale.edu

Baseball Bullets
Niagra Falls and
Baseball Hall of Fame

NIAGARA FALLS: CANADA
Tourism Bureau
5400 Robinson Street
Niagara Falls, Ontario, Canada
L2G2A6
(800) 563-2557
www.niagarafallstourism.com

NIAGARA FALLS: USA
Tourism Bureau
345 Third Street, Suite 605
Niagara Falls, NY 14303
877-FALLS US (325-5787)
www.niagara-usa.com

BASEBALL HALL OF FAME
25 Main Street
Cooperstown, NY 13326
(888) HALL-OF-FAME
www.baseballhall.org

LAKE FRONT MOTEL
10 Fair Street
Cooperstown, NY 13326
(607) 547-9511
www.lakefrontmotelandrestaurant.com

COOPERSTOWN CHAMBER OF
COMMERCE
31 Chestnut Street
Cooperstown, NY 13326
(607) 547-9983
www.cooperstownchamber.org

Baseball Bullets
Woodstock

BETHEL WOODS CENTER
FOR THE ARTS
200 Hurd Road
Bethel, New York 12720
(866) 781-2922
www.bethelwoodscenter.org

My Ballpark Rankings

1. San Francisco Giants, AT&T Park
   Splash hits into the beautiful Bay.
2. Pittsburgh Pirates, PNC Park
   Take a water taxi to the game.
3. Boston Red Sox, Fenway Park
   The Green Monster.
4. Baltimore Orioles, Oriole Park
   BBQ with Boog at original retro park.
5. Detroit Tigers, Comerica Park
   Cobb, Kaline and Horton in the outfield.
6. Minnesota Twins, Target Field
   Take Light Rail from airport to the park.
7. Colorado Rockies, Coors Field
   Great view of the Rockies.
8. St. Louis Cardinals, Busch Stadium
   The Arch is awesome.
9. Philadelphia Phillies, Citizens Bank Park
   Take the subway with the fanatic fans.
10. Cleveland Indians, Progressive Field
    Heritage Park.
11. Chicago Cubs, Wrigley Field
    Ivy-covered walls and Bleacher Bums.
12. New York Yankees, Yankee Stadium
    Legendary park blends old and new.
13. Seattle Mariners, Safeco Field
    Environmental jewel.
14. San Diego Padres, Petco Field
    Giant sandbox for the kids.

15. Arizona Diamondbacks, Chase Field
      Only swimming pool in MLB.
16. Los Angeles Dodgers, Dodger Stadium
      Sunshine and palm trees.
17. Houston Astros, Minute Maid Park
      Center field on a slope.
18. Cincinnati Reds, Great American Ball Park
      Riverfront view.
19. Atlanta Braves, Turner Field
      Dynamic downtown skyline.
20. Texas Rangers, Rangers Ballpark in Arlington
      Bold and beautiful.
21. Washington Nationals, Nationals Park
      A presidential race during every game.
22. New York Mets, Citi Field.
      Big improvement over Shea.
23. Milwaukee Brewers, Miller Park
      Watch the hot dog races.
24. Kansas City Royals, Kauffman Stadium
      Fabulous fountains.
25. Los Angeles Angels of Anaheim, Angel Stadium
      Bullpen blocks the view.
26. Chicago White Sox, U.S. Cellular Field
      Missing a neighborhood feel.
27. Toronto Blue Jays, Rogers Centre
      Impressive when the roof opens.
28. Oakland A's, Oakland–Alameda County Coliseum
      A football stadium.
29. Florida Marlins, Sun Life Stadium
      Another football stadium.
30. Tampa Bay Rays, Tropicana Field
      No sunshine in the Sunshine State.

Acknowledgments

I want to begin by thanking my wonderful wife, Carol, for her love and support. She held down the fort when Matt and I were on the road and provided travel tips, encouragement and plenty of creative ideas in the formation of this book.

My daughter, Sarah, a terrific writer in her own right, gave me inspiration to follow my passion in pursuing this endeavor. I am so proud of you and everything you do.

Matt was my catalyst who pushed my buttons and forced me to live outside of my comfort zone – and in so doing, opened up new pathways for awareness. You are my baseball buddy for life.

I also want to thank my mother-in-law, Liz Kruidenier, a Smith College English major, for coming up with the title for this book. She also served as my first editor and prodded me to explain the nuances of baseball to people who don't follow the sport. Peter Kruidenier, Ollie McNamara, Richard and Joan Meyers and Wendy and Philip Wilkinson all offered support and encouragement.

To my sister Andrea, brother-in-law, Fred Fenton, and to my brother, Russell – thank you for providing a home on the road and being part of my journey. I have truly enjoyed taking your kids to the ballpark – and playing whiffle ball in the backyard.

To my best friend, Marty Gonzalez, thank you for sharing part of the journey with me in St. Louis, San Francisco and Oakland. It's always fun to be at the ballpark together. And thanks also to Peter Golenbock and Ron Hyde for your baseball anecdotes, insights and stories about the game. I'd like to give a special thanks to Ken Smith for your extra editing highlights. Finally, thanks to Jack Broudy, Robert Drabant, Scott Morris, Bill Reich, Bob Reich, Rick Sarner and Herb Weisbaum for your eternal friendship.

And to Mom, Dad and Roberta, I miss you each and every day.

Author Biography
Mike Luery

Mike Luery is a member of SABR, the Society for American Baseball Research and an award-winning journalist, with more than two decades of broadcasting experience. Currently, he is the investigative and political reporter for CBS 13 in Sacramento, California, where his "On The Money" television reports air multiple times each week. Luery's stories provide an in-depth look at the connection between money and politics.

Previously, Luery served for three years as NBC's Capitol Bureau Chief in Sacramento, where he covered Governor Arnold Schwarzenegger and reported political stories daily for a dozen NBC television stations across California and Nevada. He also worked for 15 years as the Call 3/Consumer Reporter for KCRA-TV in Sacramento, providing viewers with important lessons each day in consumer protection.

Early in his career, Luery was a television reporter for KMOL-TV (now WOAI) in San Antonio, Texas, and WPTV in West Palm Beach, Florida. His five-part series documenting the 1980s resurgence of the Ku Klux Klan in Florida earned an Outstanding Achievement Award for Investigative Reporting from United Press International. UPI also awarded Luery an Outstanding Achievement Award for Investigative Reporting for his multi-part series on cocaine abuse in Florida.

Luery began his broadcasting career in radio. He was the news anchor for WPLR-FM in New Haven, Connecticut, after serving as news director and news anchor at KZOZ-FM in San Luis Obispo, California, and general manager of KSPC-FM, the Pomona College radio station in Claremont, California.